AF621471

INTERSECTIONALITY IN THE ARTS PSYCHOTHERAPIES

of related interest

Creative Arts Therapies and the LGBTQ Community
Theory and Practice
Edited by Briana MacWilliam, Kristin Long, Dana George Trottier and Brian T Harris
ISBN 978 1 78592 796 6
eISBN 978 1 78450 802 9

Using Art Therapy with Diverse Populations
Crossing Cultural Abilities
Paula Howie, Sangeeta Prasad and Jennie Kristel
Foreword by Mercedes B. ter Maat and Gaelynn P. Wolf Bordonaro
ISBN 978 1 84905 916 9
eISBN 978 0 85700 694 3

Cultural Humility in Art Therapy
Applications for Practice, Research, Social Justice, Self-Care, and Pedagogy
Louvenia C. Jackson
Foreword by Dr Melanie Tervalon
ISBN 978 1 78592 643 3
eISBN 978 1 78592 644 0

Gender Issues in Art Therapy
Edited by Susan Hogan
Foreword by Diane Waller
ISBN 978 1 85302 798 7
eISBN 978 1 84642 372 7

INTERSECTIONALITY in the ARTS PSYCHOTHERAPIES

EDITED BY

Jessica Collier and Corrina Eastwood

Jessica Kingsley Publishers
London and Philadelphia

First published in Great Britain in 2022 by Jessica Kingsley Publishers
An imprint of Hodder & Stoughton Ltd
An Hachette Company

1

Copyright © Jessica Kingsley Publishers 2022
Foreword Copyright © Savneet K. Talwar 2022
Chapter 8 Copyright © Sejal Chad 2022

All rights reserved. No part of this publication may be reproduced, stored in a retrieval system, or transmitted, in any form or by any means without the prior written permission of the publisher, nor be otherwise circulated in any form of binding or cover other than that in which it is published and without a similar condition being imposed on the subsequent purchaser.

A CIP catalogue record for this title is available from the
British Library and the Library of Congress

ISBN 978 1 78775 434 8
eISBN 978 1 78775 435 5

Printed and bound in the United States by Integrated Books International

Jessica Kingsley Publishers' policy is to use papers that are natural, renewable and recyclable products and made from wood grown in sustainable forests. The logging and manufacturing processes are expected to conform to the environmental regulations of the country of origin.

Jessica Kingsley Publishers
Carmelite House
50 Victoria Embankment
London EC4Y 0DZ

www.jkp.com

Endorsements

An exceptional and timely book which succeeds in unpacking the complexities of intersectional thinking within art psychotherapy, while at the same time demonstrating its role in challenging the unconscious bias, privilege and occlusions that can often deny authentic connection. The value of art as a tool for building recognition across the multiple identity positions that we each inhabit is explored throughout in case studies that exhibit remarkable scholarship, intimacy and deep compassion. (Dr Daniel Baker)

Daniel Baker is an artist, curator and researcher. A Romani Gypsy, born in Kent, he holds a PhD on the subject of Gypsy aesthetics from the Royal College of Art, London. Baker curated FUTUROMA at the 58th International Art Exhibition at the Venice Biennale in 2019. He acted as exhibitor and adviser to the first and second Roma Pavilions, 'Paradise Lost' and 'Call the Witness', at the 52nd and 54th Venice Biennales respectively. Baker's art and writing examine the role of art in the enactment of social agency through an eclectic practice that interrogates contemporary art discourse and its social implications via the reconfiguration of elements of the Gypsy aesthetic. His work can be found in collections worldwide. Publications include *We Roma: A Critical Reader in Contemporary Art*, *Ex Libris* and *FUTUROMA*. Former Chair of the Gypsy Council, Baker currently lives and works in London.

The richness of the varied contributions to this much-needed text interrogating intersectionality provides a wealth of experiences for the reader. The wide range of contexts, discourses and varied clinical work explored here will be invaluable to all arts therapists as they seek to develop their practice and frameworks in contemporary society. The importance of this text cannot be overestimated; it is both innovative and timely, and will inspire practitioners from a broad range of professions. While being challenging, it invites the reader to articulate their own position in the work as well as that of their clients. (Dr Elizabeth Coombes)

Elizabeth Coombes is the Course Leader of the MA in Music Therapy at the University of South Wales. She has presented internationally on the topic of music therapy, cross-cultural working and practitioner identity, and has many peer reviewed publications.

In this comprehensive text, Intersectionality in the Arts Psychotherapies, *the contributors bring together multiple personal perspectives that acknowledge and honour the intersections of social and historical oppression in our work as therapeutic practitioners who use the creative arts, the body and metaphor. The reader will be challenged in their understanding of intersectionality and empowered in their practice as contemporary arts psychotherapists.* (Eugene Ellis)

Eugene Ellis is an integrative arts psychotherapist and has worked for many years with severely traumatized children and their families in the field of adoption and fostering. He is also the Director and founder of the Black, African and Asian Therapy Network (BAATN), the UK's largest independent organization to specialize in working with Black, African, Caribbean and South Asian people. Eugene has a particular interest in facilitating dialogues about race and the body, within organizations and in psychotherapy trainings. His book, *The Race Conversation: An Essential Guide to Creating Life-Changing Dialogue*, explores not just the cognitive and historical development of the race construct, but also focuses specifically on the non-verbal communication of race, both as a means of social control and as an essential part of navigating oppressive patterns.

The contemporary moment is providing ample evidence that mental health problems can only be fully understood by factoring the effects of inequality, marginalization and disempowerment. The societal structures driving those experiences have antecedents beyond any individual and so affect both the users and providers of therapy services. This much-needed book challenges any presumption that professional therapy training might confer practitioners with some kind of blanket immunity to the historical forces at play in our cultures. Instead it proposes an update to the professional model where the therapist foregrounds their own unique points of intersection within those historical forces. This auto-ethnographic approach to cultural competence avoids problematic generalizations about groups. The reader is instead offered a process whereby the arts can be used to reflexively identify cultural assumptions which might blind therapists to opportunities for more effective therapeutic encounters. I welcome the transparent authorial style used by the art therapist practitioners who demonstrate how social ownership can form the basis of a coherent therapeutic stance for our turbulent times. (Dr Neil Springham)

Neil Springham is a consultant art therapist, and Executive Director of Therapies and Patient Experience at Oxleas NHS Foundation Trust, London.

Contents

List of Figures and Tables

Foreword

SAVNEET K. TALWAR

The profession of the arts psychotherapies[1] has been shaped by theories of individual growth and the ideology of neoliberalism. The onus on wellness has rested on the individual, in the belief that if one works hard enough obstacles can be overcome. An intersectional approach takes into account the multiple dimensions of social identity and the layered forms of oppression that impact health inequities and life outcomes (Dill & Zambrana, 2009). Intersectionality, therefore, is a methodological tool that critiques capitalist, neoliberalist, global, economic and social welfare systems that contribute to the vast divide between the rich and the poor (Collins & Bilge, 2016; Crenshaw, 1989; Dill & Zambrana, 2009; Kuri, 2017; Talwar, 2010). Neoliberal policies understand poverty and suffering as moral failures, placing the responsibility of success on individuals. Neoliberal ideology, focusing on personal effort, engenders systemic inequalities as individual problems rather than intersectional ones. Arts psychotherapies education has relied on individualized models of treatment that focus on art-making to engage with abstract concepts of the self, on affect regulation and self-expression; it has created a one-size-fits-all approach that fails to confront the power structures that produce difference (Gipson, 2017; Kuri, 2017; Talwar, 2019). Intersectional markers – race, class, gender, sexuality, disability and religion, among other vectors of difference – have been overlooked in favour of universal paradigms of human development (Collins & Bilge, 2016; Talwar, 2010). As Kelly (2019) emphasizes, danger arises when moderate educators embrace the language of intersectionality, radical liberalism and social justice, only to bend it to serve capitalistic, institutional and neoliberal ideologies that reinforce the social order rather than serve

1 I use the term arts psychotherapies and creative arts therapies interchangeably. In the US, the collective term for art, drama and music therapy is creative arts therapies, while in the UK it is arts psychotherapies.

justice. Educational scholar Bettina Love (2019) argues that our educational systems, in normalizing structural racism and inequality, continue to reproduce whiteness and the status quo.

This book, edited by Jessica Collier and Corrina Eastwood, illustrates how arts psychotherapies can be enriched by engaging in an intersectional framework. Focused primarily on the work of arts psychotherapists in the United Kingdom, the authors engage with intersectional feminism from various points of view: as an assessment methodology to embody a self-reflexive approach, to contextualize the role of feelings and emotions from intersectional markers, and to contextualize mental health stigma and shame. They take up the limitations of the *Diagnostic and Statistical Manual of Mental Disorders* (*DSM*) and diagnosis, as well as the importance of decentring Whiteness in art therapy education and treatment modalities.

Arts psychotherapies, like other therapeutic professions, stand at a critical juncture in the wake of COVID-19, the Black Lives Matter (BLM) protests for racial justice of 2020, and the rise in White nationalism globally. The COVID-19 pandemic, a global health crisis, has disproportionately impacted racial and ethnic minorities. Research has long indicated that systemic inequalities, such as poverty and limited access to healthcare, have a direct correlation to life expectancy (Dill & Zambrana, 2009). Intersectional scholars Dill and Zambrana (2009), in their book *Emerging Intersections: Race, Class, and Gender in Theory, Policy, and Practice*, illustrate the impact of inequality on communities of colour and how public policies reinforce systemic inequality. Engaging in intersectionality as a methodological tool brings professions like arts psychotherapies closer to advocating for change and social justice.

In a recent article in *Voices*, Gipson, Williams and Norris (2020) write about the historical and systemic neglect Black communities in the United States face at the hands of the medical and therapeutic communities. That poor and working-class people the world over have been at increased risk of getting sick and dying from COVID-19 urgently requires art therapists to recognize that wellness and healing need to be a social and intersectional concern. Gipson, Williams and Norris call on creative art therapists to reflect on their role as therapists and global citizens in the midst of the pandemic and BLM protests. They question why creative art therapists have remained silent in the face of White supremacy and anti-Black racism, questioning the complicity of creative art therapists in racial capitalism that has enabled the mental health industrial complex. They ask for a radical re-centring of Black lives by naming anti-Black racism and state-sanctioned violence in the senseless killings of George Floyd, Breonna Taylor, Ahmaud Arbery and many others. Now a national and global movement,

BLM demands that we recognize intersectionality to contextualize the embodiment of intergenerational trauma, violence, anger, hate and fear, if we want to envision methodologies of care and restorative justice. Similarly, Grzanka and colleagues (2020) have called on psychologists to examine the role of justice and challenge the boundaries in science that are complicit in reproducing inequities. They argue for the centralizing of intersectionality and social justice scholarship in the face of COVID-19, BLM protests for racial justice, and the global rise of White nationalism.

Intersectionality demands that creative art therapists engage with the social and material context of life to avoid reinforcing ideologies of neo-liberalism. In the last two decades, creative art therapists have challenged positivist epistemologies and advocated for an urgent need to consider social, cultural and political dimensions in therapeutic practice (Awais & Yali, 2013; Boston & Short, 1998; George, Green & Blackwell, 2005; Gipson, 2019; Gipson, Williams & Norris, 2020; Hedley, 2013; Ravichandran, 2019; Sajnani, 2016; Talwar, 2010, 2019; Talwar, Iyer & Doby-Copeland, 2004; Tillet & Tillet, 2019; Yi, 2019). A responsible model for intersectionality rests on 'citation practices that reflect intersectionality's origins in Black feminist thought and women of colour scholar-activism, as well as through analyses that reflect intersectionality's commitment to reflexivity, structural critique, and complexity' (Grzanka *et al.*, 2020, p.304).

Naming and citational practice

Intersectionality has become commonplace in our vocabulary. It is critical that creative art therapists reference and name the labour of intersectional scholars of colour, as is done throughout this book. Briefly, intersectionality arose out of the lived experiences and intellectual work of Black feminists, Latinas, lesbians of colour, and queer and disability studies scholars (Anzaldua, 1987; Crenshaw, 1989; Collins, 1990; Thompson-Garland, 2011; Weber, 2001, among others). Although the term 'intersectionality' was coined by Kimberlé Crenshaw (1989), the analysis of systemic racism and oppression began formally with the work of the radical Black feminist group Combahee River Collective (CRC) in the 1970s (Taylor, 2017). Black feminists of the CRC, such as Barbara Smith, Beverly Smith and Demita Frazier, spoke directly of oppression and how multiple intersecting identities result in new forms of suffering for Black women. Other important contributions to intersectional feminism are: Audre Lorde's (1984) essays on anti-racism and sexism and her experiences as a Black lesbian; Patricia Hill Collins's *Black Feminist Thought* (2000); Gloria Anzaldua's *Borderlands/La Frontera* (1987); Gloria Anzaldua and Cherrie Moraga's *This Bridge Called My Back:*

Writings by Radical Women of Color (1981); and Chandra Mohanty's (1994) and Gayatri Spivak's (1988) contributions to global feminism and critiquing post-colonial theory to foreground the writings of non-Western feminists. Black feminists and women of colour have contributed to resisting oppressive representations of identity and difference by articulating the complexity of their lived experiences under systemic oppression.

In similar ways, Black women and women of colour, along with some White women scholars in art, drama and music therapy, have contributed to intersectionality and its discourse, among them ones whose intellectual contributions have gone unrecognized. Three Black art therapists – Lucielle Venture, Sarah MacGee and Georgette Powell – worked to combat the impact of racism, racial violence, poverty and mental health in the 1970s (Gipson, 2019); Hiscox and Calisch (1998) published the first book on multiculturalism in the United States, *Tapestry of Cultural Issues in Art Therapy*; while Campbell and colleagues (1999) published *Art Therapy, Race and Culture* in the UK, along with Hogan (2000), who published *Feminist Approaches to Art Therapy*. For the past two decades, art therapists of colour have made a concerted effort to advocate for the recognition of difference through their contributions to and dialogues on cultural competence (Boston & Short, 1998; George *et al.*, 2005; Talwar *et al.*, 2004), social justice (Gipson, 2015, 2017; Talwar, 2010, 2019), racial justice (Gipson, 2015; Williams, 2018) and cultural humility (Jackson, 2019).

Self-reflexivity and critical consciousness

Self-reflexivity has increasingly gained attention in the arts psychotherapies and is a focus of each chapter of this book. Self-reflexivity is a method of knowledge construction in the therapeutic process that is bi-directional, using the 'self' as a point of reference. A reflexive approach implies that therapists question the cultural, political and social forces that have shaped their understanding of cultural difference, and it needs to be distinguished from countertransference, which refers to the emotional reactions of the therapist. The concepts of the 'unconscious' and 'countertransference' hold tremendous power as therapeutic concepts for accessing the unknown layers of the mind. Many believe that the visual imagery produced in a therapy session is an objective means of reaching the unconscious or unknown parts of the self. An intersectional analysis questions the relationship between knowledge production and practice – that is, questioning how we know what we know. The unconscious and countertransference, from a psychological perspective, are 'closed off' to the client and therapist (Talwar, 2010). If a social and cultural analysis is centralized, the therapeutic relationship becomes a bi-directional one that accounts for the social positioning of the therapist and client and the social and historical locations that have shaped their lived experiences (Talwar, 2019). 'This means understanding how culture, society, politics, and institutions work to shape our interactions and understanding of cultural difference' (Talwar, 2019, p.67). Lévesque (2007) argues that by recognizing prevailing power structures, art therapists can become advocates and reduce the impact of oppressive systems that entrap the people we serve. Developing self-reflectivity is therefore directly linked to moving towards critical consciousness; it is achieved by uncovering our implicit biases, cultural beliefs, and the values that are embedded in, and the power of, historical and social systems oppressing those we serve.

Intersectionality and structural critique

Intersectionality has often been confused with identity politics. Conservatives and liberals exploit the confusion to argue for the politics of identity without any analysis of power, privilege or oppression. Intersectionality demands that we examine the social construction of the art therapies and the historical discourses that have shaped our professions and 'reinforced the normative versus the deviant body' (Talwar, 2019, p.19). By doing so, art therapists will be better equipped to help clients understand mental health stigma and the cultural forces that produce emotions of shame, guilt and fear. Although it is critical to engage in self-reflexive practice and social positioning, it is equally important to decentre Whiteness on the institutional and structural level to challenge the epistemological frameworks that have shaped art therapy practice, education and mental health (Eastwood, 2021; Hamrick & Byma, 2017). If our professions are to remain viable fields of inquiry, we need to critique the methodological and epistemological frameworks that have shaped them, to ask who benefits from the positivist and apolitical stance undergirding therapeutic practice. We need to hold our national organizations, like the American Art Therapy Association and the British Association of Art Therapists, accountable for the policies and initiatives that have caused harm to non-normative bodies and people of colour (George *et al.*, 2020). Decentring Whiteness is a moral issue for mental health practitioners, and fighting White supremacy an ethical imperative (Eastwood, 2021; Hamrick & Byma, 2017; Spanierman & Smith, 2017).

With the rise of White nationalism across the globe, Grzanka, Gonzalez and Spanierman (2019) ask that mental health professionals assess their tools for combating White supremacy. Offering a critical conceptual framework, the authors ask for a commitment to anti-racist and anti-oppressive praxis in 'research, psychotherapy and advocacy' (Grzanka *et al.*, 2019, p.481), one that focuses on intersectionality, identifying racial affect and allyship. As such, it is critical that the training of arts psychotherapists and creative arts therapists include a sustained focus on 'Whiteness, racism, [and] White Supremacy' (Grzanka *et al.*, 2019, p.482). A structural critique arising from lived experience focuses on the embodiment of the social and material conditions of daily life, the laws and policies that have reinforced inequality, and the insidious impact of trauma and violence in the lives of poor, racialized, working class, disabled and sexually minoritized people – all topics that this book addresses. Understanding structural critique and complexity is an act of radical empathy and caring that is illuminated in this book. Chapters in this book examine arts psychotherapies rooted in a social justice praxis that examines trauma not just as a psychological issue, but an intersectional one. This book adds to the cultural turn in the creative arts therapies and arts psychotherapies, a much-needed critical engagement.

References

Anzaldua, G. (1987). *Borderlands/La Frontera*. San Francisco, CA: Aunt Luke Books.

Anzaldua, G. & Moraga, C. (1981). *This Bridge Called My Back: Writings by Radical Women of Color*. Bloomington, IN: Third Woman Press.

Awais, Y. J. & Yali, A. M. (2013). A call for diversity: The need to recruit and retain ethnic minority art therapy students in art therapy. *Art Therapy: Journal of the American Art Therapy Association, 30*(3), 130–134. doi:10.1080/07421656.2013.819284.

Boston, C. & Short, G. (1998). Art Therapy: An Afrocentric Approach. In A. Hiscox and A. Calisch (eds) *Tapestry of Cultural Issues in Art Therapy* (pp.36–48). London: Jessica Kingsley Publishers.

Campbell, J., Liebmann, M., Brooks, F., Jones, J. & Ward, C. (1999). *Art Therapy, Race and Culture*. London: Jessica Kingsley Publishers.

Collins, P. H. (1990). *Black Feminist Thought: Knowledge, Consciousness, and the Politics of Empowerment*. London: Routledge.

Collins, P. H. & Bilge, S. (2016). *Intersectionality*. Cambridge: Polity Press.

Crenshaw, K. (1989). Demarginalizing the intersection of race and sex: A black feminist critique of antidiscrimination doctrine, feminist theory and antiracist politics. *University of Chicago Legal Forum, 1*(8), 139–176.

Dill, B. T. & Zambrana, R. E. (eds) (2009). *Emerging Intersections: Race, Class, and Gender in Theory, Policy, and Practice*. New Brunswick, NJ: Rutgers University Press.

Eastwood, C. (2021). White privilege and art therapy in the UK: Are we doing the work? *International Journal of Art Therapy*. doi:10.1080/17454832.2020.1856159.

George, J., Greene, B. & Blackwell, M. (2005). Three voices on multiculturalism from the art therapy classroom. *Art Therapy: Journal of the American Art Therapy Association, 22*(3), 132–138.

George, J., Yancy, G., Sharpe, D. & Moore, A. (2020). Taking a pulse of the American Art Therapy Association's values: A study of a nonprofit organization in conflict. *The Psychologist-Manager Journal*. Advance online publication. http://dx.doi.org/10.1037/mgr0000109.

Gipson, L. (2015). Is cultural competence enough? Deepening social justice pedagogy in art therapy. *Art Therapy: Journal of the American Art Therapy Association, 32*(3), 142–145. doi:10.1080/07421656.2015.1060835.

Gipson, L. (2017). Challenging neoliberalism and multicultural love in art therapy. *Art Therapy: Journal of the American Art Therapy Association, 34*(3), 112–117. doi: 10.1080/07421656.2017.1353326.

Gipson, L. (2019). Envisioning Black Women's Consciousness in Art Therapy. In S. K. Talwar (ed.) *Art Therapy for Social Justice: Radical Intersections* (pp.96–120). New York, NY: Routledge.

Gipson, L., Williams, B. & Norris, M. (2020). Three Black women's reflections on COVID-19 and creative arts therapies: Then and now. *Voices, 20*(2), 1–5. https://doi.org/10.15845/voices.v20i2.3115.

Grzanka, P., Flores, M. J., VanDaalen, R. A. & Velez, G. (2020). Intersectionality in psychology: Translational science for social justice. *Translational Issues in Psychological Science, 6*(4), 304–313. https://dx.doi.org/10.1037/tps0000276.

Grzanka, P., Gonzalez, K. A. & Spanierman, L. A. (2019). White supremacy and counseling psychology: A critical-conceptual framework. *The Counseling Psychologist, 47*(4), 478–529.

Hamrick, C. & Byma, C. (2017). Know history, know self: Art therapists' responsibility to dismantle white supremacy. *Art Therapy: Journal of the American Art Therapy Association, 34*(3), 106–111.

Hedley, S. (2013). *Experiencing Race as a Music Therapist: Personal Narratives*. Gilsum, NH: Barcelona Publishers.

Hiscox, A. R. & Calisch, A. C. (eds) (1998). *Tapestry of Cultural Issues in Art Therapy*. London: Jessica Kingsley Publishers.

Hogan, S. (ed.) (2000). *Feminist Approaches to Art Therapy*. London: Jessica Kingsley Publishers.

Jackson, L. (2019). *Cultural Humility in Art Therapy*. London: Jessica Kingsley Publishers.

Kelly, L. (2019). How moderate teachers perpetuate educational oppression. Retrieved 10 August 2020 from https://medium.com/@mslisamkelly/how-moderate-teachers-perpetuate-educational-oppression-fc9479a661a7.

Kuri, E. (2017). Toward an ethical application of intersectionality in art therapy. *Art Therapy: Journal of the American Art Therapy Association, 34*(3), 118–122. doi:10.1080/07421656.2017.1358023.

Lévesque, F. (2007). *Critical Art Therapy: A Third Perspective*. Retrieved 10 August 2020 from www.researchgate.net/publication/355032101_Critical_Art_Therapy_a_Third_Perspective.

Lorde, A. (1984). *Sister Outsider*. Trumansburg, NY: Crossing Press.

Love, B. (2019). *We Want to Do More Than Survive: Abolitionist Teaching and the Pursuit of Educational Freedom*. Boston, MA: Beacon Press Books.

Mohanty, C. (1994). *Feminism Without Borders: Decolonizing Theory, Practicing Solidarity*. Durham, NC: Duke Press.

Ravichandran, S. (2019). Radical Caring and Art Therapy: Decolonizing Immigration and Gender Violence Services. In S. K. Talwar (ed.) *Art Therapy for Social Justice: Radical Intersections* (pp.144–160). New York, NY: Routledge.

Sajnani, N. (2016). Borderlands: Diversity and social justice in drama therapy. *Drama Therapy Review, 2*(1), 1–3.

Spanierman, L. B. & Smith, L. (2017). Confronting White hegemony: A moral imperative for the helping professions. *The Counseling Psychologist, 45*, 727–736. doi:10.1177/0011000017719550.

Spivak, G. (1988). Can the Subaltern Speak? In C. Nelson (ed.) *Marxism and the Interpretation of Culture*. Champaign, IL: University of Illinois Press.

Talwar, S. (2010). An intersectional framework for race, class, gender, and sexuality in art therapy. *Art Therapy: Journal of the American Art Therapy Association, 27*(1), 11–17. doi:10.1080/07421656.2010.10129567.

Talwar, S. (2019). *Art Therapy for Social Justice: Radical Intersections*. New York, NY: Routledge.

Talwar, S., Iyer, J. & Doby-Copeland, C. (2004). The invisible veil: Changing paradigms in the art therapy profession. *Art Therapy: Journal of the American Art Therapy Association, 21*(1), 44–48. doi:10.1080/07421656.2004.10129325.

Taylor, K. Y. (2017). *How We Get Free*. Chicago, IL: Haymarket Books.

Thomson-Garland, R. (2011). Integrating Disability, Transforming Feminist Theory. In K. Q. Hall (ed.) *Feminist Disability Theory* (pp.13–47). Bloomington, IN: Indiana University Press.

Tillet, S. & Tillet, S. (2019). 'You Want to be Well?' Self-Care as a Black Feminist Intervention in Art Therapy. In S. K. Talwar (ed.) *Art Therapy for Social Justice: Radical Intersections* (pp.123–143). New York, NY: Routledge.

Weber, L. (2001). *Understanding Race, Class, Gender and Sexuality: A Conceptual Framework.* New York, NY: McGraw-Hill.

Williams, B. (2018). Unapologetically black: Seven questions and poems that explore how race performs in clinical practice. *Drama Therapy Review, 4*(2), 223–232. doi:10.1386/dtr.4.2.223_1.

Yi, S. (2019). Res(crip)ting Art Therapy: Disability Culture as a Social Justice Intervention. In S. K. Talwar (ed.) *Art Therapy for Social Justice: Radical Intersections* (pp.161–177). New York, NY: Routledge.

Introduction

JESSICA COLLIER AND CORRINA EASTWOOD

The idea to create this book came while we were both visiting lecturers on an art psychotherapy postgraduate programme in the UK. We found ourselves frustrated by the absence of robust and embedded critical thinking in our profession surrounding systemic oppression and discrimination, the complexity of social inequalities, and the power hierarchy inherent in the therapeutic relationship and the institution. Recommended reading lists across the arts psychotherapies programmes, perhaps reflecting the profession as a whole, continue to include outdated, often intrinsically racist and misogynistic principles. These are rarely contextualized or critiqued to make the content and theories more useful or relevant to contemporary arts psychotherapy practice. We felt that a deeper analysis of what has been overlooked is vital if we are to respond to ever louder calls for the arts psychotherapies professions to meaningfully understand and adapt to the needs of clients and colleagues who may not fit the historical dominant norm.

This apathy towards questioning the status quo seems rooted to some extent in the idea that heterosexual, cisgendered, White, middle-class women and men, who represent the majority of the profession in the UK, are not in a position, nor have a responsibility, to discuss inequity and discrimination, and that this should be left to the minority of colleagues in our field who identify as a 'different' race, class, gender, sexuality or other intersecting identity. In contrast to this, we felt the discussion needed to be had by everybody practising, teaching, training, researching or simply curious about the arts psychotherapies in the UK and worldwide, even if – especially if – this might feel difficult, tentative or erroneous. If we undertake arts psychotherapy practice without embracing uncertainty or potential discomfort; if we cannot accept that we might get things wrong; if we don't question our own prejudices and experiences and how they influence our practice, then we are not reflecting on our inherent position of power seriously enough.

Intersectionality has travelled a long way both academically and colloquially in areas of feminist theory, gender, race and queer studies, activism, psychotherapeutic thinking and more recently in popular culture. The term was first used by Kimberlé Crenshaw, an American civil rights advocate and law professor, in her influential paper 'Demarginalizing the intersection of race and sex: A Black feminist critique of antidiscrimination doctrine, feminist theory and antiracist politics' (1989), in which she suggested the metaphor of a crossroads to examine race and gender discrimination combined. This paper considered the difficulties in establishing the origins of an accident if it were to occur at such an intersection, and argued that a true understanding of the oppression of Black women could only be understood at the 'intersect' of being both Black and a woman. Crenshaw's term named core principles already defining the social justice actions of many autonomous movements led by women of colour in the US earlier in the twentieth century; movements that challenged colonialism, racism and sexism (Collins & Bilge, 2016).

Thus, the primary concerns of intersectionality were born of activism and social justice work prompted by social inequalities. They focused on issues of social context and complexity, as well as the relationality of power. Women of colour specifically felt the impact of occupying multiple social locations and of falling between the gaps of equality movements and groups that were designed to support their oppression. Crenshaw (1989) notes that Black women's experiences were much broader than the general categories that discrimination discourse provided. Previously, Black feminist writers such as Toni Cade Bambara (1970) and Frances Beal (1969) were exploring the experiences of Black women using intersectional frameworks that considered issues of race, gender and class as they were simultaneously experienced, albeit using different vocabularies at the time. Indeed, Sojourner Truth's speech 'Ain't I a Woman?', given to an audience of White feminists at a women's rights convention as long ago as 1851, also asserts strong intersectional sentiments.

In the late 1970s and 1980s, shared vocabularies began to emerge to suggest a more collective use of intersectionality within social movements. Educational institutions were transformed by 'bottom-up' social movement politics, hastening the development of intersectionality as a form of critical inquiry within academia. Later, more visible social protest against exclusion occurred 'outside' institutions and gave way to 'insider' activism. Institutions responded by recruiting the very people they once excluded – feminist women of colour, who brought a social movement ethos with them. Alongside this was an understanding of the importance of identity politics and the multi-dimensional ways in which identity markers intersect to impact experience within societal systems of power. 'Had social movements not fought for the inclusion of women of colour in colleges and universities, conceptions of intersectionality advanced by social movement actors were unlikely to have emerged within the academy' (Collins & Bilge, 2016, p.78).

There followed a time of challenge, with institutional transformation and the survival of critical inquiry originating in social movements appearing to depend on an adherence to the existing norms in academia. This often included a need to defend social justice and political sensibilities within any academic context, in the first instance. 'Scholars engaged in building programmes in women's studies, ethnic studies and in lesbian, gay, bisexual and transgender studies have had their intellect, their scholarship, their professionalism and even their sanity questioned' (Dill, 2009, p.229). Collaboration between the various new fields of study brought multiple histories of social inequalities and oppressions. The overarching terminology or framework that intersectionality provides seemed to address many of these challenges of coalition and, in turn, academic legitimacy and incorporation.

Crenshaw is credited with naming intersectionality, and in giving it legitimacy in the field of academic inquiry. She formulated clear narratives illustrating structural power, while simultaneously honouring intersectionality's foundations in social movement settings. Her focus on the experiences of women of colour as a Black feminist, and the building of her argument from a 'ground-up' perspective, drew directly from the experiences of women of colour in relation to their complex social locations and mirrored existing areas in academia, as it adapted to this new context. A further irony surrounding structural power and normative practice is the consequential distancing of intersectional thinking as critical inquiry, now part of institutional and academic incorporation, from intersectional practice drawn from grassroots politics. The simplistic attributing of the founding of intersectionality to Crenshaw alone, without acknowledging the contextual social and historical complexities of its inception as a form of critical inquiry and practice, fails to practise what we hope to preach. However, it does also give a clear example of the way in which dominant thinking in practice, and normative practices in academia, can be steadfast and systematic in silencing the voices of the 'other'.

Arts psychotherapists have long advocated for greater consideration of identity, politics and social justice in their work (Talwar, Iyer & Doby-Copeland, 2004; Talwar, 2010; Hogan, 2012; Kapitan, 2015). Some have noted the way in which the profession continues to resist the contextualizing of clinical thinking and experience within a social and political framework that examines identity markers such as race, sexuality and gender in relation to professional practice, training and research. As practitioners, we have an ethical obligation to explore the unconscious motives and biases that may lead us to avoid examining uncomfortable issues of identity. In considering the unconscious, we could note Crenshaw's less well-known metaphor of the 'basement' (1989), which explores social hierarchies and systemic injustice. Crenshaw invites the reader to imagine a deep basement containing disadvantaged people, stacked with feet on shoulders; those at the bottom experiencing the full array of disadvantages with no clear view of what is above them. The heads of those at the top brush against the basement ceiling. In efforts to correct some issues of domination, those on the ground floor may admit those from the basement who are nearest the ceiling. For those at the bottom however, the ground floor, even the ceiling, remains out of reach. Carastathis (2016) reflects on the significance of the overlooking of this metaphor, acknowledging societal structures of dominance and subordination in relation to intersectionality's ability to travel more 'comfortably'. Kuri (2017) encourages the predominantly White demographic of arts psychotherapists worldwide to avoid co-opting intersectionality in 'comfortable' ways, and instead become critically aware of theories and histories of how Whiteness continues to influence current values and biases in arts psychotherapy. This could be applied to all areas of privilege.

As arts psychotherapists working within the creative, visual and metaphorical realm, we are well equipped to ask ourselves what happens to intersectionality if we detach it from the 'basement'. Crenshaw continues to outline her ongoing belief that without naming a problem, it cannot be visible, stating that if the problem is not visible, then it cannot be solved. Detaching from the metaphorical 'basement', and avoiding naming the problem, corresponds elegantly with the primary aim of the psychodynamic art psychotherapies in which 'unknowable' or 'unnameable' unconscious patterns that manifest detrimentally can be made conscious and 'knowable' through the making of images and narratives which alert the maker to the problem they were previously oblivious to. Intersectionality regards the naming of an un-named problem as an essential part of the discourse and a possible means of pursuing a greater understanding of identity, oppression and difference.

Each chapter in *Intersectionality in the Arts Psychotherapies* is written with a varying degree of focus on the key principles of intersectionality and its foundations. Namely, the intersecting ways in which identity markers meet to form an individual's unique experiences; self-reflexivity in relation to individual and collective social location; its roots within social change activity; and the contextualizing of social, cultural and political power.

Collins and Bilge (2016) write of the varied and sometimes contradictory ways in which intersectionality is understood, and this book may illustrate the ambiguity and adaptation of intersectional approaches in arts psychotherapy practice, from the unique locations of the therapist authors and the individuals they work with.

In the opening chapter of the book, Corrina Eastwood highlights the importance of bringing together reflexive psychodynamic and intersectional thinking. Both these ideas foreground the centrality of understanding the unconscious as a primary aspect of the therapeutic relationship. Throughout this personal and emotive chapter, Eastwood further elucidates the necessity for the therapist of exploring, acknowledging and integrating their own identity and narrative honestly, including using personal art-based inquiry or art-based auto-ethnography as a means of self-reflexivity, so as to better recognize unconscious motivations and provocations the therapist may have internalized, and that may come alive in the therapeutic encounter.

Historical narratives, and the immeasurable, transgenerational consequences that supervene traumatic histories experienced by oppressed peoples, are also the focus of Chapter 2, in which Wabriya King reconsiders attachment theory. While this is widely accepted by arts psychotherapists as a foundational principle on which interpersonal relationships can be understood, King asks how we have come to pathologize family bonds that do not conform to the White, middle-class standards conceived and established as 'normal' by practitioners and researchers. How is it, wonders King, that we have created a universally accepted formulation of human connection in the absence of any consideration of the effects of race and racism and the violent subjugation of millions of families? S. J. Langer also reflects on the intergenerational effects of trauma and describes, in Chapter 3, his reaction when a student points out his overlooking of the toxic effects of slavery in the US during a seminar. Langer uses this oversight to examine his countertransference through an intersectional lens. This includes an emphasis on the importance of humility and tolerance of the therapist's discomfort, and the essential recognition that knowledge, or access to knowledge, may not be enough to avert countertransferential resistance, prejudice or the limits of our own observations. Indeed, reflecting further on his own practice and experience, Langer suggests that we must acknowledge our resistance to examining our countertransference as a signal of disruption. We should consider it the very means to avoid the rhetoric of privilege, thereby promoting cultural competence while practising with varied and diverse clients, with an emphasis in this chapter on transgender and genderqueer experience.

In Chapter 4, Georgina Evans focuses on the body. Many of the individuals we work with as arts psychotherapists may describe a feeling of psychic fragmentation. Evans uses her own experience, growing up as a woman of colour on two different continents, as a starting point for discussion around responses to outward perception and the notion of identity in relation to social context. She constructs her argument using a trilateral framework of the 'medical body', the 'cultural body' and the 'psychological body', and explores these ideas through a wide-ranging survey of philosophical and intersectional ideas and an illuminating clinical vignette. Sarah Furneaux-Blick also places her own experience at the heart of Chapter 5. Arguing against neoliberal ideology, which she suggests suppresses the possibility of true diversity or equality, Furneaux-Blick reflects on the dichotomy of simultaneously possessing privileges and oppressions. Through self-reflection and the examination of the countertransference she felt within a therapeutic relationship with an underprivileged young boy, she shines a light on the importance and complexity of recognizing and accepting internalized feelings of both guilt and shame at her White, working-class background, and the ways in which these feelings are manufactured externally in our social structures. Corrina Eastwood continues this analysis of internalized shame in her moving case study in Chapter 6, once again highlighting the centrality of self-reflexivity as a key principle of intersectional thinking. Retrospectively, Eastwood notes the gaps and blinkered spots in her practice, including the denial of her own social privation as a woman from the Gypsy, Romani, Traveller community. In a detailed case study, she acknowledges that while she could make use of her feminist principles to examine the gender disadvantages she and her client might share, she was less able to comprehend mutual oppressions of race or ethnicity. Eastwood writes of her developing awareness regarding her own identity and the parallels this internal realization had with her client's experience. Using imagery in the sessions, including intuitively drawing portraits, enabled both the client and the therapist to feel properly seen and heard, while tolerating uncertainty and the complexity of their work together.

This book would not exist without the generous consent of the people the authors have worked alongside. In Chapter 7, Jessica Collier questions the notion of consent from a different perspective – in relation to sexual violence and rape mythology. In her broad inquiry, Collier draws from her own experience to consider the potential risk of unconscious retaliation when the therapist works with a sex offender and has themselves been a victim of sexual assault. She considers the shift in the power hierarchy that may take place between victim and perpetrator, both interpersonally and intrapersonally, and the shared internalization of shame embodied in both positions. She then reflects on how this may be complicated further if the therapist has also experienced homophobia in relation to sexual violence, intensifying the invalidation of identity and agency. Collier further considers the potential equivocality of consent, exacerbated by the wide cultural acceptance of sexual violence, while simultaneously considering the disadvantages experienced by the sexual offender she worked with. Chapter 8 also considers shame and sexual violence from the perception of the survivor therapist. Applying the important observation that we must not collude in the cultural silencing of sexual trauma, and using vignettes from groups to demonstrate her ideas, Sejal Chad's thoughtful, deeply researched and revealing chapter asks important questions about therapist disclosure. Chad explores the potential effects disclosure might have on clinical work, including the influence on boundaries, transference responses and client tolerance of exposure. She also considers the consequence for survivors of contemporary societal expectations, and the ongoing remnants of Freud's repudiation of his own patients' sexual traumas and his characterization of these women as fantasists. The undercurrents of this disavowal, argues Chad, can still be felt in psychotherapy trainings today, where sexual trauma is contemplated only as the experience of the client and not of the therapist.

Eleni Tsolka introduces Chapter 9 with an eloquent analogy that music, like identity, exists only as an intersection of different components coming together. She goes on to describe the multiple elements embedded in her work as a music therapist in the Palestinian territories, feeling culturally out of her comfort zone – literally in a war zone – but also working with unfamiliarity and the unconscious. Tsolka, a Greek national trained in the UK, explores the myriad intersections of the group she worked with, including differences relating to the social expectations around gender, social class, language, religion and ethnicity and the everyday infringement of basic human rights. She examines her position retrospectively as potentially being perceived as an 'oppressor' opposed by the group. She also reflects on her unconscious internalization of the position of woman and immigrant in the group, manifest initially in her passive musical responses and becoming conscious only when thought about reflexively. Jaspal Kaur Lotay also writes about culture, highlighting the significance of faith and religion. In Chapter 10, she reflects on her experiences developing arts psychotherapy practice within her own community, as a Sikh Punjabi woman. She describes the resistance she encountered when setting up an arts psychotherapy pilot project; feeling marginalized from outside her community by her training university and tutors, as well as from within her community when challenging patriarchal norms and naming gender inequalities. Kaur Lotay notes the impossibility of embodying and translating Western psychoanalytic concepts into a language her community can give meaning to, as both a concrete example of outsider misunderstanding, and an example of different culturally specific ways of thinking, learning and knowing. She equates this with her strong countertransference feelings that she is perceived as 'difficult to reach', mirroring the experience of her clients as seen from the White institution. Kairo Maynard further discusses the experience of being perceived as 'difficult' in Chapter 11, where she describes a young Black girl's struggle to realize her own identity within the context of a systemically racist institution. Maynard underlines the many ways in which Black people, and Black girls, are more susceptible to mental health issues due to societal disadvantage, but also through the racist and misogynist stereotyping they must navigate to be accepted. This includes the damaging double-bind Black girls and women face when they are perceived as either 'subordinate' or 'angry', and is highlighted here when Maynard's client is described as challenging and 'scary', merely for expressing her emotions. This essential chapter emphasizes the importance of representation in the dramatherapy room, but simultaneously observes the contradiction and complexity that while Maynard herself is a Black woman, she cannot speak for all Black girls and women. In the therapeutic relationship, Maynard astutely suggests, there is both a sameness *and* a difference; the ultimate difference of self and other.

The repudiation of difference between male and female experience, and the horrifying prevalence of gendered violence and its cultural acceptance, is the basis of Chapter 12. Jessica Collier explores the damage done when entrenched misogynistic myths and systems are internalized and colluded with by society, and by the marginalized women they are intended to oppress, particularly women who have already transgressed socially sanctioned standards of femininity as a consequence of their disadvantage. Collier seeks to understand better the unconscious mechanisms that underlie pervasive sexism and misogyny and the widely held assumption that gender hierarchy is natural or biological. Through an expansive discussion incorporating sociological and psychoanalytic concepts, an arts psychotherapy clinical vignette and reflection on what we can learn through the thoughtful appreciation of work by established artists, Collier considers the profoundly harmful consequences the tolerance of violence towards and subjugation of women has on the whole of society.

Intolerance of gender diversity, neurodiversity and disability, and the damage discrimination does to people with these intersecting identities, is the subject of Chapter 13. Informed by her own experiences as a music therapist, Naomi Rowe reveals the continued prejudice faced by LGBTQ+ (lesbian, gay, bisexual, transgender, queer/questioning and others) individuals and highlights the double discrimination encountered by transgender and bisexual people who may be excluded by both straight and gay communities. Rowe also considers the pressure that conforming to constricting concepts of gender identity and sexuality has on neurotypical and neurodiverse people, offering troubling statistics showing the significant impact on their mental and physical health. Rowe highlights the frequency with which LGBTQ+ individuals are pathologized, and the shocking lengths heteronormative medical and psychological practice has gone to 'fix' them. This includes attempts to surgically 'correct' the bodies of intersex infants, conversion therapy to 'cure' homosexuality and behavioural therapy designed to make children on the autism spectrum appear 'normal'. Rowe offers her thoughts on how arts psychotherapists might challenge their own unconscious biases so as to practise safely and inclusively. The fundamental necessity of inclusion, intersectional, feminist values and social action are at the heart of Chapter 14, in which Noa Yeheskel Baum, Gillian W. Datlen, Corrina Eastwood and Charlotte Elliston write, from different perspectives, about the founding of Outskirts, an intersectional art therapy charity. In addition to a focus on the ethically informed values and ethos of their work, the authors accentuate their practice as conceived within a complex societal system in which the use of intersectional approaches might promote vigilance in respecting every individual's experiences and trauma as well as engaging clients who might otherwise be excluded. Particularly significant to this chapter is the inclusion of the voice of the client herself. The final chapter calls for a more inclusive learning experience of collective inquiry, participation and the addressing of social inequality. Hayley Berman challenges the pedagogical and professional presumption that academic 'knowledge' must prevail, instead advocating for the interchange of ideas and the discovery of ways of coming together through the explicit invitation to name, make overt and engage with feelings of otherness and sameness. Berman considers this through a personal lens, in the context of her experience of growing up in South Africa and coming to the UK, and also through a group analytic framework in which traditional forms of leadership are disrupted, while a psychosocial, democratic, holding and containing space from which to acknowledge economic, familial and social injustices is offered. Berman suggests that, to be meaningfully inclusive, leadership should not be hierarchical, but collaborative and relational.

Intersectionality in the Arts Psychotherapies is intended as a starting point for discussion and the sharing of ideas and experiences by those interested in developing arts psychotherapies theory and practice as a socially inclusive shared endeavour. We thank all our contributors and the individuals they worked with who so generously gave their permission for their stories to be included. This book is dedicated to them.

The matter of language as language matters

Throughout this book, the language chosen has been considered by each of the contributors and used in the way that feels most faithful to their personal experiences and the ideas they are communicating. Acronyms have been used by some authors, although it is accepted that these can be reductive and neglect the complexity of the diverse minorities they attempt to describe. BAME (Black, Asian and Minority Ethnic) in particular is coming to be seen as problematic in that it recognizes some communities, while overlooking others, and merges divergent minority ethnic groups together. For some Black people, it does not adequately highlight the damaging impact of colourism, and for many White-passing groups, such as GRT (Gypsy, Roma Traveller), the acronym invalidates their experiences of racism. In some chapters, capitalization is used to describe ethnic groups and also Whiteness, thereby inviting the reader to understand this not as a passive adjective to describe skin colour, but to make Whiteness visible as a politicized construction. Other contributors choose not to capitalize 'black', commenting on and historically contextualizing a lens of politicized Blackness in ways appropriate to their chapters and subjective experience. Some authors explicitly challenge language use, for example clarifying terminology such as 'transgender' as an adjective and the complexities surrounding this, or the potentially imperialistic and outdated nature of terminology such as 'ethnic minority'. Others may tentatively use this terminology, while acknowledging 'minority' in the context of societal power dynamics rather than those who are fewer in number, or propose alternative terms such as 'global majority' to describe any community of people that isn't the White 'norm'. The word survivor has been used when writing about those who have experienced abuse. We recognize that some people may prefer alternative terms, but have used survivor for the purpose of clarity and continuity, while acknowledging difference of preference and perspective. We also note that language such as the word Gypsy should be recognized as a racial slur, used only by those from the GRT community and of Romani descent, if they choose to self-identify this way. As with all language that marginalizes or is persecutory, this is due to the historical and current use of the word to dehumanize and oppress. We wish to highlight the importance of language and the ways in which it can be used to mark, hoard, concede and abuse power, and the importance of a willingness to accept challenge, debate and change. We understand the choices of language used throughout this book may be wrong for some. Nevertheless, they represent an attempt at finding acceptable shared vocabularies at the time of writing.

A note on content

The chapters in this book explore complex material which some may find disturbing, including discussions around racism, misogyny, homophobia and transphobia, poverty and intergenerational trauma. In addition, experiences of addiction, violence and sexual abuse are shared in some of the case vignettes.

References

Bambara, T. (1970). *The Black Women: An Anthology*. New York, NY: Signet.

Beal, F. (1969). Double Jeopardy: To be Black and Female. In B. Guy-Sheftall (ed.) *Words of Fire: An Anthology of African American Feminist Thought* (pp.146–155). New York, NY: New York Press.

Carastathis, A. (2016). *Intersectionality: Origins, Contestations, Horizons*. Lincoln & London: University Press.

Collins, P. H. & Bilge, S. (2016). *Intersectionality*. Cambridge: Polity Press.

Crenshaw, K. (1989). Demarginalizing the intersection of race and sex: A Black feminist critique of antidiscrimination doctrine, feminist theory and antiracist politics. *University of Chicago Legal Forum, 1*(8), 139–176.

Dill, B. T. (2009). Intersections, Identities, and Inequalities in Higher Education. In B. T. Dill and R. Zambrana (eds) *Emerging Intersection: Race, Class and Gender in Theory, Policy and Practice*. New Brunswick, NJ: Rutgers University Press.

Hogan, S. (2012). Postmodernist But Not Post-Feminist: A Feminist Postmodernist Approach to Working With New Mothers. In H. Burt (ed.) *Art Therapy and Postmodernism: Creative Healing Through a Prism*. London: Jessica Kingsley Publishers.

Kapitan, L. (2015). Social action in practice: Shifting the ethno-centric lens in cross-cultural art therapy encounters. *Art Therapy: Journal of the American Art Therapy Association, 32*(3), 104–111.

Kuri, E. (2017). Toward an Ethical Application of Intersectionality in Art Therapy. *Art Therapy: Journal of the American Art Therapy Association, 34*(3), 118–122. doi:10.1080/07421656.2017.1358023.

Talwar, S. (2010). An intersectional framework for race, class, gender, and sexuality in art therapy. *Journal of the American Art Therapy Association, 27*(1), 11–17.

Talwar, S., Iyer, J. & Doby-Copeland, C. (2004). The invisible veil: Changing paradigms in the art therapy profession. *Art Therapy: Journal of the American Art Therapy Association, 21*(1), 44–48.

Chapter 1

Intersectional Reflexivity: Art Psychotherapy Practice and Self

— CORRINA EASTWOOD —

Introduction

This chapter will consider self-reflexivity from both personal and professional perspectives, exploring key principles of intersectional thinking. In honouring the origins of intersectional thought, that being in grassroots women-of-colour-led social justice movements (Collins & Bilge, 2016), and for the context of this chapter, I define these key principles as: a focus on identity, using self-reflexivity to explore the ways in which identities can meet and interact for individuals; acknowledging social and political life in relation to Self; centralizing considerations of social justice and giving voice to marginalized communities; and understanding the relational nature of power, in individual, societal and organizational realms (Carastathis, 2016; Collins & Bilge, 2016).

Talwar (2019) notes that intersectionality begins with a focus on identity, and this chapter will model considerations of intersectional thinking as a practice framework in art therapy, by using Self as a starting point of reference for intersectional analysis of social location (Talwar, 2019). I will attempt to illustrate self-reflexivity and share personal accounts of how cultural stories have been symbolized within the visual and conceptual realms of my personal art practice, and have also supported my making of meaning, and explorations of racial, cultural identity awareness (Doby-Copeland, 2013). Art-based inquiry (Chiltern & Scotti, 2014; Kapitan, 2014; McNiff, 2013; Seregina, 2019) and art-based auto-ethnography reveal the conscious and potentially unconscious ways in which lived experience connected to identity has influenced my career as an arts therapist. I give context to the evolution of my theoretical approaches as an art therapy practitioner and my desire to create safe spaces to explore trauma related to structural and relational abuses of power in response to a developed understanding of power as a relational entity. I will explore the connections between my interest in intersectionality as a tool to analyse power and frame human experience, and my own lived experiences of both marginalization and privilege, reflecting on how this may have impacted my approach to therapeutic work. In doing so, I aim to model the complex ways in which art therapists may reflect on the entanglements of their own identities, and how this may impact on therapeutic relationships and potential responses to visual media, symbols and narratives that may relate to familial and cultural influences. I will illustrate a metaphorical stepping-in-and-out (Brown, 2017) of different parts of the Self to ethically explore the individually determined focus, agendas or potential biases in art therapy work. In exploring existing intersectional approaches utilized by art therapy practitioners, and the presence of explorations of social and political considerations in literature, discourse and curriculum, I will highlight the importance I believe such approaches may have in post-modern art therapy practice.

Intersectional reflexivity, art-based inquiry and art therapy practice

As I sit on the train travelling to visit my father in hospital, I dip into Maxine Borowsky Junge's chapter 'The Art Therapist as Social Activist: Reflections on a Life' (Junge, 2007). I am drawn to read it again in a way I avoid examining. My dad is dying of cancer and I am distracted and often lose my place when reading. I ask myself how I am going to write this chapter when my dad is dying. I consider which commitments I can reschedule, what space I can create for grieving and how I can compartmentalize enough to write. I ask myself, is writing this chapter more important than giving these feelings of grief and loss the time they deserve? Before attempting to answer this question for myself, I glance back to the book *Art Therapy and Social Action* (Kaplan, 2007):

> It has always seemed to me that a good therapist has to understand the existential world of the client as much as possible. I also believe that the good clinician not only understands the client's culture but works in the 'real world' to make it a more enhancing and nurturing environment. (Junge, 2007, p.50)

I think again about writing this chapter, my interest in intersectionality and my own and my clients' places in this 'real world'. I consider my journey in seeking theory to understand the interconnected nature of identity markers for the benefit of my clients and myself. I reflect on my past motivations and on my increased questioning of the disparities and oppressions that exist in society and the way they contribute to the trauma and distress felt by many clients, but also to the ways in which trauma is understood and 'treated' from perspectives of socially dominant epistemology and ontology.

I consider the need I had to find a way to survive this difficult work around seven years after qualifying. I was working with women with a diagnosis of borderline personality disorder, one of four art therapy posts I held at the time. I continued then, as I do now, to utilize psychodynamic theories and place importance on the understanding of unconscious processes. I sought the guidance of three supervisors in providing support for my clients, through facilitating the creation of, and bearing witness to, the processing of artworks that explored multiple, intersecting stories of injustice, abuse and trauma. I needed to find a way to understand the complexities and enmeshments of human experience in relation to identity and the part this plays in a wider social and political consideration of experience and trauma. This kind of thinking was often discouraged in supervision, where clinical focus would be brought back to the individual and family. Despite this, I needed to find a way to feel I could support personal change, but also social change in my work, and that without this dimension, art therapy had begun to feel futile.

Tillet and Tillet (2019) draw parallels between personal self-care, political organizing and the foundations of community care as a Black, feminist intervention in art therapy. For me at that time, a pursuit of social justice felt crucial to my pursuit of personal wellbeing as a practitioner, and became intrinsically linked with my art therapy work, particularly when considering gender-related oppression.

As I continued on my train journey to visit my dad, it occurred to me that the solution was not to organize myself a space to write, distinct from my grief. I did not need to separate my feelings about my dad, my loss or my identity from my practice as a therapist to coherently convey my interest in working with clients in a way that could accommodate a more nuanced understanding of client subjectivity and experience (Weber, 2001). I didn't need to find a way to write this chapter *in spite* of my experience right now, in the 'real world'. Just as with my choice to be a therapist, I find ways to work, *because of* my experiences there.

In 1998, I went to art school. Although I received a sound primary school education, I did not attend any examinations, gaining no qualifications and leaving full-time education at the age of 11. Years later, I secured a place on a BA Fine Art course on the strength of a portfolio. On the course, we were given the option to take an introduction to art therapy, run by an art therapist who I will refer to as Claire. I had taken part in some art therapy as a child. I had valued this, and drawing on my experiences of mental health services and care systems in childhood and adolescence, I felt that this was something for me.

Claire ran our first experiential session. We were asked to create artwork about family and I chose to depict a story my dad had told me since childhood. It had always been my favourite family story, passed down through generations. I am Romani Gypsy, from the Gypsy, Romani Traveller (GRT) community, and I grew up with my family keeping archetypal feeling tales alive through storytelling. Many Romanichal (English Romani) only sporadically attend formal education due to complex reasons that go beyond the practicalities of nomadic lifestyles. These include feelings of restlessness and avoidance of permanence and containment due to experiences of persecution, racism and inter- and trans-generationally transmitted trauma. Due to this, the creation of archives of Traveller experiences are also unusual. I reflected on this as I made a drawing depicting the narrative of the meeting of a baby and a snake.

My dad's childhood was spent travelling the UK. Most of his tales were about hop picking: the backbreaking work, the sense of freedom, but also the racism and exclusion he experienced in every town. He would recount narratives of being denied access to services or to enter shops or pubs, including violent acts of hate crime. These stories resonated for me and felt both similar to and different from my own experiences of growing up Romani, a generation later. He would also communicate the cultural rules and resulting mentalities that he had developed and been taught in response to societal powers and oppressions, that would protect him physically and emotionally. I observed and experienced this through the way he would interact with others, the way he modelled existence in the world and navigated through it, and through his and my mum's parenting.

Dad would tell the story of the baby and the snake as if it meant everything and nothing. He would describe that while working in the fields, the mothers would leave their babies in prams under bushes. The babies would be left with milk bottles to feed from. Once, a particular child would not settle. The baby would cry and the mother would return, seeing that the child had drunk all its milk. Yet it still cried for more. The mother discussed this with others, saying that the baby seemed starved, yet she was doing her best to feed it and the milk was always drunk. One day, on responding to her child's cries once again, the mother was horrified to find a snake near the baby, suckling from the bottle and stealing the baby's milk. The mother then realized that the milk she was doing her best to provide was being stolen from her and her baby day after day, as her child grew more and more distressed.

In a tutorial with Claire, as we discussed essay writing support due to my lack of secondary school education, I described the story behind the image I had created. I commented that it was just a Traveller story and that I didn't know if it were true or not. I gave it little significance, and my sense of the potential of this narrative to symbolize that which is stolen from persecuted communities, impacting on their abilities to grow healthy and thrive, existed only on the very edges of my awareness. Claire responded with a lingering gaze, commenting, 'It feels very true, doesn't it?'

We discussed the support I might be able to access at the university and again Claire commented on my dad in this same measured way: 'He didn't go to school...' She paused. '...and you didn't go to school.' I remember thinking that art therapists are very strange, then asked myself why Claire would imply these things are meaningful and connected when they just weren't!

Over 20 years later, I began to make the connections and unravel the entanglements that Claire had pointed me towards and acknowledge the intersect of where my experience had met my dad's, and where we had both met a wider cultural and political history of intolerance of difference and prejudice. Talwar (2010) observes that knowledge is situated within its historical and geographical context. Knowledge can be a basis of power, and power gained via knowledge is never a static entity, but relational (Talwar, 2019) and liable to shifts and change. Indeed, epistemology can be culturally determined, with the capacity to 'define' often being the prerogative of those in power. As I confided in Claire my dad's telling of a culturally important story, she allowed us the space for racial and cultural empowerment, through the defining of our own narratives. I had recounted a story that used symbolism to convey a possibly coded, possibly unconscious testimony of oppression, and at that moment multiple personal, social and political systems impacted on my ability to process a potentially transformative awakening to a shared predicament (Hocoy, 2007). I also simultaneously experienced positions of both privilege and marginalization and was enabled to engage meaningfully in a process of defining/redefining, as an empowering and subversive creative activity. In 1998, I was in the last cohort of students in the UK to undergo means testing to secure government fee payment enabling access to higher education for those from low-income families (Anderson, 2016). Due to this political/social context, I was the first in my family to attend university and engage in this specific process of coming to know. The tide of marketization which has flowed in one direction since has ensured that to date I am the last.

Many years after qualifying as an art therapist, I began the process of taking my art practice into filmmaking. I decided to film my dad and other family members to capture the story of the baby and the snake. I wanted to archive the experience of GRT marginalization and use the story to juxtapose other stories I had been told of societal and institutional racism and violence, experienced, witnessed and sometimes re-enacted for generations in my community. Research conducted by The Traveller Movement, compiled in the report *'The last acceptable form of racism?'* (The Traveller Movement, 2017), illustrates the prejudice GRT people face in their everyday lives in the UK. The report findings show that 91 per cent of us have experienced discrimination because of our ethnicity and 70 per cent have experienced discrimination in education.

This kind of data is tangible evidence of the experiences of GRT people, yet I wanted the final cut of *The Baby And The Snake* (Figure 1.1) to explore something more tacit and less directly verbally communicable. Much like the making of unconscious processes conscious in psychodynamic therapy practice and the use of art to discover alternative meaning, I hoped exploration through film would be a way to embody less academically traditional structures of knowledge (Seregina, 2019).

Figure 1.1: Poster for the film *The Baby And The Snake*

In 2015, I was asked to take part in the International Institute for Visual Arts event 'Say No to Identity Theft – Issues Surrounding the Politics, History and Current Situation of English Gypsy Romani Identity in the UK'. I showed a trailer of *The Baby And The Snake*. This event prompted the emergence of a new process of personal exploration in my response to racial cultural identity, through a more in-depth critical art-based inquiry:

'...art-based research requires a different attitude toward knowledge-creation from both researcher and audience, pointing to an epistemology that is interaction and experience oriented. The approach further necessitates continuous reflexivity, breaking one's assumptions and making one question existing meaning' (Seregina, 2019, p.2).

In highlighting the interactions between the personal and political, and private and public (Talwar, 2019), the event raised my consciousness of feelings surrounding my own experiences of direct, inter- and trans-generational trauma caused by racism. The questions and answers at the event had emphasized my unconscious fears, ambivalence and shame in owning my identity as a Romanichal woman, without defending against difficult feelings through deflection and denial. I became acutely aware of my internalization of my parents' shame and fear surrounding the revealing of my ethnicity in certain social contexts and my use of filmmaking to create a distanced exploration of this for myself. My light skin and education seemed to bear testament to both my parents' explicit and implicit instruction to avoid the truth about my ethnicity and to perpetuate denials.

Following this event, I further explored through my art practice the feelings evoked in my family dynamic and in wider society surrounding my multiple social locations and racial, cultural identities. This included an intersectional exploration of the impact of my gender identity and sexuality. This creative process was motivated by a desire to document and research cultural experience, but also to find personal meaning, self-reflect and create therapeutic containment for difficult feelings.

In collaboration with artist Mia Hawk, I completed The Pedestal Project, a self-portraiture project utilizing costume, props and family and cultural narratives that hold significance (Figure 1.2). Seregina (2019) notes the way in which art-based research utilizes artistic practice in order to explore phenomena by engaging with audiences. They further illustrate the way that the methodology can shift focus from the product of research to the process of research, much like the art therapy making process and resulting artworks. They note that this gives 'room for experience-based, interpersonal, and dialogical engagement' (Seregina, 2019, p.2).

In reflecting on this process, Mia and I agreed that what seemed evoked by the enactments and photographic archiving was a sense of integration and grief but also an ultimate defiance. Resonating with the process of active imagination (Jung, 1969), where part of the personality enters into fantasy material and the other observes the process, I reflected on how myth and fairy tale may amplify what resonates with the archetypal atmosphere of the material (Schaverien, 2005). The exploring of costume and makeup becomes representative of identity formation, photographed as a visual narrative and cultural archive. This process was paralleled by my sharing with Mia a verbal narrative of life experience and desire to be 'all of myself at once'. In this image, pheasant skins gifted to me by my dad from birds he had killed to eat may in part represent the tensions between middle-class appearance and working-class origins. The rawness of the attempted integration seems to be illustrated in the bloodied attachment/detachment of the skins. The theatrical makeup may represent war paint and the absurd, commenting on my pale skin and feelings of alienation and difference felt from within and outside my community; as well as symbolizing disguise as a form of self-protection. The word 'slut' is scrawled across my chest responding to patriarchal shaming that exists for women within my community and beyond, and also comments on the complexities of sexuality. Trinkets inherited from family adorn my costume; I am about to eat caviar from an over-sized silver spoon.

Figure 1.2: Brazen Chavi/Silver Spoon

In considering the politics of words, Corradi states that 'Gypsy' still represents the radical 'other'. 'Gypsy was (and is even now) an insult, synonymous with vagabond, lazy, dirty, unable to work, unreliable, false, and cunning' (Corradi, 2018, terminological note).

I had always owned my identity as Romani by choosing wisely when not to mention it. This silence is culturally embedded and feels relevant to my place as a woman within a traditional patriarchal community, and my place in English society as Romanichal. The creative process and resultant product of the project in part reclaims and reappropriates as a way of challenging the normative power of stereotypes, enabling 'discursive practices of re-signification – a crucial terrain of agency and symbolic warfare' (Corradi, 2018, p.XVIII).

I had never acknowledged the damage of internalizing an inherent sense of being 'other' (Trinh, 1989) and the impact of the unfairness felt by the necessity of ethnic death (Quintanales, 1983) to 'thrive'. I had not before created safe spaces beyond personal therapy to acknowledge the trauma caused by societal hate and institutionally sanctioned racism, or to stay with the feelings evoked by the stories of hate I was told and was part of. I had not contextualized the parenting I received that responded to inter- and trans-generational transmissions of trauma. The story of the baby and the snake had begun to extend in meaning for me through the use of art-based inquiry. It also began to feel like a communication from my parents about the limitations on parenting and attachment under circumstances where they had no capacity to understand or control just how much nourishment a racist society steals from their children. The Traveller Movement's research shows that 76 per cent of GRT people have actively hidden their ethnicity to avoid discrimination or prejudice (The Traveller Movement, 2017). When considering this and my art therapy practice as simultaneously held, I can reflect on Hocoy's thoughts on the illuminating of the therapist's shadow in honour of ethical practice. He asks, 'Do we silence in our clients the voices of difference that we have been socialized to silence in ourselves?' (Hocoy, 2007, p.9).

I unconsciously began a process of challenging normative powers and silencing; despite my personal denials, before this point I had begun to challenge denials of unfairness impacting my clients or those like my clients, through the connected activities of activism, art-making and art therapy practice. This included considerations of the ways I worked in the therapeutic space and relationship, in part guided by a questioning of whether the theories I practised were chosen to conceal unrecognized needs or conflicts within myself that I could begin to understand through intersectional art-based research. I began to question that which I may have silenced in my clients while unconsciously defending against my own identity-related feelings of shame. This extended to my active questioning of the norms I found within the institutions I worked and in my teaching on MA Art Therapy trainings.

Collier (2015) writes of being changed by her clients, and the need to be able to suffer when projections hurt, rather than act on the countertransference.

Fundamental to intersectional thinking is self-reflexivity. I continue to value the psychodynamic foundations of my practice and reflect on the potentiality that activism may be acting on countertransferential feelings to avoid bearing the pain our clients bring. However, for me, this shift in my clinical thinking represented the change we should be able to suffer, that Collier observes.

In 2012, I wrote the article 'Art therapy with women with borderline personality disorder: A feminist perspective'. I stood on the shoulders of art therapists such as Hogan (1997), Burt (1997) and Talbott-Green (1989) to see a way to respond to the personal, societal and political injustice I found being experienced by my clients, paralleled and re-enacted within institutional dynamics and policy. I discovered the work of feminist therapists such as Veldhuis (2001), Brown (2010) and Lerman and Porter (1990) and enriched my clinical thinking to integrate an explicit examination of power, continuously questioning the power dynamics in the therapeutic relationship (Eastwood, 2012). I endeavoured to increase my understanding of diversity issues and my potential unconscious biases, to reflect on in personal therapy and supervision. I took the risk of allowing myself to make mistakes and tried to consciously position myself as ally and not saviour in the therapeutic relationship, questioning my agendas and the potential to be seduced by the gained power inherent in enactments of care. Primarily, I began to question art therapy as a profession and ask what are the potential cultural assumptions, identity-related norms, values and constructions that art therapy has privileged as a profession and used to shape practice and policy (Hocoy, 2007; Talwar, 2019). Burt (2012) notes how meaning and knowledge are constructed with a focus on who is asking the questions about whom. I began to embark on a process of questioning the questions, of challenging my own ambiguous ethical concerns and of exploring the meaning of meanings (Talwar, 2019).

Intersectionality and the art therapy profession

Intersectional thinking is complex and cannot be clearly defined or neatly organized. The advocating of systems thinking to enhance understanding of the complexities of human experience in some ways complicates that which we seek to clarify. We are guided to embrace an understanding of a world of entanglements rather than separations. For me, this corresponds well with psychodynamic therapeutic thinking and our need as art therapists to tolerate the ambiguity of practice. Intersectionality does not provide certainty, instead it challenges it.

Intersectionality was conceived before it was named by Kimberlé

Crenshaw (1989), in the work of many Black women and a framework born from social change activity in the United States, prompted by social inequalities. Preceding this chapter, art therapists have addressed issues of identity and social justice (Burt, 2012; Hogan, 2012; Kapitan, 2015; Talwar, 2019; Talwar, Iyer & Doby-Copeland, 2004). However, to date, few have gone beyond exploring identity markers in isolation. This includes my own article (Eastwood, 2012) that focused solely on the analysis of gender in binary ways. I can question this now and know that during the time of writing I was aware of the specific race/gender intersects of my clients. Yet to explore beyond gender into the realms of race specifically, for me as a woman with White privilege (McIntosh, 1989), at the time felt personally uncomfortable and professionally risky. Intolerable feelings and risk aversion I have since been able to greater challenge in my practice and writing, in part as an act of social action (Eastwood, 2021).

When considering auto-ethnography, Vidal-Ortez (2004) clarifies the term 'white person of colour' where the auto-ethnographer is a 'boundary-crosser' with regard to dual identity. Miles (1989) critiques the defining of racialization often in somatic terms, and I hold all perspectives at once as I continue on my journey of ever shifting responses to identity formation. My journey has included self-reflexivity and sense-making of the connections between my personal experience and professional focus. Yet my understanding of my simultaneous marginalizations and privilege, and my ability to contextualize my sense of White privilege within my life experiences, lacked clarity. I had yet to fully acknowledge shame surrounding my ethnicity or my internalized racism, and so was also yet to acknowledge my experiences of racism, the insights they gave me, or my potential to re-enact racism in complex ways. An intersectional approach to self-reflexivity and social and cultural inquiry, in part through art-based inquiry, has made some such acknowledgements possible.

Talwar's (2010) observations regarding a lack of intersectional thinking in art therapy practice in the US resonate a great deal. I have faced resistance in the UK to integrating a more intersectional approach. The resistance to integrating explorations of our privileges, power or prejudices as art therapists, trained within Eurocentric, cishet patriarchal traditions in a profession dominated by White, middle-class women, has felt present in my teaching and is often reinforced by existing focus in art therapy curriculum.

I completed my train journey to visit my dad. I soon moved back to my childhood home to support my mum with his end-of-life care. During this time, I continued to write this chapter and work on my art-based inquiry related to identity, creating the sculptural piece entitled 'It feels very true, doesn't it?': Removed to/Must accept (Figure 1.3).

Figure 1.3: 'It feels very true, doesn't it?': Removed to/Must accept

The piece is created from casts of my parents' hands made on my father's return home from hospital to die. It consists of a nest woven from gold threads gifted to me by my aunt, and tyre tread, a material that would cover our kitchen floor in my childhood as my dad would cut the treads on the car tyres he traded in. The nest is cradled by the hands and contains an identity card my dad still possessed, issued to him at the age of three, a card that was issued to all GRT children stating each time the card owner was 'Removed to' their next stopping place. In addition, the nest contains a section of my school report, saved by my mum. It states: 'Constant absences and truancies from school have clearly hampered her progress. She must accept that unless she attends regularly, success in GCSE work will slip out of her grasp.' The torn report is curled and nestled inside my dad's identity card, pinned in place. All components sit in a box my dad made for me in prison. I completed the weaving of the gold thread that restricts, embellishes and holds the nest together as I sat by my dad's bedside at home, in the hours after his death.

Conclusion

An intersectional framework cannot be placed over any given project without dynamic thinking. However, intersectional exploration as illustrated above through my use of Self and art-based inquiry can provide a tool for the linking of experience, theory and practice in art therapy in a way that can enrich and inform therapeutic thinking and explorations of visual media. I hope to have illustrated the subversion of normative power, insight gained and transformative qualities of art-making for me personally. Nevertheless, I also want to note my experiences of transformation through psychodynamic therapy from a client and therapist perspective. Reflecting on the political climate at the time of writing, where the UK government continues to create policy that deliberately discriminates and eradicates the rights of GRT people (Gov.UK, 2019; O'Neill, 2020), it is easy to focus only on the negative impact of my identities that lead to oppression. In considering art therapy practice, I am reminded of the possibilities of the transformation of perceptions to process trauma and empower. As therapists, there are always limits to our abilities to individually or collectively make social change. Yet often, the potential to empower clients to view their struggles from different perspectives can feel endless, or at least equal to hopelessness on bad days.

In his contribution to *We Roma: A Critical Reader in Contemporary Art*, philosopher Albert Atkin writes, 'Roma nomadism is not only an action *in* the world, it is a way of *seeing* the world' (Atkin, 2013, p.46). He continues to note this cultural epistemology, as acting as a lens. He asserts that nomadism as a lens 'means that nothing is complete or settled – there are no laurels to rest on. It means nothing is solved, problems are only problems in a particular place, solutions are those things that allow us to move forward to the next place' (Atkin, 2013, p.47). This interpretation of Romani cultural difference and ways of seeing resonates with my approach to my art therapy practice – the need to tolerate uncertainty and ambiguity from psychodynamic perspectives and the acknowledgement of the impact of the ever-changing intersects of identity, power dynamics and social location. This reminds me of the value of my difference in relation to a majority society and within my profession, value I have struggled to see in the past, but can now subvert meaningfully through artistic and therapeutic exploration, challenging racism and societal pressures to assimilate. I believe there is much potential to support clients in subverting personal perspectives to become empowered, while also acknowledging that there has always been, and may continue to be, need for social change in response to individual experiences of trauma.

Central to the purpose of working at the intersections has been to gain understanding to enable the empowerment of marginalized communities that can then guide resistance and action for change. This relationship to social change has been important to my thinking as an art therapist. As Collins and Bilge note, 'Intersectionality is not simply a method for doing research but a tool for empowering people' (2016, p.37).

Acknowledgements

I would like to thank my husband Gavin for all his support and to dedicate this chapter to my mum and dad.

Atch on Dad, Kushti Boc and dik you down that bavvel drom.

References

Anderson, R. (2016). University fees in historical perspective. History & Policy. Accessed 13/11/19 at www.historyandpolicy.org/policy-papers/papers/university-fees-in-historical-perspective.

Atkin, A. (2013). Reconstruction, Recognition, and Roma. In D. Baker & M. Hlavajova (eds) *We Roma: A Critical Reader in Contemporary Art*. Utrecht: BAK & Amsterdam: Valiz.

Brown, L. S. (2010). *Feminist Therapy*. Washington DC: American Psychological Association.

Brown, P. (2017). Verbal quote, Hertfordshire University MA Art Therapy experiential module guidance.

Burt, H. (1997). Women, Art Therapy and Feminist Theories of Development. In S. Hogan (ed.) *Feminist Approaches to Art Therapy*. London & New York, NY: Routledge.

Burt, H. (2012). Multiple Perspectives: Art Therapy Postmodernism and Feminism. In H. Burt (ed.) *Art Therapy and Postmodernism: Art Therapy Through a Prism*. London: Jessica Kingsley Publishers.

Carastathis, A. (2016). *Intersectonality: Origins, Contestations, Horizons*. Lincoln & London: University Press.

Chilton, G. & Scotti, V. (2014). Snipping, gluing, writing: The properties of collage as art based research practice in art therapy. *Journal of American Art Therapy Association, 31*(4), 163–171.

Collier, J. (2015). '3 man unlock: out of sight, out of mind': Art psychotherapy with a woman with severe and dangerous personality disorder in prison. *Journal of Psychoanalytic Psychotherapy, 29*(3), 1–19.

Collins, P. & Bilge, S. (2016). *Intersectionality*. Cambridge: Polity Press.

Corradi, L. (2018). *Gypsy Feminism: Intersectional Politics, Alliances, Gender and Queer Activism*. Oxford: Routledge.

Crenshaw, K. (1989). Demarginalizing the intersection of race and sex: A Black feminist critique of antidiscrimination doctrine, feminist theory and antiracist politics. *University of Chicago Legal Forum, 1*(8), 139–167.

Doby-Copeland, C. (2013). Practicing Multicultural Competent Art Therapy. In S. Prasad, P. Howie & J. Kristel (eds) *Using Art Therapy with Diverse Populations: Crossing Cultures and Abilities*. London: Jessica Kingsley Publishers.

Eastwood, C. (2012). Art therapy with women with borderline personality disorder: A feminist perspective. *International Journal of Art Therapy, 17*(3), 98–114.

Eastwood, C. (2021). White privilege and art therapy in the UK: Are we doing The Work? *International Journal of Art Therapy*. https://doi.org/10.1080/17454832.2020.1856159.

Gov.UK (2019). *Government Consults on New Police Powers to Criminalise Unauthorised Encampments*. Accessed 23/07/20 at www.gov.uk/government/news/government-consults-on-new-police-powers-to-criminalise-unauthorised-encampments.

Hocoy, D. (2007). Art Therapy as a Tool for Social Change: A Conceptual Model. In K. Kaplan (ed.) *Art Therapy and Social Action*. London: Jessica Kingsley Publishers.

Hogan, S. (1997). Problems of Identity: Deconstructing Gender in Art Therapy. In S. Hogan (ed.) *Feminist Approaches to Art Therapy*. London & New York, NY: Routledge.

Hogan, S. (2012). Postmodernist but Not Post-Feminist! A Feminist Postmodernist Approach to Working with New Mothers. In H. Burt (ed.) *Art Therapy and Postmodernism: Creative Healing Through a Prism*. London: Jessica Kingsley Publishers.

Jung, C. G. (1969). *General Aspects of Dream Psychology*. London: RKP.

Junge, M. (2007). The Art Therapist as Social Activist: Reflections on a Life. In K. Kaplan (ed.) *Art Therapy and Social Action*. London: Jessica Kingsley Publishers.

Kapitan, L. (2014). *Introduction to Art Therapy Research*. New York, NY: Routledge.
Kapitan, L. (2015). Social action in practice: Shifting the ethno-centric lens in cross-cultural art therapy encounters. *Art Therapy: Journal of the American Art Therapy Association, 32*(3), 104–111.
Kaplan, F. (2007). *Art Therapy and Social Action*. London: Jessica Kingsley Publishers.
Lerman, H. & Porter, N. (1990). *Feminist Ethics in Psychotherapy*. New York, NY: Springer Publishing Company.
McIntosh, P. (1989). White privilege: Unpacking the invisible knapsack. *Peace and Freedom*, July/August, 8–10.
McNiff, S. (2013). *Art as Research: Opportunities and Challenges*. Bristol: Intellect.
Miles, R. (1989). *Racism*. London: Routledge.
O'Neill, G. C. (2020). I'm a Romany Gypsy: Why is racism against us still acceptable? *The Guardian*. Accessed 23/06/20 at www.theguardian.com/commentisfree/2020/jun/15/romany-gypsy-racism-britain-prejudice-roma-travellers.
Quintanales, M. (1983). I Paid Very Hard for My Immigrant Ignorance. In C. Moraga & G. Anzaldua (eds) *This Bridge Called My Back: Writings by Radical Women of Color*. New York, NY: Kitchen Table: Women of Color Press.
Schaverien, J. (2005). Art and active imagination: Reflections on transference and the image. *International Journal of Art Therapy, 10*(2), 39–52.
Seregina, U. (2019). Co-creating bodily, interactive, and reflexive knowledge through art-based research, consumption markets and culture. *Consumption Markets & Culture*. Accessed 28/06/19 at https:/doi.org/10.1080/10253866.2019.1634059.
Talbott-Green, M. (1989). Feminist scholarship: Spitting in the mouths of the gods. *The Arts in Psychotherapy, 16*, 253–261.
Talwar, S. (2010). An intersectional framework for race, class, gender, and sexuality in art therapy. *Journal of the American Art Therapy Association, 27*(1), 11–17.
Talwar, S. (2019). *Art Therapy for Social Justice: Radical Intersections*. New York, NY: Routledge.
Talwar, S., Iyer, J. & Doby-Copeland, C. (2004). The invisible veil: Changing paradigms in the art therapy profession. *Art Therapy: Journal of the American Art Therapy Association, 21*(1), 44–48.
The Traveller Movement (2017). 'The last acceptable form of racism?' The pervasive discrimination and prejudice experienced by Gypsy, Roma and Traveller communities. Accessed 13/11/19 at https://travellermovement.org.uk/phocadownload/userupload/equality-human-rights/last-acceptable-form-of-racism-traveller-movement-report.pdf.
Tillet, S. & Tillet, S. (2019). 'You Want to Be Well?': Self-Care as Black Feminist Intervention in Art Therapy. In S. Talwar (ed.) *Art Therapy for Social Justice: Radical Intersections*. New York, NY: Routledge.
Trinh, T. (1989). *Women, Native, Other: Writing Post Coloniality and Feminism*. Bloomington, IN: Indiana University Press.
Veldhuis, C. B. (2001). The Trouble With Power. In E. Kaschak (ed.) *The Next Generation: Third Wave Feminist Psychotherapy*. New York, London, Oxford: The Haworth Press.
Vidal-Ortiz, S. (2004). On being a white person of color: Using autoethnography to understand Puerto Ricans' racialization. *Qualitative Sociology, 27*(2), 179–203.
Weber, L. (2001). A conceptual framework for understanding race, class, gender and sexuality. *Psychology of Women Quarterly, 22*(1), 13–32.

Chapter 2

Colonialized Attachment: A Dramatherapy Perspective

WABRIYA KING

Introduction

When I began writing this chapter, I wondered what my motivation was. I had no great passion to write. I find academia terrifying and came up with several reasons to back out of the opportunity. Running parallel to this journey, with the murders of Breonna Taylor and George Floyd, the racial and cultural seas have been churned up, setting in motion a global tidal change that I hope will be considered here, on the shores moving forward as the tides reconnect in a new rhythm. With this parallel process in mind, it seemed essential that I write.

I want to pose questions about how environment, culture, race and social class might play a part in how we form attachments, and the impact history has had on the Eurocentric conception of developmental theories deemed to be typical and representative. Despite the dominance and wide acceptance of modern attachment theory, there is little evidence to suggest that the way infants develop early relationships is universal. Further, I want to explore to what extent the dramatherapy space acts as a microcosm of unconscious social bias.

As a second generation Black British Jamaican studying dramatherapy, I quickly became aware that concepts of attachment seemed to have a predominantly White and middle-class undercurrent. Photographs in the suggested textbooks, both good and bad, invariably showed well-dressed White babies with their White mothers, effortlessly conjuring up stereotypical affluent White heteronormative families. Despite living in a diverse and multicultural city, I found that at conferences and development days, presentations were inevitably given by White women, often discussing Black patients. I was feeling uncomfortable about the ease with which highly skilled dramatherapists failed to connect the dots of past culture to present behaviour, and it occurred to me that a colonialized way of practising is standard.

As a student, while undertaking a placement in a medium secure hospital, I observed many patients with histories of insecure or disrupted attachments, but noted that this was assessed in the context of Western cultural expectations. When I weighed up my own ancestral history, it was clear that my foremothers had no choice but to create what would now be deemed disordered attachments with their children. It is therefore imperative that a number of issues that arise from this Western developmental assumption are challenged. These include: how much importance dramatherapy training gives to the idea of different cultural attachments and the impact this may have on the people we work with; how ignorance of different cultural attachment styles might affect the therapeutic relationship; and how the lack of knowledge or thinking around ingrained colonialized social behaviours might unconsciously be played out in the dramatherapy space. In exploring these themes, I will foreground the significance of prioritizing a White majority and the resulting neglect of different groups who find themselves in our care. I will focus on race and culture from a West Indian perspective.

Encountering prejudice

As a child, I was the only Black girl in my primary school class and was often described as stern or angry by teachers, when in truth I was often scared or hurt. Eberhardt asserts:

> ...blacks are so strongly associated with threat and aggression that this stereotypic association can even impact our ability to accurately read the facial expressions of black people. For example, a black man who is excited might appear angry. Fear can be misread as outrage. Silence taken as belligerence. (Eberhardt, 2019, pp.35–36)

I wonder now if this misconception was influenced by my inability to express such emotions effectively, or if my teacher's compassion had fallen prey to racist societal stereotypes. In hindsight, I realize how harsh and damaging these labels were for a child of primary school age. My White counterparts were seemingly allowed to show these emotions without such characterization. More recently, during my first year of dramatherapy training, while in group therapy I shared my debilitating experience of the 'angry Black woman' stereotype. Iyanla Vanzant highlights the damage such stereotypes inflict when she states:

> There are dangerously false stereotypes about black women that not only diminish our humanity but also distort our self-image. While it is perfectly natural and acceptable for human beings to engage in a variety of emotional expressions, when a black woman's expression makes others uncomfortable, the labels given to those expressions become her identity...her behaviour becomes who she is in the sight of others. She is assumed to be easy to trigger and difficult to control. The label silences the natural, organic expression to feelings of overwhelmingness, fear and the experience of being stripped of personal power or private space. (Vanzant, 2017)

I continue to be scared of being identified with this label, as I frequently was in school. The dramatherapist leading the group, a White woman, said that she wasn't aware of this particular stereotype, and another White member of the group stated she had Black friends and that she was not aware this was 'a thing'. Maybe, she suggested, it was my own stuff. The following week, she apologized, as having spoken to her friend, she was informed it was definitely a common stereotype.

Reflecting on this instance, I thought momentarily that perhaps my observations were wrong. Maybe this was 'my stuff': the commonly referred to 'chip' that non-Black groups use to discredit the prejudice experienced by the Black community. But surely, I thought, as qualified and training art therapists, there should be a deeper awareness and understanding of such emotionally debilitating social constructs?

My frustrations accumulated during my forensic placement in the second year of training. I attended the Forensic Arts Therapies Advisory Group (FATAG) conference, and was faced with a discussion about patients, predominantly from ethnic and lower social class groups, who were described as having disordered or insecure attachments. The conference attendees were predominantly White art therapists. I recall maybe two other Black therapists. I was conscious of this disparity throughout the discussion of a demographic that had historically been, and by some groups continues to be, considered 'lesser' than the White norm. The debris of post-colonialism felt very present and I felt compelled to share my thoughts and feelings with the group. What I shared in that discussion was my belief that popular psychological teachings of attachment derive from a White middle-class 'secure' perspective. Teaching of different cultural attachment styles was lacking in my experience during training. Indeed, the 2005 John Bowlby Memorial Conference addressed the notable gap in the development of attachment theory manifest in the absence of any consideration of the effects of race and racism (Laschinger, 2006). 'In recent centuries...racism, in its underpinning of power inequality in relationships, has been primary in the distortion, denial and destruction of attachment bonds' (ibid, p.5). I was aware of the fundamental attachment disruption among many of my patients within the forensic unit and will explore this further later in this chapter. Nevertheless, I am aware that this kind of attachment disruption is not unique to or limited to only Black or Black mixed-heritage patients. Race and racism is vast and varied. However, as I am solely writing from my own perspective as a therapist who is of Black Caribbean descent, I will continue to keep the points of discussion to this demographic, while wishing to highlight that multiple intersects of disadvantage, including gender, class, sexuality, physical ability and poverty, as well as race, add to the higher statistical percentage of people who may encounter the mental health system. It is likely that people from Black and Black mixed heritage are more likely to be from lower income backgrounds than their White counterparts, again increasing their chances of interactions with the mental health system.

> BAME communities are also often faced with disadvantages in society. They are more likely to experience poverty, have poorer educational outcomes, higher unemployment, and contact with the criminal justice system, and may face challenges accessing or receiving appropriate professional services... Each of these can act as risk factors for the development of mental health problems. (Mental Health Foundation, 2019)

Prejudice and mental health

The Mental Health Foundation provides a number of concerning statistics and data regarding the experiences of Black African, Caribbean and Black British people. For example, the Adult Psychiatric Morbidity Survey (Mental Health Foundation, 2019) found that Black men were more likely than their White counterparts to experience a psychotic disorder in the last year, and that the risk of psychosis in Black Caribbean groups is estimated to be nearly seven times higher than in the White population. Of course, the impact of higher rates of mental illness is that people from these groups are more likely than average to encounter mental health services. Detention rates under the Mental Health Act during 2017/18 were four times higher for people in the Black or Black British group than those in the White group. A figure that starkly confirms the societal impact of prejudice. The Count Me In Census (Care Quality Commission, 2011), which collects information on inpatient care, found higher than average admission and detention rates for Black groups in every year from 2006 to 2010. In addition, Black men were reported to have higher rates of drug use and drug dependency than other groups, and while the White Caucasian population experienced the highest rates for suicidal thoughts, completed suicide rates were higher among young men of Black African, Black Caribbean origin, and among middle-aged Black African, Black Caribbean and South Asian women, than among their White British counterparts (Mental Health Foundation, 2019).

These statistics suggest that, institutionally, the medical profession is still unable to interpret the cultural, emotional nuances of the Black population. The medical sector is not alone in its possible prejudice; the NHS, Metropolitan Police and education sectors all have statistics that would suggest a negative bias towards Black employees and students. A Bristol University national study of Statutory Assessment Tests (SATs) of teacher/student assessments versus the official 'blind' marked test results found that, on average, White students were scored 3.3 points lower than their actual result, in comparison to Black Caribbean and African pupils who were scored 5.6 and 6.4 points lower respectively.

Contrastingly, the same study revealed that Indian and Chinese students tended to score higher than their actual result (Akala, 2018). This seems to show that teachers had much lower expectations for their Black students and, possibly feeding into another stereotype, much higher expectations of Indian and Chinese students. Akala states that, 'In short, the study confirmed that teachers are human beings and that they project their biases and those of our society onto children' (Akala, 2018, p.82). The result of hundreds of years of anti-Black propaganda and fear mongering has allowed and normalized a seemingly instinctive unconscious prejudice to become enmeshed in the core fabric of Britain's institutions.

Dokter (2016) indicates in a small study that more Black and minority groups tend to access dramatherapy than their White counterparts (Dokter & Khasnavis, 2008 cited in Dokter, 2016). She also highlights the figures of the dramatherapist cultural background survey taken from the British Association of Dramatherapists (BADth) Analysis of Dramatherapy Equal Opportunities Survey. The results from 2015 show that only 2 per cent of the dramatherapists who took part in the survey identified as Black in contrast to nearly 70 per cent who identified as White. During my own dramatherapy training I observed 45 trainees on the course. Across the three groups, ten of us identified as Black or mixed heritage, making our yearly average approximately three out of fifteen, which might suggest a small increase since the survey of 2015. Nevertheless, despite this suggested growth in numbers, the figures remain low. There will be numerous factors influencing this, but I feel the financial expense might result in fewer students from low-income backgrounds undertaking the training, in addition to the lack of acknowledgement in the curriculum regarding racism – an aspect which may also deter minority groups.

Art therapists and social and unconscious bias

Given the high number of non-Black, historically culturally privileged art therapists working in mental health and the statistically high number of Black patients being treated for mental illness, it is inevitable that the positions of power will sit with White professionals. As art therapists we can be integral to the care of the patients and clients we encounter, but without the essential culturally inclusive training we are not perhaps 'culturally competent' (Maynard, 2018, p.37). It is important, therefore, that we consider to what extent we are aware of the possible unconscious social biases, stigmas and stereotypes we hold towards our patients and our patients hold towards us. Art therapists are not without their own individual unconscious biases. Without a robust training that consciously and rigorously aims at meeting and examining this, and without personal therapy that gives us a safe place to explore our own prejudices, discrimination will continue to slip through the net and art therapists of all backgrounds will find their biases unowned in the therapeutic space and relationship.

Colonialism: A brief history

Seebohm (2011), a White dramatherapist, discusses themes of post-colonialism and apartheid present in a description of her sessions with a Black male patient in a medium secure unit. She describes the patient calling her 'Mistress' and re-enacting the figure of the shackled man as they walked to the therapy room. Like Seebohm, when working in a medium secure unit, I too questioned the power dynamic of the key-holding therapist and patient, so obviously with limited access or control of their movements and choices within the unit, and how this dynamic might change depending on the key holder being Black or White. I often looked around the multidisciplinary team during art therapy meetings as we discussed each patient and wondered to what extent these 'experts' considered the trauma and historical attachment disruption within some of the patients: '...if one seeks to understand the social dynamics of today, one must trace the major processes of history' (Manley, 1974, p.45 cited in Arnold, 2012, p.23).

The 1661 Barbados Slave Code or Act, and the subsequent Jamaican Slave Act of 1696, saw not only the enslavement of Africans in the West Indies as a 'legally sanctioned and regulated institution' (Olusoga, 2017, p.69), but marked the beginning of the concept that 'negro' and 'slave' were to be one and the same. This ideology was then used to define them from their 'White', indentured 'servant' counterparts. The Act sanctioned considerably more brutal punishments for 'slaves' than 'servants', for minor crimes or as means to quell and regulate the 'heathenish brutish and uncertain dangerous pride of people, whose nature required that they be subject to rigorous and "punishionary laws"' (Black, 2015, p.46 cited in Olusoga, 2017, p.70). Black people endured body mutilation including nostril slitting, the branding of the cheeks or forehead, and even castration. Conversely, an extension to their indentured sentence (Olusoga, 2017) was considered punishment enough for the White criminals who worked alongside the enslaved Africans of the West Indies, whose only crime was to be Black. The separation of Black people from White was extended to all human qualities, they were property no more than livestock, and considered to lack the emotional capacity to have feelings (Arnold, 2012). Slaves cultivating civilized family structures were seen by some plantation owners as criminal and punishable. Legislation enabled slave owners to forcibly rape and breed from their slaves, and gave them the liberty to separate or remove babies from their mothers as they would the other animals they owned. Arnold (2012) retells the life of enslaved African Mary Prince, who had several of her children removed and sold to other plantations, before being sent to England to take care of her master's children. For enslaved women who were allowed to keep their children, some were permitted to carry them tied to their backs in the traditional African custom while they were at breastfeeding age. Mostly, they were left with an older slave who could no longer tend the fields, to be trained, not nurtured, for work on the plantation. This could start from as young as three years old (Hogg, 1979 cited in Arnold, 2012).

Enslaved Africans were forbidden from speaking in their native language at any point. Considering the cultural and personal isolation and erosion of emotional expression experienced under such extreme brutality, I wonder what effect this had on 'attachment'. So normalized was the persecution of enslaved Black people that numerous accounts, from personal journals to nationalized manuals, uncover the brutality meted out. The diary of a mid-seventeenth-century British slave owner in Jamaica, Thomas Thistlewood, told of punishing a slave by whipping, followed by gagging him for hours with his mouth full of faeces. Over the course of 30 years, Thistlewood's diaries also describe nearly four thousand acts of sexual intercourse with 136 enslaved women (Manjapra, 2018). Both Arnold (2012) and Fletchman-Smith (2018) write of the frequent infanticide enslaved women undertook to save their children from the torture of slavery. Arnold (2012) extends the theme of parenting to the more recent Caribbean migration of the Windrush generation, who were named after the *SS Windrush*. The 1948 docking of this ship carried 492 of what would be the first of many West Indian *British* subjects between 1948 and 1971. I highlight *British*, as having grandparents of this generation, I witnessed the pride they had in being part of the British Empire and their high regard for England. To finance this prodigious move, many migrants left their children behind until they had the means to accommodate and care for them in their new 'home'. Arnold (2012) describes the long hours in underpaid menial jobs undertaken by these initial West Indian migrants, and the limited and at times substandard living and childcare options left open to them, including the social services and residential nurseries established during the war, in rural safe areas far from the city and potential risk of bombing. For post-war migrants – often new mothers who had no means to travel – visiting their children was difficult or impossible, leaving them and their children in a strange, all-White, new world: '...the long-term consequences of the separation of young children from their mothers had not been considered' (Arnold, 2012, p.51). From the beginning of slavery to at least 1971, the official end of the Windrush generation, the continued strain and disruption on attachment faced by West Indian mothers and their children have undoubtedly left lasting scars within the community.

Colonialism and attachment theory

Attachment theory, developed by John Bowlby and further expanded by Mary Ainsworth, is now a generally recognized hypothesis and is often seen as the foundation of therapeutic studies. The accepted attachment patterns are described below.

- Secure attachment – characterized by secure trust in the primary caregiver, which enables the child to confidently seek physical proximity after moments of stress or anxiety. This is further enhanced by the infant's security to explore their environment.
- Insecure attachment: ambivalent – characterized by the child flitting between avoiding or approaching the primary caregiver after moments of separation or distress; avoidant – characterized by the child exhibiting seemingly content behaviours in moments of stress.
- Disorganized attachment (developed and added to by Mary Main and Judith Soloman) – characterized by a collection of avoidant and ambivalent behaviours, with the child often seeming confused, dazed, unsure or cautious when in the presence of their primary caregiver.

When held up against this popular psychological model, enslaved African mothers of the West Indies would stand little chance of achieving relationships with their children that the West would recognize as secure attachment. Dalal (2006, p.18) asserts, 'Problematic attachment histories lead to the generation of avoidant, ambivalent or disorganized patterns of relating to others.' Within the horrendous boundaries of colonialism, insecure and disorganized attachment patterns between West Indian mothers and their offspring would have flourished. The same tragic state of affairs would have existed for many during the Windrush years, and indeed continue now for millions of migrants and enslaved people globally. Keller states, 'The population in which this model is adaptive is Western, middle-class families, representing less than five percent the world's population' (Keller, 2018, p.13). And yet, these criteria colour the judgement on attachment universally. Taking a more inclusive approach, Dalal (2006) brings the concept of culture and attachment together and states that 'the infant's developmental process is formed and mediated through the cultural systems in which they take place. It follows then that each cultural system will generate its own forms of attachment which legitimate different ways of being together' (Dalal, 2006, p.20). He suggests that the Western notion of the 'secure base' should be known simply as 'the base'. It has always been my thinking that mothering or parenting is passed down from one generation to the next. If we consider parenting in the context of colonialism, we may see the transgenerational trauma of enslavement and discrimination manifesting in styles of caregiving and consequent attachment patterns. Dalal's notion of 'the base' opens the door to considering attachment theory within wider cultural histories. 'We do not just attach to people,' writes Dalal, 'but we also attach to categories' (ibid, p.25). I believe this to be true when thinking about attachment and culture.

Intercultural dramatherapy practice and the importance of diverse teaching in training

As Seebohm (2011) reflects on the colonialized themes that played out during her sessions with a Black patient, James, also a White dramatherapist, asserts that:

> Historically, what might be described as western white colonial dominance has attacked and undermined many cultures, their values, attitudes and belief systems. A treatment programme offered by a white therapist to a black person must, I believe, take this into account if it is going to be truly effective in the aim and intention to heal or repair. (James, 1998, p.209)

James reflects that it took four years of working alongside her client to become conscious of her own ignorance about the experience of being a Black immigrant. Through this raised consciousness, their time together allowed her increased levels of insight and empathy. James's work with her client supports the benefits of dramatherapy within this context, but it also emphasizes the need for rigorous, diverse and inclusive attachment teaching within the curriculum. James was able to come alongside her client as she explored loss, grief, belonging and what it is to be a mother or to mother, but I wonder how much deeper this work might have gone if James had had increased insight and empathy from the beginning. Nevertheless, over a four-year period a therapeutic bond clearly formed, and when asked about her decision to have a White therapist, her client replied:

> In choosing a therapist I trust the invisible antenna that reaches much deeper than personality. The kind of black therapist I wouldn't go to was one who had their own agenda about colour, who wanted to crusade about colour. A white therapist has helped me to feel proud and more connected with the fact I am Black. (James, 1998, p.208)

It seems important to explore this negative outlook on the possibility of a Black therapist by James's client who, having had an abusive mother, may have unconsciously been wary of the idea of a Black therapist holding the therapeutic space in which she could safely feel vulnerable or frightened. She may have felt that processing trauma with a Black therapist might reactivate the trauma she experienced from her Black mother. It may be that the client's response illustrates something of the internalized racism that comes with living in a racist society and perhaps her desire to validate her White therapist, although this is obviously supposition, and shared ethnicity may not be the foundation of a successful therapeutic relationship. James's client does poignantly state, 'The arts can work cross-culturally because they offer so many languages to be able to understand' (James, 1998, p.210). Carr (2016) literally demonstrates this in her work with clients who have English as a second language. I use this example as I believe that being Black is to embody a racial foreign language. She writes of 'the central importance of the mother tongue to identity, and of affirming clients' linguistic history and repertoire' (Carr, 2016, p.17).

Conclusion

In 2018, I went to hear Christina Sharpe read an excerpt from her book *In the Wake: On Blackness and Being*:

> Wakes are processes; through them we think about the dead and about our relations to them; they are rituals through which to enact grief and memory. Wakes allow those among the living to mourn the passing of the dead through ritual; they are the watching of relatives and friends beside the body of the deceased from death to burial and the accompanying drinking, feasting, and other observances, a watching practiced as a religious observance. But wakes are also 'the track left on the water's surface by a ship; the disturbance caused by a body swimming, or one that is moved, in water; the air currents behind a body in flight; a region of disturbed flow; in the line of sight of (an observed object); and (something) in the line of recoil of (a gun)'; finally, wake means being awake and, also, consciousness. (Sharpe, 2016, p.21)

I was moved by the powerful imagery of Black people living in the wake of our histories, but I would suggest that we are all somehow living in the wake. It is how we learn to consider and negotiate this within society and in the therapeutic space that is our learning.

The legacy of the systematic dehumanization of Black people for the purpose of enslavement has facilitated racism and ignorance within British communities and institutions that continues today, from the stories of Teddy boys retold to me by my grandad; to the shooting of Dorothy Groce by the police in a search of her home and which sparked the 1985 Brixton riots experienced by my mother's generation; from my childhood memories of the tragic racially motivated murder of Stephen Lawrence to the recent unexplained death of Simeon Francis in police custody. The list is endless.

I acknowledge the constant battle in keeping this chapter focused on intersectionality and on attachment theory and not a retelling of Black and minority discrimination and destruction throughout history. And yet, it is vital that we acknowledge how discrimination, bias, prejudice and the imbalance of power have influenced the pedagogy of psychological therapies, the foundation of which is the unquestioned acceptance of attachment theory.

So, where does this leave dramatherapy in the context of intersectionality? Progress is slow, but change is happening and I am aware of the momentum within the dramatherapy community to continue learning. The use of sensitive terminology, for example, is important. 'Ethnic minority' is an outdated, imperialistic term used to describe any community of people that isn't the White norm. Within many 'ethnic minority' circles, the more accurate term of 'global majority' is used in its stead. I would like to see this used within the language of dramatherapists.

Nevertheless, the culture of dramatherapy and its teaching has changed and improved over the years. There is an acknowledgement from the course convener at the training I attended that more needs to be considered moving forward, and a willingness to adapt to ensure that diversity in training promotes an awareness to future therapists. I cannot speak for every institution, but I do encourage them to take a closer look at how 'inclusive' their trainings really are.

Christine Mayor wrote a piece entitled 'Playing with race: A theoretical framework and approach for creative arts therapists' (Mayor, 2012) in which she highlights the familiar olive branch that arts therapies extend when using language suggesting that the arts transcend difference. She states, 'I have watched issues of race emerge and be avoided by the creative arts therapy community in our writing, research and training' (Mayor, 2012, p.14). I would argue, based on my training experience, this is unfortunately still the case.

'For the most part we do not first see, and then define, we define first and then see' (Lippmann, 1922 cited in Eberhardt, 2019, p.33). Holding Lippmann's statement in mind, diversity and cultural bias awareness must become integral to our training and applied to how we hold the therapeutic space. Once practising, cultural supervision – a supervision that looks at culture and the therapist's stance within that – should be an expectation. I believe these should be considerations when thinking about not only attachment, but the global majority in teaching.

As a dramatherapist, I feel that the possibilities in the space I safely hold for my clients and patients are endless – out of this world or realm. But if my cultural understanding is limited or unconsciously biased, then how can I openly walk alongside them?

Acknowledgements

This chapter is dedicated to my grandparents Joyce and George and my mother Carol.

References

Akala (2018). *Natives: Race and Class in the Ruins of Empire*. London: Two Roads.

Arnold, E. (2012). *Working with Families of African Caribbean Origin: Understanding Issues around Immigration and Attachment*. London & Philadelphia, PA: Jessica Kingsley Publishers.

Care Quality Commission (2011). *Count Me In 2010*. Accessed 29/04/20 at https://webarchive.nationalarchives.gov.uk/20110504143648/http://www.cqc.org.uk/_db/_documents/Count_me_in_2010_FINAL_(tagged).pdf.

Carr, M. (2016). Dramatherapy Across Languages: Experiences, Drawbacks and Opportunities for Dramatherapists and their Clients Working in a Second Language. In D. Dokter & M. Hills De Zarate (eds) *Intercultural Arts Therapies Research, Issues and Methodologies* (pp.15–33). London & New York, NY: Routledge.

Dalal, F. (2006). Racism: Processes of Detachment, Dehumanization and Hatred. In K. White (ed.) *Unmasking Race, Culture, and Attachment in the Psychoanalytic Space* (pp.10–35). London: Karnac Books.

Dokter, D. (2016). Developing Intercultural Good Practice Guidelines in Dramatherapy. In D. Dokter & M. Hills De Zarate (eds) *Intercultural Arts Therapies Research, Issues and Methodologies* (pp.93–110). London & New York, NY: Routledge.

Eberhardt, J. L. (2019). *BIASED: Uncovering the Hidden Prejudices that Shape Our Lives*. London: Windmill Books.

Fletchman Smith, B. (2018). *Mental Slavery: Psychoanalytic Studies of Caribbean People*. London & New York, NY: Routledge.

James, J. (1998). Remembering: Intercultural Issues in Integrative Arts Psychotherapy. In D. Dokter (ed.) *Arts Therapists, Refugees and Migrants: Reaching Across Borders* (pp.206–215). London & Philadelphia, PA: Jessica Kingsley Publishers.

Keller, H. (2018). Introduction: Understanding Relationships – What We Would Need to Know to Conceptualize Attachment as the Cultural Solution of a Universal Developmental Task. In H. Otto & H. Keller (eds) *Different Faces of Attachment: Cultural Variations on a Universal Human Need* (pp.1–24). Cambridge: Cambridge University Press.

Laschinger, B. (2006). Attachment Theory and the John Bowlby Memorial Lecture: A Short History. In K. White (ed.) *Unmasking Race, Culture, and Attachment in the Psychoanalytic Space* (pp.5–9). London: Karnac Books.

Manjapra, K. (2018). When will Britain face up to its crimes against humanity? *The Guardian*, 29 March. Accessed 10/07/20 at www.theguardian.com/news/2018/mar/29/slavery-abolition-compensation-when-will-britain-face-up-to-its-crimes-against-humanity.

Maynard, K. (2018). To be Black. To be a Woman. Can dramatherapy help Black women to discover their true self despite racial and gender oppression? *Dramatherapy, 39*(1), 31–48. Accessed 20/04/20 at https://doi.org/10.1080%2F02630672.2018.1432668.

Mayor, C. (2012). Playing with race: A theoretical framework and approach for creative arts therapists. *The Arts in Psychotherapy, 39*(3), 214–219. Accessed 20/07/20 at www.sciencedirect.com/science/article/abs/pii/S0197455611001298.

Mental Health Foundation (2019) Black, Asian and Minority Ethnic (BAME) communities. Accessed 23/04/20 at www.mentalhealth.org.uk/a-to-z/b/black-asian-and-minority-ethnic-bame-communities.

Olusoga, D. (2017). *Black and British: A Forgotten History*. London: Pan Books.

Seebohm, H. (2011). On Bondage and Liberty: The Art of the Possible in Medium-Secure Settings. In D. Dokter, P. Holloway & H. Seebohm (eds) *Dramatherapy and Destructiveness: Creating the Evidence Base, Playing with Thanatos* (pp.120–132). London & New York, NY: Routledge.

Sharpe, C. (2016). *In the Wake: On Blackness and Being*. Durham, NC: Duke University Press.

Vanzant, I. (2017). *The Myth of the Angry Black Woman*. Accessed 22/06/20 at www.huffpost.com/entry/the-myth-of-the-angry-black-woman_b_11897252.

Chapter 3

Knowing and Acting: On Intersectionality and Countertransference in Clinical Work in the United States

S. J. LANGER

Introduction

Writing this chapter at this moment in time could not have been more appropriate. I have been writing this chapter through the spring and summer of 2020 in New York. It is in the middle of a pandemic which is disproportionately infecting and killing people of colour, the poor, the disabled and the elderly in my country. Riding out the surge in New York, to then watch its needlessness crest across the country, creates a sense of hopelessness and fear. Our government is seemingly bent on allowing the pandemic to carry out passive eugenics by way of inaction and misinformation on the US population. Our death toll will likely be beyond double what it is now, by the time you are reading this chapter. The murders of George Floyd and countless others ignited a global protest movement against individual and institutional racism in the name of Floyd among so many others, including trans, Black, Indigenous, people of colour (BIPOC). We have felt the urgencies of their deaths. The US President has repealed protections in healthcare for transgender and non-binary (TGNB) people, opening the way for providers to refuse care, any type of healthcare, during a pandemic and beyond.[1] The Trump administration has also repealed any legal recognition of transgender identity at the federal level, protections for trans youth in education, and access to serve in the military. It saw the largest protest rally (15,000 people) in support of Black Trans Lives in US history in

1 Currently there is an injunction in Walker v. Azar in the United States District Court for the Eastern District of New York, so the repeal is stayed for now (Riley, 2020).

Brooklyn, New York (Patil, 2020). Then at the Republican National Convention speakers attacked trans youth and spread the myth that trans people are sexual predators of minors in restrooms. And there are still refugee children, kidnapped from their parents, traumatized and likely never to be united, imprisoned around the US. This is my localization.

We are practising in a context in which many of our patients are not just excluded or oppressed by government and institutions, but actively being annihilated by them across multiple intersections. We see the corrosive effects of violence, personal and political, enacted on our patients, more deeply than most people. White supremacy, patriarchy and gender conformity are interwoven tactics to keep those in power, in power (Feinberg, 1996). Colonialism is the structure from which eugenics developed and then found its peak, or so we thought, in the early twentieth century. The goal was the norming of the population from the stance of breeding able-bodied, white, heteronormative, gender-conforming people (Talwar, 2010). Forces of destruction also work from an intersectional structure.

Intersectionality in theory and practice

Intersectionality and unconscious bias are propelled into the collective discourse and not only reserved for academia. But how do clinical principles intersect with protest and politics? Are they useful to our work? Should we be staying in our own lane, working only on an individual level? How does our countertransference disrupt our ability to act intersectionally? We need to be able to hold these realities. If we do not hold them, we are in danger of denying them. We will be unable to be the 'good enough' mirrors our patients require. We know we cannot avoid countertransferential reactions, but we can be disciplined in our self-interrogation and practised in humility in order to act well. Countertransference in Freudian and Winnicottian definition is the patient's unconscious effect on the therapist, the therapist's feelings which could interfere with the treatment but also the understandable reactions to the patient's presentation, clinically and objectively (Freud, 1910; Winnicott, 1994). Since the beginning of psychoanalysis, Freud asked clinicians to engage in a personal analysis to manage their countertransference, and to keep it up every five years (Freud, 1912, 1937).

Countertransference locates the problem mostly within the therapist. Intersectionality weaves into our work the need to understand ourselves in relation to how we understand the other and what is provoked by our own identity or experience. If we have not understood our own privilege and oppression, how will we bring patients further into their own understanding? Only when the therapist has processed their own feelings can they provide a treatment tailored for the patient and not towards the therapist's needs (Winnicott, 1994).

The framework I will be working from is located within intersectionality that Crenshaw (1989) has developed, but also drawing from a predecessor of hers, Bayard Rustin.[2] He instructed us about inter-relationship. From his perspective, civil rights did not grant access to freedom. He asked us, what good is it to gain access to public accommodations ending Jim Crow[3] if one did not have the money, the economic equality, to use them (Rustin, 1965)? He understood the inter-relationship between race, poverty, education and employment and that there was no such thing as a single-issue fight. This is why the 1963 march was framed as The March on Washington for Jobs and Freedom. He also understood that 'self-help' alone would not provide freedom for people of colour, quipping that for every sex worker the Muslim movement of self-empowerment in Harlem reformed, the institutional racism and conditions of the 'ghetto' would replace with two more (1965). In 2009, Litwak was still discussing that whites continued to believe that opportunity was equal, and disparities lie in a certain lack in the disenfranchised; not that systemic racism in our economic, education and justice systems conspire against people of colour, communities with lower incomes, gender non-conforming people, invisibly yet in plain sight.

Another new approach to examining intersectionality has been proposed by de Vries (2015). His multidimensional prism is a method for examining race, gender, sexuality, class, nationality, ability, language, religion, culture, ethnicity, body size and age in a more dynamic intersectional frame. It is a dodecahedron with 12 pentagons holding each of these categories. Within each category are specific details which affect it. For example, the pentagon for gender has legal gender, identity, expression, perceived and normative/variant within it; whereas race has perceived, identity, legal race and physical attributes. It was developed out of qualitative interviews with primarily BIPOC transgender people in the community. If you turn the prism, you shift the focus to highlight a different aspect, but the other dimensions are still visible in the background.

2 Rustin was the organizer of the March on Washington for Jobs and Freedom in 1963, the civil rights leader and educator who taught MLK about the principles of non-violence and sidelined in his place in civil rights history as an out gay, Quaker, Black man.

3 Jim Crow laws were laws passed in the American South in which there were different rules for Blacks and whites in public life enshrining segregation and oppression for Blacks in America post reconstruction (Packard, 2002).

Clinical and societal context

I will highlight here an intersectional revolutionary approach to clinical work drawing from these interdisciplinary thinkers. This structure requires not only examination of the intersectionality within the person in their social context, but that we think about our clinical interventions from an extra-therapy perspective. It is meaningful to my patients and my clinical work that I attend Trans Day of Remembrance[4] or Black Lives Matter and Trans Rights protests. It means something to our treatment if my patients see me there, as either part of the community or supporting the community. Mirroring the existence of reality. However, whether my patients see me there or not, sharing in a community experience not only enables a capacity for empathy but also provides nuance and specificity to the questions I can ask about a patient's experience. A 'qualitative transformation of fundamental institutions' (Rustin, 1965, p.4) societally, culturally, interpersonally and intrapsychically. Although we may not be involved in policy development, we need to know the policies which affect the people with whom we work. When the president revokes trans people's ability to serve in the military, that news affects the sessions I will conduct that day. It is complicated to restructure a patient's self-esteem when their government tells them they are unfit to serve and that economic opportunity is limited for them. When hate crimes against BIPOC, Jewish, TGNB and queer people began to rise after the 2016 election, assessing paranoia, hypervigilance and realistic safety plans shifted from other times in my practice. The threat was more real and thus the intervention needed to be more concrete. For instance, with one patient who was a transwoman early in transition, who already felt unsafe on the street, we talked about taking a self-defence class in conjunction with our work regulating her anxiety and social phobia.

Educating therapists

A movement of multiculturalism in counselling arose with the first civil rights movement in the US (Arrendono & Perez, 2003; Hurley & Gerstein, 2013). Incorporating difference initially took the form of identity-specific classes in the early 1970s, eventually taking the framework of 'multicultural classes' and 'cultural competence' trainings (Abrams & Moio, 2009; Jani *et al.*, 2011; Kirmayer, 2012). Although this was, and is, directed out of good will and effort to address the problem, it also seems to be a recreation of

4 Trans Day of Remembrance occurs on 20 November to honour the TGNB people who have died due to violence and oppression against the community. Most, if not all, of those people are BIPOC. It can involve vigils, invited speakers and opportunity for community members to share about someone they lost or about their own fears.

ghettoizing the groups who have their own classes. It also assumes that everyone in the class is white, American (here in the US), heterosexual, cisgender and other majority statuses. This approach boils groups down with little or no approach of intersectionality.

There is also the concept of ethno-cultural matching of clinicians with clients (Kirmayer, 2012). This is a reductionist intervention. It assumes same group members can automatically understand each other. It diminishes actual clinical skills to identity. It forces people to be identified by their identities, and most importantly, it lets out-of-group clinicians off the hook as they do not need to make the effort to work intersectionally.

'Cultural responsiveness' (Sue *et al.*, 1991), 'cultural humility' (Tervalon & Murray-Garcia, 1998) and 'cultural safety' (Papps & Ramsden, 1996) continue to attempt to address these issues. Cultural safety was developed in New Zealand in the 1980s, in response to poor medical care of the Maori people. It builds on cultural competence to include examination of institutional racism, colonialism and discrimination and how they affect healthcare, particularly emphasizing interrogating power.

Tummala-Narra (2014) details a list of approaches to culturally competent therapists, but what is more useful here is her recognition that the patterns of behaviour, transference and countertransference are essential for examining prejudices and assumptions. We may have the knowledge of group differences, but our ability to act in the clinical moment is more likely hampered by countertransference, not knowledge. Stroumsa and colleagues (2019) quantified this in their study on the effects that educating health providers about trans and gender diverse content had on their thoughts about trans patients. It found that knowledge of trans health did not have an effect on reducing clinician transphobia.

The therapist's ability to tolerate uncomfortable feelings is what will enable patients to feel safe to explore in session (Tummala-Narra, 2014). Furthermore, the therapist's tolerance of their own discomfort will enable them to act. Most therapists know what the right action is, but supervision sessions are usually spent exploring why the therapist was resistant to taking that action, what their countertransference was and how it interfered with the work.

Additionally, we need to work against a binary framework in our approach to non-conforming behaviour: pathological or non-pathological (Talwar, 2010). This must be across identities, be it pathologizing the behaviour of Black children as 'angry' (Wilkins *et al.*, 2013) or gender non-conformity as mental illness (Langer & Martin, 2004). Talwar encourages us to use the principles of countertransference with the self-reflexive tasks of working intersectionally (2010), while Anthias understood intersectionality more broadly as a heuristic tool for understanding power, privilege and boundaries (2013).

Early on in teaching my class on clinical theory and practice to our first semester art therapy graduate students, I was covering intergenerational trauma. We were reviewing the literature I had assigned on the intergenerational effects of the Holocaust, primarily studied in Israel. Then, the only African-American student raised her hand and simply, without accusation, asked, 'What about slavery?' A shock ran through me at the recognition of my unconscious bias (Eberhardt, 2019). I was grateful that the student spoke up and felt comfortable enough to do so in my class. I immediately thanked the student and acknowledged my glaring gap and that it was likely in no small way related to being white. I may also have uttered an audible 'ugh', my visceral response to this realization that, despite all my allyship, reading and action in my teaching, it was not as anti-racist as I thought. I am grateful I did not react with defensiveness, but rather with humility and was forgiven for my failure. We need to appreciate the burden we impose on students, when we do not do the work ourselves.

This is imminently important to the clinical work these students are doing and will do in their careers, since many of their patients will be descendants of 12 generations of official enslavement in this country, with many more years of terror following through Jim Crow and other forms of institutional racism. I took an informal poll that day of the demographics of the students' internship caseloads and it seemed to be about 80–90 per cent African American. So, why had I not found the literature on the intergenerational trauma of slavery? My research skills are not lethargic. I had been fallible to what Lazarre (1996) described of Americans as our ability to tangle with European genocide and barely acknowledge the violence in our own country. As much as I do not feel a part of America, I am still a product of her. As much as my efforts to be a global and educated citizen in a disavowal of American exceptionalism, my countertransference in relation to being a product of America and recipient of the privilege it grants whites caught me in the place between knowledge and knowing, interrupting my ability to act.

In terms of research literature, the discussion of slavery's effect in clinical literature is lacking and one has to be creative and interdisciplinary. It is also an effect of institutional racism that this kind of research is not financially and institutionally supported in the US in the manner in which studying the Holocaust is in Israel. The Holocaust is not Israel's shame and crime the way slavery is in the US. The US has barely been able to confront it.

The setting

Butler (2019) discusses Blackness as being speechless, atopic and placeless in the consulting room, since that room is historically a white room. White people are indoctrinated into entitlement, privilege, superiority and the idea that whiteness is *the* world perspective (Suchet, 2007). I would add that the consulting room is a cisgender, male, heteronormative and ableist room as well. This applies to clinical moments in the room, as well as the physical space. It took a decade of prodding the management in my office space for them to finally 'un-gender' the restrooms.

If the environment cannot imagine or hold an image of a child, how can mirroring and thus attachment be formed? How do we create the Winnicottian 'potential space' or, as Butler (2019) examines, the ability for Winnicott's 'going-on-being' (Winnicott, 1956)? This has been explored by Butler (2019) for the BIPOC patient and Langer (2016, 2019) for the TGNB patient. The patient develops a Winnicottian 'false self' to accommodate for the other's inability to reflect and hold them. Obviously, this rupture is compounded in the BIPOC, TGNB patient. Education alone does not enable a clinician to positively mirror their TGNB patients of colour. If we assume the setting is apolitical then its 'violence remains unchecked' (Butler, 2019, p.156).

Suchet's (2007) introspective account of whiteness and its effect on clinical work is a strong example of examining one's privilege, position and countertransference. She weaves her early life living as a white person in apartheid South Africa with clinical examples of working with BIPOC patients in a very honest account. When paired with her 2011 article on clinical work with a transman, it reveals how even the most expert clinician can be hampered by her other privileges, in this case her cis-privilege. In the 2011 article, Suchet discusses her analysis with a transman prior to his transition. Her countertransference to his trans identity was due to her over-identification with him, since he presented as a lesbian at the time. She directed the treatment in the manner that he needed to accept his 'femaleness' and work through his sexual abuse history. She confused trauma with being causative of trans identity, which is ironic since this has been, and continues to be, an interpretation perpetrated on lesbians with a trauma history. She viewed his need to express masculinity through her own cis-privilege, that trans identity and expression are a deviation from the norm of cisgender existence. Her patient repeatedly confronted her on this stance, but she still had difficulty examining her own countertransference. She refused to even read the literature the patient suggested to her and did not seek out expert supervision for this case. These two examples highlight how even the most intelligent and introspective clinician can remain tangled in their own countertransference. Additionally, it illustrates how knowledge or access to knowledge alone is insufficient to dismantle countertransferential resistance. If Suchet had been in supervision with someone adept at working through gender with a patient, she may have been directly and consistently challenged by this supervisor on her biased perspective on trans identity and defensiveness towards learning more about it. It would also have taken the burden off the patient to fight for their right to exist within their own analysis.

'Apocalyptic concrete jungle'

I am an interloper to art therapy. I do have a background in filmmaking and writing, but I am not a licensed art therapist. However, as a licensed clinical social worker, I have had the good fortune of being adopted into the art therapy programme at the School of Visual Arts (SVA) to teach general clinical theory and practice and work as a thesis advisor. I am a grateful adoptee, who has learned spectacularly from my colleagues and students.

A colleague of mine collaborates with a non-profit organization which works with young people involved in the juvenile justice system in New York City to develop art therapy opportunities for their participants. The typical manner in which institutions and young people interact is that the institution offers an hour with art materials and the young people accept it or not. DelliCarpini (2020) pivots to offer the institution – the location – as a material for the art therapy, as opposed to a privileged place in which the young people should feel lucky to be. She appreciates their feelings of not being welcome in an expensive Manhattan neighbourhood as valid, and not as resistance. 'Apocalyptic concrete jungle' is the theme the participants gave the second project cycle in which they took ownership of the studio space in our department, transforming the walls into murals they designed expressing their views and feelings about living in New York City as young people of colour (ibid, p.17). As she says, she works from Owens's theory of representation – it is an act, it is not a neutral or static object (1992).

There is not enough space here to describe the entire project, but I direct you to her article for that exploration. I do want to highlight the clinical reframing and countertransferential work of DelliCarpini, as well as the experience of a student intern with this project.

DelliCarpini discusses approaching resistance not as an intrapsychic defence, but as the signal of disruption in power and privilege. She suggests this as a clinical tool to upend reliance on a medical model which especially pathologizes BIPOC people's behaviour when viewed through white, hetero/cisnormative lenses. She is careful not to intrude on the participants, but consistently and unobtrusively offers herself for clinical work.

When a participant refuses her help on their part of the mural, she does not provide a heavy-handed interpretation, but respects their wishes. Her repeated attempts are eventually rewarded.

Our countertransference needs to be examined in order to avoid falling back onto these tropes of privilege. It is not only knowledge of this fact that prevents us from repeating the mistake, but the reflection that DelliCarpini enacts on her own privileged position, which makes action in the direction of true intersectionality possible. She reflects on her own countertransference to reframe clinical interventions and how to lend her social capital to the young people. She asks participant artists to speak as paid SVA guest lecturers, and offers support towards attending SVA as undergraduates (DelliCarpini, 2020). This is a keen example of clinical interventions being approached from an intersectional frame on the individual and institutional level.

A student intern joined this project two years into it. She described that she was not seen as an 'ops' (oppositional adult) by the youth, and believed this was because she was a woman of colour. The youth questioned her on her ethnicity, thinking she was 'Hispanic or mixed', although she was Egyptian. Through their curiosity of her ethnicity, they were able ultimately to explore their own ethnic and racial identities. For instance, while working on the mural, they discussed the risks of living in the world as BIPOC people (Ibrahim, 2019). Other clinical material was opened up through identification, whereas DelliCarpini, who is white, provided opportunity for different clinical material to be processed.

'My Gender is No Thank You'

Trans research, which centres trans clinical work, is usually focused on what studying white trans people can teach us about white cisgender people, completely ignoring BIPOC trans people, making this next example so vital (de Vries, 2015). At times it does take a clinician from within intersectional experiences to weave these into dynamic clinical opportunities.

In our graduate department, master's candidates must complete a thesis which can be either research or a document of clinical work. One art therapy student created a fibre studio group for gender non-conforming and non-binary youth at an LGBTQ centre as part of their thesis (Roland-Waring, 2019). The Ali Forney Center is a drop-in centre in New York City for LGBTQ youth who are experiencing homelessness. The fibre studio group consisted of between two and seven young people from the programme, aged between 21 and 25 years old. They identified as Black, mixed race, Southeast Asian and (my favourite) mestizo or American enough to fit in. Gender was described as non-binary, agender, transwoman, androgynon, chaotic and evolving by the group members and the art therapist. Roland-Waring understood that how one expresses their gender non-conformity in dress exposes one to danger socially (Gordon & Meyer, 2007; Harrison, Grant & Herman, 2012). However, there is the mental health risk of not living in one's affirmed gender which overrides this physical danger (Connelly *et al.*, 2016). The ability to tangibly fashion one's gender expression is a life-saving intervention given the high suicide rates in TGNB youth, especially of young people of colour with family rejection in their history (James *et al.*, 2016). As fashion photographer Bill Cunningham said, 'Fashion is the armor to survive the reality of everyday life' (Press, 2010). Gender-affirmative interventions and mirroring are suicide prevention for TGNB youth of colour in the inner city, in a homeless drop-in centre.

During the sessions, one young person created a small tulle bandeau from a beige skirt and he painted the word 'Fluid' on it. There were members who received positive mirroring of their skills and they began to see their skills as marketable, by seeing their work online. Language was exchanged and explored: 'I'm learning so much here. It's just...if your pronouns can be "bad bitch", then mine can be "soft boy"' (Roland-Waring, 2019, p.23). The group had a cultural privacy to use language and slang without having to explain it to anyone. The format of a closed group protected members from microaggressions, misgendering and harassment which can occur in LGB spaces that TGNB people inhabit (Alxndr, 2018). These young people are often marginalized within their marginalized group. Another member processed their anger at barriers to top surgery, due to the lack of full medical coverage and chronic illness, by embroidering 'My Gender is No Thank You', 'stabbing' the anger into the material.

This group and the directives appreciated and provided healing on an intersectional basis. It addressed the needs of these young people based on their age (if they were developmentally on target); race (compositionally and language); economic status (if they could afford to buy new wardrobes or have access to healthcare to have top surgery); size (larger-sized clothes were lacking in donations); gender (if they had space to explore and to tangibly create their genders and ability); and emotional and skill-based support. They departed from viewing services for TGNB youth as only centred on transition and only binary, and managed their identification with their clients in support of the clinical work.

Conclusion

So many of our intersectional positions are social constructions, including race, gender and disability. Intersectionality is about being suspicious and curious. We do not take for granted that we know another's experience; we are suspicious about how a research question is being framed and by whom. Are the theorists or practitioners or researchers self-reflective? Students are ahead of us. We should listen to them. Incorporating intersectionality is a collective construction. This is why we need diversity in the student and faculty body.

It is foundational humility that is needed to examine countertransference from an intersectional frame *and* to be able to act. The humility to tolerate the rupture in the transference when a patient calls us out on our ignorance or assumption. Humility to preface our interventions or hypotheses with the admission that we may not know. 'But we can agitate the right questions by probing at the contradictions which still stand in the way' (Rustin, 1965). We are in the business of questions, but questions which are useful in their ability to transect multiple dimensions. This is intersectionality in action. When a question, either individual clinical moments or directive design, can address intersectional levels, conscious and unconscious material, then those are the revolutionary acts.

References

Abrams, L. S. & Moio, J. A. (2009). Critical race theory and the cultural competence dilemma in social work education. *Journal of Social Work Education, 45*(2), 245–261. doi:10.5175/JSWE.2009.200700109.

Alxndr, T. (2018, February 6). *Nonbinary folks are still invisible, even in queer spaces*. Available at www.them.us/story/nonbinary-invisibility-queer-spaces.

Anthias, F. (2013). Intersectionality what? Social divisions, intersectionality and levels of analysis. *Ethnicities, 13*(1), 3–19.

Arredondo, P. & Perez, P. (2003). Expanding multicultural competence through social justice leadership. *The Counseling Psychologist, 31*(3), 282–289. doi:10.1177/0011000003031003003.

Butler, D. G. (2019). Racialized bodies and the violence of the setting. *Studies in Gender and Sexuality, 20*(3), 146–158. https://doi.org/10.1080/15240657.2019.1641935.

Connelly, M. D., Zervos, M. J., Barone, C. J., Johnson, C. C. & Joseph, C. L. M. (2016). The mental health of transgender youth: Advances in understanding. *Journal of Adolescent Health, 59*(5), 489–495.

Crenshaw, K. (1989). Demarginalizing the intersection of race and sex: A Black feminist critique of antidiscrimination doctrine, feminist theory and antiracist politics. *University of Chicago Legal Forum, 1*(8), 139–176. Available at https://chicagounbound.uchicago.edu/uclf/vol1989/iss1/8.

DelliCarpini, E. (2020). Breaking Bars: Community based art therapy mural project. *Art Therapy: Journal of the American Art Therapy Association, 37*(4), 185–193.

de Vries, K. M. (2015). Transgender people of color at the center: Conceptualizing a new intersectional model. *Ethnicities, 15*(1), 3–27.

Eberhardt, J. L. (2019). *Unconscious Bias: Uncovering the Hidden Prejudice That Shapes What We See, Think, and Do*. New York, NY: Viking.

Feinberg, L. (1996). *Transgender Warriors.* Boston, MA: Beacon Press.
Freud, S. (1910). The Future Prospects of Psychoanalytic Therapy. In J. Strachey (ed.) *Standard Edition, 11,* 141–151. London: Hogarth Press.
Freud, S. (1912). The Dynamics of Transference. In J. Strachey (ed.) *Standard Edition, 12,* 97–108. London: Hogarth Press.
Freud, S. (1937). Constructions in Analysis. In J. Strachey (ed.) *Standard Edition, 23,* 257–269. London: Hogarth Press.
Gordon, A. R. & Meyer, I. H. (2007). Gender nonconformity as a target of prejudice, discrimination, and violence against LGB individuals. *Journal of LGBT Health Research, 3*(3), 55–71.
Harrison, J., Grant, J. & Herman, J. (2012). A gender not listed here: Genderqueers, gender rebels, and otherwise in the National Transgender Discrimination Survey. *LGBTQ Policy Journal 2,* 13–23.
Hurley, E. J. & Gerstein, L. H. (2013). The Multiculturally and Internationally Competent Mental Health Professional. In R. L. Lowman (ed.) *Internationalizing Multiculturalism: Expanding Professional Competencies in a Globalized World* (pp.227–254). Washington, DC: American Psychological Association.
Ibrahim, R. (2019). *An Intersection of Art Therapy and Cultural Contexts with Minority Youth.* Master's thesis, School of Visual Arts, MPS Art Therapy, New York.
James, S. E., Herman, J. L., Rankin, S., Keisling, M., Mottet, L. & Anafi, M. (2016). *The Report of the 2015 U.S. Transgender Survey.* Washington, DC: National Center for Transgender Equality.
Jani, J., Pierce, D., Ortiz, L. & Sowbel, L. (2011). Access to intersectionality, content to competence: Deconstructing social work education diversity standards. *Journal of Social Work Education, 47*(2), 283–301. doi:10.5175/JSWE.2011.200900118.
Kirmayer, L. J. (2012). Rethinking cultural competence. *Transcultural Psychiatry, 49*(2), 149–164. doi:10.1177/1363461512444673.
Langer, S. J. (2016). Our body project: From mourning to creating the transgender body. *International Journal of Transgenderism, 15*(2), 66–75.
Langer, S. J. (2019). *Theorizing Transgender Identity for Clinical Practice: A New Model for Understanding Gender.* London: Jessica Kingsley Publishers/Hachette.
Langer, S. J. & Martin, J. I. (2004). How dresses can make you mentally ill: Examining gender identity disorder in children. *Child and Adolescent Social Work Journal, 21*(1), 5–23.
Lazarre, J. (1996). *Beyond the Whiteness of Whiteness: Memoir of a White Mother of Black Sons.* Durham, NC: Duke University Press.
Litwak, I. F. (2009). *How Free is Free: The Long Death of Jim Crow.* Cambridge & London: Harvard University Press.
Owens, C. (1992). *Beyond Recognition: Representation, Power, and Culture.* Berkeley, CA: University of California Press.
Packard, J. M. (2002). *American Nightmare: The History of Jim Crow.* New York, NY: St. Martin's Press.
Papps, E. & Ramsden, I. (1996). Cultural safety in nursing: The New Zealand experience. *International Journal of Quality in Health Care, 8*(5), 491–497.
Patil, A. (2020). How a March for Black Trans Lives Became a Huge Event. *The New York Times,* June 15, 2020. Available at www.nytimes.com/2020/06/15/nyregion/brooklyn-black-trans-parade.html.
Press, R. (Dir.), Gefter, P. (Prod.) (2010). *Bill Cunningham.* New York, NY: Zeitgeist Films.
Riley, J. (August 17, 2020). Federal judge blocks Trump administration rule removing transgender health care protections. MetroWeekly. Available at www.metroweekly.com/2020/08/federal-judge-blocks-trump-administration-rule-stripping-away-transgender-health-care-protections.
Roland-Waring, A. (2019). *Transcending the Gender Binary: Exploring Gender Identity with Gender Nonconforming Youth.* Master's thesis, School of Visual Arts, MPS Art Therapy, New York.
Rustin, B. (1965). From protest to politics: The future of the Civil Rights Movement. *New York: Commentary Magazine,* 2 February, (39), 25–31.

Stroumsa, D., Shires, D. A., Richardson, C. R., Jaffee, K. D. & Woodford, M. R. (2019). Transphobia rather than education predicts provider knowledge of transgender health care. *Medical Education, 53*(4), 398–407. doi:10.1111/medu.13796.

Suchet, M. (2007). Unraveling whiteness. *Psychoanalytic Dialogues, 17*(6), 867–886.

Suchet, M. (2011). Crossing over. *Psychoanalytic Dialogues, 21*(2), 172–191. doi:10.1080/10481885.2011.562842.

Sue, S., Fujino, D. C., Hu, L. T., Takeuchi, D. T. & Zane, N. W. (1991). Community mental health services for ethnic minority groups: A test of the cultural responsiveness hypothesis. *Journal of Consulting and Clinical Psychology, 59*(4), 533–540.

Talwar, S. (2010). An intersectional framework for race, class, gender, and sexuality in art therapy. *Art Therapy: Journal of the American Art Therapy Association, 27*(1), 11–17.

Tervalon, M. & Murray-Garcia, J. (1998). Cultural humility versus cultural competence: A critical distinction in defining physician training outcomes in multicultural education. *Journal of Health Care for the Poor and Underserved, 9*(2), 117–125.

Tummala-Narra, P. (2014, May 5). Cultural competence as a core emphasis of psychoanalytic psychotherapy. *Psychoanalytic Psychology, 32*(2), 275–292. https://dx.doi.org/10.1037/a0034041.

Wilkins, E. J., Whiting, J. B., Watson, M. F., Russon, J. M. & Moncrief, A. M. (2013). Residual effects of slavery: What clinicians need to know. *Contemporary Family Therapy, 35*(1), 14–28.

Winnicott, D. W. (1956). Primary Maternal Preoccupation. In L. Caldwell & H. Taylor (eds) *The Collected Works of D.W. Winnicott: Volume 5, 1955–1959*. Oxford: Oxford University Press.

Winnicott, D. W. (1994). Hate in the counter-transference. *The Journal of Psychotherapy Practice and Research, 3*(4), 348–356.

Chapter 4

Skin to Paper: The Body in Art Psychotherapy

GEORGINA OBAYA EVANS

Introduction

The body is not neutral but powerful and vulnerable. It is part of a dynamic 'body-mind' complex: fundamental to our formation of self as integrated intersubjective beings; able to feel, think, imagine and act to create and destroy the world.

As an art psychotherapist with a background in bodywork and visual cultures, I am interested in exploring the performative presence of the body in art psychotherapy. While training in the profession, I was aware of the animated presence of bodies in the room while engaged in clinical work. This was particularly evident when I was working in a hospital setting with people diagnosed with personality disorder (PD). Personality disorder can now be understood in terms of attachment disorder (Bateman & Fonagy, 2006). Most clients with this diagnosis are trauma survivors, whose worlds have in some ways been destroyed. This emotional devastation often leads to a loss of symbolic function and sense of self. The body becomes the primary means of communication, and intolerable feelings are 'acted out' (De Zulueta, 1993). The body also becomes the vehicle for emotional self-regulation through enacted behaviours, such as drug and alcohol use and the complex issue of self-harming. Self-harm is defined as 'the act of deliberately causing harm to oneself either by causing a physical injury, by putting oneself in dangerous situations and/or self-neglect' (National Self Harm Network, 2021). In this context, self-harm can be understood as an embodied expression of psychological distress, as well as a means of regulating emotions (Morgan *et al.*, 2012).

PD is diagnosed according to subcategories outlined in the World Health Organization's *International Classification of Diseases* (ICD-10) and the American *Diagnostic and Statistical Manual* (DSM-5). Both are used to diagnose mental health disorders in the UK. Interestingly, women are more frequently diagnosed with borderline personality disorder (BPD), which is often co-morbid with depression, anxiety, eating disorders, post-traumatic stress disorder and bipolar disorder (NICE, 2009). With a lower prevalence of PD reported among 'black' patients compared with 'white' patients in the UK (Gilloway *et al.*, 2010), race also makes a difference. The important point here is that social classifications of difference matter.

The treatment of BPD has moved away from the traditional psychoanalytic approach towards mentalization-based treatment, which aims to directly address the compromised symbolic functioning and emotional dysregulation associated with attachment disorders (Bateman & Fonagy, 2006). Mentalizing is the process by which we make sense of each other and ourselves, implicitly and explicitly, in terms of subjective states and mental processes (Bateman & Fonagy, 2006). Art psychotherapy has been evidenced to support the development of mentalizing capacity in BPD (Springham *et al.*, 2012).

For many who come into contact with mental health services when their world is shattered and they are unable to cohere, art psychotherapy can be effective in facilitating multilayered communication between client and therapist. Indeed, clients who cannot be helped elsewhere are frequently referred to the arts psychotherapies. Often, difficult unconscious material can arise, facilitating new paths of healing. Through the creation of an art product that can be thought about with both concrete and symbolic meanings, art psychotherapy offers an inherently embodied process: client and therapist are engaged in kinetic actions of art-making, moving around the room, looking together from different perspectives, talking and coming into 'being' together within the architectural space (Skaife, 2008).

Incorporating social constructions of meaning that frame and influence clinical work more widely is central to this discussion about the body in art psychotherapy. I am a mixed-heritage woman of colour, who grew up with the experience of being perceived differently in different continents: as 'white' in Africa and 'black' in Europe. My embodied experience was of being neither one nor the other: neither 'black' nor 'white' but brown! Having to respond to dramatically different external perceptions of myself was profoundly challenging and a catalyst for developing a multilayered understanding of identity in relation to social context. This informs my critical enquiry of notions of 'self' in clinical practice and my exploration of the body in therapeutic practice.

In this chapter, the 'performance' of the body is explored in the clinical art psychotherapy setting by adopting an overarching lens of intersectionality (Crenshaw, 1989). Coined by Crenshaw to conceptualize the double oppression of African American women on grounds of both race and sex, intersectionality offers a framework for thinking beyond an 'either/or' binary to a 'both/and' perspective (Collins & Bilge, 2016). This makes for a more complex view. For example, a client's gender, ethnicity and sexuality are all considered alongside the clinical diagnosis when considering treatment options. Drawing from theoretical research and my clinical experience of working with people diagnosed with personality disorder, I will explore the body from three perspectives: the 'medical body' – the body in the medical setting; the 'cultural body' – the body from a cultural perspective; and lastly, the 'psychological body' – the body from a more integrated intersectional perspective. I hope to draw attention to the presence and performance of bodies in art psychotherapeutic practice and to bring occluded bodies out of the shadows and into view.

The body in therapeutic practice

The somatic presentations of his patients were instrumental to Freud's psychoanalytic theorization and his mapping of our landscapes of the mind (Orbach, 2009). Modern medicine emerged in the philosophical milieu of the early enlightenment period. During this era, the ideas of philosopher René Descartes inaugurated the split between mind and matter which had a profound influence on Western culture, including the development of psychoanalysis (Blackman, 2008). 'Man' was aligned with 'mind', thought and scientific self-determinism: the 'norm' against which variance came to be measured. 'Woman' was aligned with the 'material body': biologically determined and ruled by 'nature' and her emotions. Thus establishing 'an unbridgeable gulf between mind and matter' (Grosz, 1994, p.7) which continues to this day, manifesting in gender bias and stereotyping. Cartesian dualism comprehends mind and reason as flexible and fluid, while the body is positioned as fixed and cut off from social influences. This too underpins binary structures of knowledge production and associated sociocultural power dynamics.

Today, the prioritization of mind over body seems to prevail (Orbach, 2003). Nevertheless, the importance of the body in our understanding of psychological work continues to grow. For example, advances made in comprehending the role of trauma in psychophysiological stress and our phylogenetically encoded mechanisms of adaptation are outlined in Porges' polyvagal theory (Porges, 2011). Similarly, research and understanding of complex post-traumatic stress disorder (C-PTSD) resulting from multiple and ongoing stresses of trauma, such as those experienced in prolonged cases of child abuse or exposure to domestic violence or the violence of war (Herman, 1992), point to the primacy of the body in our understanding of psychological distress and the need for trauma-informed approaches to treatment (Van der Kolk, 2014). Orbach (2003) advocates a view of 'the body as body', highlighting a need for the therapist to meet the challenge of bringing their own body into the therapeutic encounter to facilitate a more potentiated healing process:

> We have to pay attention. We have to look, listen, feel and interrogate ourselves. And, if we pay the same kind of attention to our body nuances and body feelings as we do to our more commonly apprehended countertransference, I think we will have a great deal to offer those with troubled bodies and body symptoms. (ibid, p.14)

The notion of 'embodiment' adopted here follows Blackman's (2008) concept of the 'communicating body', an emergent body which connects and communicates that which 'cannot be captured by the concept of cognition' (ibid, p.35). This approach to embodiment challenges the Cartesian separation of mind and body and highlights the presence of the body in everyday, intersubjective communication, including the process of thought itself (Damasio, 2000).

Until recently, theories of the body in the practices and processes of art psychotherapy have remained relatively under explored. Nonetheless, some art psychotherapists have touched on the subject: Melliar and Bruhka (2010) adopt a phenomenological framework to explore how experiences of self are made possible within a therapeutic community (TC) residential setting; Whitaker (2004) explores body awareness and motion within the context of art psychotherapy practice; and Skaife (2001, 2008) offers a useful philosophically informed discussion and phenomenological theorization of the body in art psychotherapy that calls for a more socially engaged perspective.

A socially engaged perspective requires us to bear in mind the specific needs and agendas of the communities we serve. However, this intention is not always followed through. It has been argued that issues of equality and difference are not sufficiently thought about nor given adequate consideration despite their significant impact on our work as psychological practitioners (Lago & Thompson, 1996). The Black, African and Asian Therapy Network was created to address this unmet need in terms of race. Britain is an increasingly diverse social environment and we need paradigms to make sense of the highly complex dynamics of our private and public selves. Encounters of gender, race, class, ethnicity and LGBTQ+ difference impact our shifting intersubjectivity and embodied interdependence. This affects our understanding of ourselves and our actions. How then do we locate the body in the theory and practice of art psychotherapy and through what frames of reference can it be understood? Discussing multiplicities of identity and difference, the Black, lesbian, feminist poet Audre Lorde wrote, '...for it is not difference which immobilises us, but silence. And there are so many silences to be broken' (Lorde, 1984, p.44). The body in therapy and issues of difference remain poorly addressed. Adopting an intersectional perspective might create new approaches for bringing often unspoken material to voice.

Intersectionality: A framework for art psychotherapy practice

An intersectional paradigm offers a way to interrogate and understand our lives beyond the Cartesian binary 'either/or' lens. Intersectionality can be understood as '(1) an approach to understanding human life and behaviour rooted in the experiences and struggles of disenfranchised people; (2) an important tool for linking theory with practice that can aid in the empowerment of communities and individuals' (Collins & Bilge, 2016, p.36).

Thus, gender, ethnicity and socio-economic background, for example, must be recognized as informing the emergence of personal and social identities within shared social frameworks of meaning. Socially constructed meaning influences our impressions of who we are: our bodies and how we 'perform' (Butler, 1990) ourselves psychophysiologically in daily life. Identity is therefore central to our mental health and wellbeing.

The feminist philosopher Grosz suggests that the body, as carrier of these socially constructed frames, is itself constructed and, as such, is a contestable and contested site of knowledge production. This creates a problem with any effort to understand the body in any given context as 'natural':

> The body, or rather bodies, cannot be adequately understood as historical, pre-cultural, or natural objects in any simple way; they are not only inscribed, marked, engraved, by social pressures external to them but are the products, the direct effects, of the very social constitution of nature itself. (Grosz, 1994, p.x)

The impact of societal inequities, difference in access to opportunities and variances of representation in the public domain requires more nuanced understanding. Issues of inclusivity go right to the heart of the therapeutic relationship, the privacy of the therapeutic room and the power dynamics of the therapeutic project at all levels. For example, the ongoing push to de-colonize the academy and curriculum in educational establishments throughout the country evidences the urgent need to address the legacy of colonialism and the politics of the neocolonialism of the 'global North'. This raises important questions about how therapists are trained and how well the training equips therapists to deal with issues of equality and difference. Therapists from all backgrounds need to be adequately prepared to offer effective inclusive treatment to clients from all socio-economic and cultural backgrounds (Alleyne, 1989) and must employ rigorous self-reflexivity to this end, including an understanding of difference conceived through the body and, in this chapter, formulated through three specific perspectives: the medical body, the cultural body and the psychological body.

The medical body: BPD and self-harm

The medical model is premised on the understanding of disease caused by biophysiological factors: pathogens and hereditary genetic mutations that must be controlled. This approach seeks to establish what is ailing a patient, the likely cause of the condition and the medical care required with reference to presenting symptoms. Prior to the adoption of the biopsychosocial model, BPD was treated according to the medical model of diagnosis, prognosis and treatment of illness, which underpinned psychiatric services. The clinician took the role of expert. The patient's view was not sought beyond their presentation of physical 'facts' used to diagnose and establish treatment. The 'body' of the patient was thus stripped of psychological subjectivity and effectively disempowered, disembodied and subjectively removed from the medical equation (Grosz, 1994). This evidences the influence of Cartesian dualism that continues to influence much contemporary evidence-based medicine and underlies contemporary art psychotherapy practice.

As noted, BPD is characterized by unstable relationships, poor self-image, volatile mood swings and self-harming behaviours. Eastwood (2012) critiques the predominantly female diagnosis of BPD as a social construction of the feminine as disempowered, excessively emotional and childlike. In art therapy with women diagnosed with BPD, she highlights the important role of feminist therapy in disrupting unequal power dynamics inherent in 'misogynist' psychoanalysis and advocates the need to reframe and prioritize the voice of the client as expert in clinical work.

Laing criticized the psychiatric use of the medical model of diagnosis as an abstracted 'non-reciprocal static model' (1976, p.37), which did not consider wider social frameworks and influences in the diagnosis of illness. Relating this to art psychotherapy research and evidence-based practice (EBP), Gilroy (2006) cautions that science as a 'social-activity' is not impartial, even though it is widely taken to be so. This, no doubt, impacts how clients, and all of us, think about ourselves:

> It shores up the vested interests of certain parties while drawing resources, attention and focus away from others... [T]he government's, and therefore EBP's, focus on the clinical and cost-effectiveness of treatments has accelerated the shift in research attention away from understanding mental health problems and exploring them in a social, cultural and political context, towards positivist approaches to treatment, that is, to outcomes. (Gilroy, 2006, p.19)

Both Laing and Gilroy advocate a non-binary approach to medical practice that aligns with an intersectional attitude to research and treatment practices.

Art psychotherapy bridges medicine and culture. As such, considering social constructions of meaning beyond the medical domain into the cultural arena may inspire different ways of thinking about psychological distress and treatment. Self-harm is particularly prevalent among people with BPD (Suyemoto, 1998) and often remains secretive and undetected for long periods of time (Mental Health Foundation, 2021). This is in stark contrast to public performances of self-injurious behaviours which can be seen and interpreted as artistic expression and inquiry in the context of the cultural arena.

The cultural body: Cutting skin in performance art

Acts of self-injury and body mutilation, as seen in conditions such as personality disorder, schizophrenia and psychosis, have been interpreted as having little meaning: '...the act itself has little symbolic meaning other than regulating affect dysregulated by loss or the threat of loss' (Bateman & Fonagy, 2006, p.27). However, from his position as a cultural psychiatrist, Favazza (1996) states otherwise: '...self-mutilation is far too complicated a behaviour to be understood by only one approach' (1996, p.xiii). He suggests that all feelings, misperceptions, anti-social and self-harming acts, symptoms and beliefs, associated with mental illness, can only be understood with reference to the psychological, social and physical integrity of the 'communal body' (ibid):

> ...an understanding of the behaviour demanded an examination of the vast array of cultural practices, attitudes and beliefs – from religion and mythology to folk healing, from infibulation to initiation rites, from artistic and literary depictions to blood customs – that form the theatre within which self-mutilation is performed. (ibid, p.xii)

Scarification and tattooing, for example, are carried out throughout the world for social and aesthetic meaning and value.

Other portals of inquiry are opened by contemporary body artists who perform body modification. For example, the artists Franko B and Ron Athey have produced performances that include ritualized bloodletting. These practices were framed by queer discourses aligned with the AIDS epidemic of the 1980s and 1990s and had significant social and political ramifications: '...the meaning of blood changed radically' (Schechner, 2009). Kira O'Reilly's work includes cutting her flesh as part of an ongoing dialogue that engages with the architecture of the body in relation to the viewer and biochemical processes and materials. Her work also thinks about the body beyond and outside language, exploring ideas that are 'lost to language' (Duggan, 2009). Cuban artist Carlos Martiel[1] uses his body as 'raw material' – cutting, piercing and rupturing his skin to interrogate existence and the ethics of humanity, to question social barriers and to critique violent racism in the USA. In these artistic practices, the body becomes the instrument of artistic expression and critique that seeks to challenge and rupture the normative understanding of an 'invisible' Cartesian or 'medical' body. The 'cultural body' of artists like O'Reilly, Franko B and Martiel seeks to disrupt the disembodied 'medical body' and create problems with contemporary views of the body: how it is perceived, understood and socially constructed. Audiences of such works are confronted by their own corporeal being and invited to reflect on their own wounds and the boundaries of socially sanctioned acts of violence.

Having witnessed a haunting performance by Franko B in which he was completely covered in white body paint and walked slowly up and down a 'catwalk' of white canvas, blood slowly streaming from his cannulated veins, I was left feeling ambivalent but also deeply touched. In Elaine Scarry's thesis *The Body in Pain* (1985), she speaks both of how pain can render us speechless, destroyed and devoid of any sense of self and also of how pain can become highly articulate as a source of the 'real' – the origin of spiritual transcendence, primal creativity and triumph over death. Does the aestheticization of pain and violence seen in some contemporary performance art serve to mask or shed light on the deeper questions of power that underlie the complex and violent underbelly of Western contemporary life (De Zulueta, 1993)? Does the work and creative practice of body artists like O'Reilly and Martiel offer us new frameworks through which to consider the destruction and violence of contemporary life or are they acting out

1 www.carlosmartiel.net/category/news

personal distress, as Lemma (2010) suggests is the case of the subcultural group The Modern Primitives?[2]

From an intersectional perspective, they are doing both: enacting and 'making visible' (Skaife, 2001) what is often hidden and shied away from in dominant cultural and medical discourses. I would argue that performance works that stretch the performer and viewers' limits of endurance offer those who choose to participate an opportunity to experience and engage in valuable social discourse at the level of intersubjective embodiment without words: a kind of 'thinking through the body', to use Blackman's (2008) apt terminology.

The psychological body: An intersectional approach

The psychological body is the body seen through an intersectional lens that draws from various influences: Grosz's (1994) notion of the 'corporeal body'; De Zulueta's (1993) inquiry of the traumatic roots of human destructiveness; Orbach's (2003) critique of the absented body of classical psychoanalytic discourse; and Alleyne's (1998) critique of 'white' feminism and dominant psychotherapeutic practices. Alleyne argues that the internalization of negative self-traits within 'black' populations in the West is due to the lack of this material being adequately acknowledged, addressed and thought about in dominant discourses. The notion of the 'psychological body' thus engenders an intersectional perspective that considers the body from multiple levels simultaneously. This complements the biopsychosocial approach of contemporary healthcare. Through an intersectional lens, the body is never 'neutral'. It engages with other bodies in the therapeutic setting, as elsewhere, as a form of communication which takes place in addition to language: this body is layered, multiple, complex and emergent. From this perspective, embodied experience can be understood more clearly as being constituted by sociocultural constructs within wider political frameworks of dominance. Access to medical treatment, education, employment and other resources is not equal and necessarily affects a person's performance

2 The term 'modern primitives' describes a community of Western individuals who have become disenfranchised with 'Western modernity'. Culturally informed body modifications such as tattooing, piercing and refiguring the body are adopted in pursuit of direct spiritual transformation and meaningful self-expression. Psychoanalyst Alessandra Lemma argues that body modifications are now widely practised and sanctioned, to a degree, in the West. She suggests cultural practices taken out of their original setting lose their collective cultural significance to become individual expressions of psychological distress. Given the increasingly dynamic cultural demographic of Western society, it now seems necessary to reconsider the socio-political complexities of how we make and communicate meaning across our embodied and intercultural lived experiences.

of self as, simultaneously, an individual, a member of various groups and society as a whole. The following clinical vignette considers how the body might be thought about and engaged with in art psychotherapy with BPD clients. All names have been changed to preserve anonymity.

Vignette: Intersectional bodies in an art psychotherapy group

The art psychotherapy session took place as part of an outpatient intensive psychological treatment service for mood disorders in an NHS setting, following the TC model. This session was co-facilitated by a group therapist from the treatment programme, Simon, and myself, then a third-year trainee art psychotherapist. The session was 90 minutes in duration, with 45 minutes each for art-making and discussion. Two of the usual five participants were present: Rena, a smartly dressed and highly psychologically minded 52-year-old woman of Caribbean and British heritage, and Gemma, a 37-year-old woman of 'white' British heritage with a quiet and insightful demeanour and a quirky bohemian dress sense. Both women had a diagnosis of BPD and had been on the programme for over a year.

On arriving for the session, both Rena and Gemma seemed to be carrying difficult feelings from an earlier group meeting. Rena gathered art materials, paper and felt pens and started work. Gemma sat down and slumped her upper body over the table.

It soon became clear that Gemma was quietly sobbing into her arm. After verbal engagement with the therapists, she started working. Her movements, initially slow and heavy, became more animated as she became absorbed in the process of painting. Gemma worked with inward drawn attention; applying paint to paper, choosing and mixing colours, getting up to gather more materials, leaning back to reflect on her work and looking up now and again to survey the room and locate other people.

Rena made an image on white paper. With a felt pen, she had sectioned her paper into four quadrants and written in each of three quadrants about her relationship with different people in her life. She started to become agitated while working on the fourth quadrant and wrote in large capital letters: 'WHAT ABOUT ME?' She then announced suddenly, 'I've got to get out of here!', and hastily left the room for a break. Gemma also left for a short break after finishing her painting. Both clients returned and the group resumed to look at the work.

Looking at the images together, Gemma seemed surprised at the suggestion that her art-making activity seemed to have calmed her down: 'I was just moving my arm really.' It was as if she hadn't tuned into the physicality of what she was doing and its impact on how she felt. It was noted that her image showed areas of colour, all merged together, and other areas where different colours seemed to be separating out, perhaps reflecting how she might have been feeling. Gemma sat quietly for a while, as if gathering her thoughts, then tentatively started to talk about a traumatic memory of 'carving' someone's name into her arm and the look of horror she saw in her parents' eyes when they discovered her. She spoke of feeling so utterly bad, abandoned, lonely and lost that she frequently used to engage in destructive behaviours as a means of escaping the mental anguish. The group held Gemma in an embrace of empathic silence as she verbalized her experience. Gemma seemed to be making links and integrating several layers of experience: her art-making activity; painful feelings towards her family; past memories of psychic distress; and her present moment experience of embodied communication with others in the art psychotherapy setting.

As Gemma spoke, Rena had been quietly, but angrily, tearing up her image. When the group's attention turned towards her, Rena spoke of always being available for others but feeling utterly unseen and unsupported herself. Suddenly, apparently overwhelmed by her feelings, she began to lash out verbally, denigrating herself and the therapy programme – it was all a 'useless waste of time' and she'd 'achieved absolutely nothing!' She made to leave but was supported to stay. Rena paced the room until she calmed down and felt contained enough to rejoin the discussion. As Gemma continued sharing her experience, Rena quietly gathered up the pieces of her destroyed image, as if gathering herself back together, and put them into an empty tissue box: a symbolic expression of containment.

Discussion

Both Gemma and Rena demonstrated embodied experiences of group art therapy as they moved between different modes of expression. The safe container offered by the therapeutic relationship, the familiar physical space of the therapy room and the group itself all contributed to the unfolding of the session and how it was utilized by the two service users. The clients moved freely between different modes of communication: making visual artwork, crying, sitting with silence, looking at work, moving around and in and out of the room, looking at and navigating each other's performing bodies, listening to and focusing on others in the group, reflecting within themselves, talking and being listened to by others. These actions contribute to what can be understood as the 'embodied language' of the session (Skaife, 2001, 2008; Whitaker, 2004) and are invaluable to our thinking and conceptualization of contemporary art psychotherapy.

However, an intersectional perspective offers a more complex reading of what might be happening in this session. From an intersectional perspective, and given the content of Rena's artwork, we can consider her experience through what McKenzie-Mavinga (2009) conceptualizes as 'recognition trauma': a painful dawning of one's own occluded and silenced experiences, perhaps activated by feeling unseen or inadequately met while the therapists' attention was, apparently, directed solely at Gemma. This allows for the historically instituted invisibility of 'black' experience in the social frameworks of a 'white world' to be meaningfully thought about. Likewise, the exaggerated enactments of Rena's 'communicating body' can be read as an effective neurophysiological discharge of negative affect, born of historic intergenerational trauma (DeGruy, 2005), which benefits from being witnessed and understood as meaningful beyond affective loss of control.

Had I been more conversant with McKenzie-Mavinga's work and specifically her 'Black Empathic Approach', I might have attempted to bring issues of race out of the shadow more explicitly and explored this further in supervision. Equipping art psychotherapists of *all* backgrounds with concepts to address socio-political issues of equality and difference would support our capacity to make visible what is often occluded through both personal and institutionalized prejudices and unconscious biases.

Conclusion

Skaife (2008) discusses a 'status quo split' in psychotherapeutic practice between mind and body, health and illness, sanity and madness. Splitting is a protective psychological defence that seems inherent to the medical model. What is the difference between the impulsive acts of mental health clients who engage in private self-harm to retrieve themselves from the abyss and body artists who cut their skin in the visibility of the cultural context? Perhaps the abject horror of incoherence itself? Western society accepts and condones violence in contexts where it is sanctioned, ritualized and culturally framed. The BPD client, as framed by the medical model, does not command such acceptance. On the contrary, their impulsive actions can induce difficult feelings among those whose job it is to treat them (Favazza, 1996).

This is well illustrated by Main (1957) in a formative paper entitled 'The ailment'. Through a series of reflective practice meetings, a clinical staff group discover that while clinicians often bear the brunt of psychological fall-out from patients, patients are similarly subject to negative transference from clinicians. Once this was brought to light and could be seen, it became possible to work with enhanced self-awareness and to operate at a level of greater clinical team integration. Incorporating an intersectional approach to reflective practice could be useful for developing greater awareness of embodied issues of equality and difference in contemporary art psychotherapy practice and training.

This chapter has considered the performative body in art psychotherapy through an intersectional lens. It suggests the historic Cartesian splitting of body and mind may underlie what occludes our therapeutic gaze. It advocates 'thinking through the body' (Blackman, 2008) from an intersectional perspective in service of more embodied and socio-culturally informed clinical practice and theory. Positioned at the intersection of art and medicine, art therapists are uniquely placed to support clients of diverse clinical and social populations to transmute psychological distress from skin to paper in their pursuit of embodied and intersubjective wellness.

References

Alleyne, A. (1989). Which Women? What Feminism? In B. Seu & C. Heenan (eds) *Feminism and Psychotherapy: Reflections on Contemporary Theories and Practices*. London: Sage Publications.

Bateman, A. & Fonagy, P. (2006). *Mentalization-Based Treatment for Borderline Personality Disorder: A Practical Guide*. Oxford: Oxford University Press.

Blackman, L. (2008). *The Body: The Key Concepts*. Oxford, New York, NY: Berg.

Butler, J. (1990) *Gender Trouble: Feminism and the Subversion of Identity*. London: Routledge.

Collins, P. H. & Bilge, S. (2016). *Intersectionality*. Cambridge: Polity Press.

Crenshaw, K. (1989). Demarginalizing the intersection of race and sex: A Black feminist critique of antidiscrimination doctrine, feminist theory and antiracist politics. *University of Chicago Legal Forum, 1*(8), 139–176. Available at https://chicagounbound.uchicago.edu/uclf/vol1989/iss1/8.

Damasio, A. R. (2000). *The Feeling of What Happens: Body, Emotion and the Making of Consciousness*. London: Vintage Books.

DeGruy, J. (2005). *Post Traumatic Slave Syndrome: America's Legacy of Enduring Injury and Healing*. Milwaukie, OR: Uptone Press.

De Zulueta, F. (1993). *From Pain to Violence: The Traumatic Roots of Destructiveness*. Chichester: Whurr Publishers Limited.

Duggan, P. (2009). The touch and the cut: An annotated dialogue with Kira O'Reilly. *Studies in Theatre and Performance, 29*(3), 307–325. Available at www.academia.edu/210296.

Eastwood, C. (2012). Art therapy with women with borderline personality disorder: A feminist perspective. *International Journal of Art Therapy, 17*(3), 1–17.

Favazza, A. (1996). *Bodies Under Siege: Self-Mutilation in Culture and Psychiatry* (second edition). Baltimore, MD: Johns Hopkins University Press.

Gilloway, A., Hall, R. E., Lee, T. & Bhui, K. S. (2010). A systematic review of personality disorder, race and ethnicity: Prevalence, aetiology and treatment. *BMC Psychiatry, 10*(33). https://doi.org/10.1186/1471-244X-10-33.

Gilroy, A. (2006). *Art Therapy, Research and Evidence-Based Practice*. London: Sage Publications.
Grosz, E. (1994). *Volatile Bodies: Toward a Corporeal Feminism*. Bloomington, IN: Indiana University Press.
Herman, J. L. (1992). *Trauma and Recovery: The Aftermath of Violence – From Domestic Abuse to Political Terror*. New York, NY: Basic Books.
Lago, C. & Thompson, J. (1996). *Race, Culture and Counselling*. Maidenhead: Open University Press.
Laing, R. D. (1976). *The Politics of the Family*. London: Pelican Books.
Lemma, A. (2010). *Under the Skin: A Psychoanalytic Study of Body Modification*. London: Routledge.
Lorde, A. (1984). *Sister Outsider: Essays and Speeches*. Trumansburg, NY: Crossing Press.
Main, T. (1957). The ailment. *The British Psychological Society, 30*(3), 129–145. https://doi.org/10.1111/j.2044-8341.1957.tb01193.x.
McKenzie-Mavinga, I. (2009). *Black Issues in the Therapeutic Process*. London: Palgrave Macmillan.
Melliar, P. & Brukha, A. (2010). Round the clock: A therapist's and service user's perspective on the image outside art therapy. *International Journal of Art Therapy, 15*(1), 4–12.
Mental Health Foundation (2021) The Truth about Self Harm. Available at www.mentalhealth.org.uk/publications/truth-about-self-harm.
Morgan, L., Knight, C., Bagwash, J. & Thompson, F. (2012). Borderline personality disorder and the role of art therapy. *International Journal of Art Therapy, 17*(3), 91–97.
National Self Harm Network (2021). The NSHN Forum. Home page. Accessible at www.nshn.co.uk.
NICE (National Institute for Health and Care Excellence) (2009). *Borderline Personality Disorder: Recognition and Management. CG78 Guideline*. Available at www.nice.org.uk/guidance/cg78.
Orbach, S. (2003). There is no such thing as a body. *British Journal of Psychotherapy, 20*(1), 3–25.
Orbach, S. (2009). *Bodies*. London: Profile Books.
Porges, S. W. (2011). *The Polyvagal Theory: Neurophysiological Foundatons of Emotions, Attachment, Communication, and Self-Regulation*. New York, NY: Norton.
Scarry, E. (1985). *The Body in Pain: The Making and Unmaking of the World*. Oxford: Oxford University Press.
Schechner, R. (2009). *Self Inflicted Wounds: Art, Ritual, Popular Culture*. Available at https://journals.openedition.org/actesbranly/445.
Skaife, S. (2001). Making visible: Art therapy and intersubjectivity. *International Journal of Art Therapy, 6*(2), 40–50.
Skaife, S. (2008). Off-shore: A deconstruction of David Maclagan's and David Mann's 'Inscape' papers. *International Journal of Art Therapy, 13*(2), 44–52.
Springham, N., Findlay, D., Woods, A. & Harris, H. (2012). How can art therapy contribute to mentalization in borderline personality disorder? *International Journal of Art Therapy, 17*(3), 115–129.
Suyemoto, K. L. (1998). The functions of self-mutilation. *Clinical Psychology Review, 18*(5), 531–554.
Van der Kolk, B. (2014). *The Body Keeps the Score: Brain, Mind, and Body in the Healing of Trauma*. London: Penguin Publishing.
Whitaker, P. (2004). Art moves: Exploring the implications of the body and movement within art therapy. *The Canadian Art Therapy Association Journal, 17*(1), 3–9.

Chapter 5

Haven't You Done Well? From Working Class to Class Blind

SARAH FURNEAUX-BLICK

Introduction

In this chapter, I will explore how the complex psychosocial considerations of class are often absent from art psychotherapy literature, training and discourse yet feel very present within the clinical setting. For the purposes of this chapter, I have struggled to define 'class'. When considering class issues in art therapy, Wood (1999) describes how explanatory definitions essentially reside in social and collective realms, noting that this is probably the reason why so little attention has been given to matters of class in the therapeutic milieu. Wood highlights that, despite difficulties in defining or acknowledging class, most people will have an idea of the class from which they originate and this 'deeply shapes their sense of identity' (Wood, 1999, p.135). I define my own class as British working class, and my intersecting identities include being a white, cisgendered, heterosexual woman. Hamrick and Byma (2017), Gipson (2015), Ryan (2014) and Wood (1999) discuss how art therapy primarily attempts to work with the internal worlds of our clients alone. In this chapter, I will illustrate, through the use of case vignettes, how the disregarding of the social, economic and politically impacted lived experiences of our clients and ourselves can reinforce ideas that mental ill-health is an issue for the individual alone, neglecting societal responsibilities of care.

Gipson (2017) notes the way in which art therapists, when struggling with uncomfortable identity-related truths, can enact a process of 'intentionally disconnecting themselves from contemporary political issues, as if art therapists stand outside of the social world that produces the issues that bring people to counselling' (2017, p.113). The meeting of shared life experiences or identities between art therapist and client is experienced routinely in art therapy practice. How we navigate these similarities and differences in the therapeutic relationship is frequently under addressed in training, with psychodynamic neutrality and the neoliberal ideology of psychotherapy appearing to operate without addressing issues of power and privilege in practice. In this context, I refer to neoliberal ideology as one that centres profit and capital within social care (Duggan, 2003; Gipson, 2017). Through this advance of capitalism in care, neoliberalism has created a one-approach-fits-all response to 'diversity' and 'equality' issues in mental health services. This often manifests in the naming of differences in individualized ways, if at all, while neglecting consideration of the impact of intersectional and institutional or societal groupings of difference, which can determine the holding of privileges and normative powers (Gipson, 2017; Kaiser, 2017; Kuri, 2017).

Therapists must acknowledge their own power, privilege and conscious or unconscious prejudices, in order to work in ways that are truly ethical and do not act out deeply held and problematic beliefs in their work. In doing so, they must also challenge neoliberal ideologies that monetize and capitalize care, promoting 'colour-blind' (Gipson, 2017) or 'class-blind' (Ryan, 2014) principles. These perpetuate myths that successes in life, including good mental health, are a result of individual determination and hard work (Gipson, 2015; Kaiser, 2017; Kuri, 2017; Ryan, 2014). These approaches can be unhelpful and potentially abusive when considering the complexities of societal oppressions and resultant traumas.

Intersectional self-reflexivity

In modelling intersectional self-reflexivity, I will offer insight from the perspective of a cisgendered woman and white art therapist coming from a working-class family from the north of England. I will examine the impact that my class-related identities and past marginalizations might have had on my current art therapy practice. I will also briefly, but importantly, acknowledge the complexity of experiencing simultaneous identity-related privileges and oppressions, including my own white privilege (McIntosh, 1989). I do this to prompt other white art therapists to acknowledge and explore how whiteness can operate in ways that reinforce positions of unnamed power and a lack of accountability in white people as they carry out their work (Hamrick & Byma, 2017). I will use two case vignettes through which to explore these ideas within psychodynamic art therapy practice. One reflects on my own personal art therapy process during my recent studies as an art therapist, on a UK-based master's training. I use this session vignette as a way of transparently exploring my internalized unconscious biases and feelings of class-related shame. The second is from my clinical work with a young cisgendered male teenage client who I will name Sam, with whom I shared some similar identity markers and lived experiences. I will reflect on how my personal realizations and explorations in therapy informed my work with Sam, helping me to make good use of our sameness in my clinical thinking, yet also potentially deny my client the space needed to address difficult issues.

Each vignette explores how intersectional thinking supports a more deeply informed and authentic therapeutic encounter, acknowledging that no therapeutic work can take place in social or political isolation.

In context: My early experience

I was born and raised in the north of England by my Irish mother and my two siblings who both left the family home when I was eight. My father was absent. Until the age of 19, when I attended art school, I acted as my mother's carer, as she experienced enduring mental health issues. Due to this, my experience at school was difficult, with a lack of family support and ability to focus. My family culture and working-class community had instilled in me a mistrust of 'middle-class' authority figures who might have offered support, and also feelings of shame and failure surrounding my economically poor and class-related locations.

In reflecting on how injurious class-related attacks can be, Ryan cites Sennett and Cobb (1972, p.256) who note that 'social differences can now appear as a question of character, of moral resolve, of will and competence' (Ryan, 2014, p.133). Written in the 1970s, these words still adequately contextualize my feelings of guilt and shame surrounding growing up in poverty in the 1980s. Tropes of 'broken homes' and those 'scrounging off the state' resonated in Thatcher's Britain at the time. Poverty was, and continues to be, seen through a neoliberal lens as individual, rather than societal, failure.

In considering the development of mental health legislation in the UK and its links to welfare provision, Wood (1999) highlights Kelvin and Jarrett's (1985) observations of the social and psychological effects of unemployment, including the impact of societal attitudes towards the unemployed. She asserts that attitudes noted in the 1349 'Parliamentary Ordinance of Labourers' that distinguished between 'sturdy beggars' and the 'deserving poor' linger in society today. 'It was out of the much-feared workhouses that the first mental hospitals developed in this country, and it does seem that the distinction between the "deserving" and the "undeserving" and prejudice towards the latter was incorporated into mental health legislation' (Wood, 1999, p.139).

In my personal and professional life, I have often found myself justifying my mother's claiming of benefits or her current and my historical need for social housing support, in relation to her poor mental health. I eventually stopped sharing such information in professional circles and began a process of editing out the circumstances in which I grew up from my own story, as a way of self-protection. I share these personal experiences to model self-reflexivity and illustrate my critical awareness of self as an art therapist, exploring my own cultural conditioning (Talwar, 2010) and internalized feelings of shame. I can acknowledge the power and insight I have gained as a therapist in allowing reflexive vulnerability and I can reflect on how clients may censor their own histories to respond to similar feelings, when their experiences may not fit the dominant narrative that determines those who are 'deserving' of our care in therapy.

University was the first time I had been in a predominantly middle-class environment. This was my peer group, yet my sense of otherness prevailed. When considering the complex psychic demands of upward social mobility on psychotherapists in practice, Ryan notes the ways in which 'Moving into a more middle-class environment exposed them to great challenges as regards their own sense of self-worth and entitlement. Along with the resulting sense of dislocation, dividedness, and multiple identities' (Ryan, 2014, p.144). At this time, my process of censoring myself included trying to 'tone down' my 'brassy' northern English accent, as a process of assimilation. Gurney (2010) explores the role class plays in the psychotherapeutic relationship and writes how an English regional accent is heard, viewed and judged within work and society. He concludes that unconscious biases are prevalent, with those with regional accents often being viewed as less intelligent, for example.

Self-reflexivity and personal art therapy vignette: 'Haven't you done well?'

I have personally heard the phrase 'Haven't you done well?' on countless occasions. Though it most often comes from well-meaning and congratulatory places, it always evokes in me something of the unsaid around societal, class-related hierarchies that intersect with issues of race, gender and economic mobility. Having 'done well', one is left to reflect on where one has transitioned from or what has been left behind or denied. There is also the assumption that one is all the wiser and better for the transition. Yet my truth is not as simplistic as transitioning smoothly from one social location to another. As with many, including our clients, those who sit bridging multiple social locations often sit comfortably in neither.

Towards the end of my training as an art therapist, I used my personal art therapy to make a mask (Figure 5.1). For me it encapsulates the personal exploration surrounding my social location and sense of economic mobility. This mask came to symbolize my unspoken belief that in order to 'do well' I must censor myself and assimilate to my new middle-class location. This censoring felt to be in relation to my ideas, political beliefs and my presentation, with a need to 'soften' my strong northern accent. While training, I felt there was a process of personal 'undoing' followed by a 'putting back together' of the pieces I had untangled and deconstructed of myself. This felt like a common and shared experience among my peers, yet I felt my mask symbolized a part of that journey that was unique to my experience.

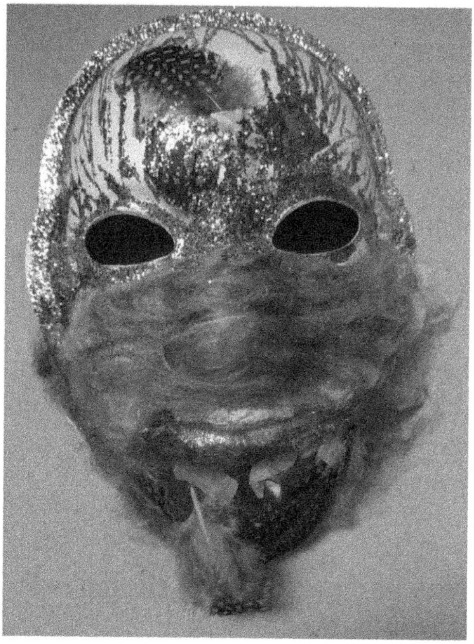

Figure 5.1: Mask

However, it became clear that there was little space on my training to acknowledge my specific journey in relation to my intersecting identities, or to explore what Collins (1986) conceives as an 'outsider within status'. At times, my training felt for me like learning how to play the part of the middle-class therapist, rather than being able to bring all of myself to my practice and utilize my lived experiences to inform my work. I often felt emotionally unsafe bringing my true self to experiential work on my course, for fear of being marginalized, or of misjudging the etiquette of professional discord in middle-class realms. This was my experience as a working-class, cisgendered, white woman entering the profession, where

I shared my whiteness with approximately 93 per cent of art therapists in the UK, as referred to in the British Association of Art Therapists workforce survey carried out in 2018. I often reflected on how alienated people of colour or transgendered people may have felt, and tried to speak to and explore such concerns. I had approached making my mask with an intention of celebration, to create a visual response to my personal and professional achievements. I wanted to create a celebration of my having 'done well'. Instead, for me, the resulting object embodied something of the bound up and suffocated: a sparkling surfaced death-mask. When I decided to try wearing the mask, my therapist commented that I looked frightening and menacing. Surprisingly, I found comfort in these comments; feeling that despite my unconscious acknowledgement of an identity 'death', I could regain some lost power through the therapeutic encounter and art-making. I could be formidable!

Reflecting on the complexities of my internalized classism and shame, I can acknowledge that hearing 'haven't you done well?' still brings me great discomfort; paradoxically, I desire it and am seduced by it, resulting in cycles of shame and unconscious bias that need to be challenged. This challenging is important to my personal wellbeing, yet its relevance to my art therapy practice in raising consciousness of my potential to act out when working with clients cannot be understated. My art-making process and the mask subverted my initial intent, showing me the 'death' inherent in a denial of true self and the resulting disempowerment experienced.

Skaife states:

> Art therapy is by nature radical. It is about empowering people. By making art, people discover their own ability to act and create originally. Art provides a mirror or comment on society, it reaches beyond the conventions of daily life. Art therapy is thus nearly always a subversive activity. (Skaife, 1995, p.2)

When I look at my mask now, I see it as an unconscious motivation toward acts of resistance. A resistance of my internalized class-related shame and a desire to challenge the words 'haven't you done well?', seeing them as politically loaded and indicative of oppression and marginalization. My mask now subverts, representing the symbolic death of the 'nice' sensibilities I have adopted in order to 'do well'; to assimilate by speaking 'properly'; being the right kind of feminine, sparkly and non-threatening and, most importantly, not 'too much'.

Clinical case vignette: Sam

The following artworks were created during clinical work with a young person, whom I will call Sam. Sam is from a working-class family. I saw him in one-to-one art therapy sessions for 12 weeks. Sam had a seemingly chaotic home life and complex learning disabilities. He was referred for art therapy due to a number of concerns, relating to both his physical and emotional wellbeing. Often, Sam's basic needs such as acceptable hygiene standards and nutrition were felt not to be adequately met in his home. Throughout the art therapy sessions, it was often uncomfortable for me to maintain close proximity to Sam, due to his poor hygiene. This acted as a powerful metaphor for me and my location and 'closeness' to our work. My initial sense was that, for Sam, his odour acted as a defence against closeness, and was an unconscious self-identification as 'bad' and not worthy of care. Class felt ever present in the context of Sam's lived experiences and social locations, not least due to the socio-economic circumstances facing the family, who occupied social housing and received support from many services.

As evidenced in the report *Health Equity in England: The Marmot Review 10 Years On* (Marmot *et al.*, 2020), the links between socio-economic positions and poor mental health outcomes are well established. Deprivation in the UK has risen in the last ten years, resulting in an increase in child poverty and homelessness. Simultaneously, the gap between wealth and poverty has widened across the country. Currently in the UK, if you are working class and economically poor, you face a bleak picture of inadequate funding for health services, and education and housing support services having experienced funding cuts of up to 31 per cent (ibid, 2020). The report also highlights the continued attitudes held in general populations towards the economically disadvantaged as lacking empathy for the 'undeserving' poor. Locating neoliberalism at the heart of social care and reform in British politics exacerbates the blame towards struggling individuals, creating division between communities, with clear winners and losers. This wrongly creates little doubt that social problems are so predisposed in some populations in society that change is not wanted or possible (ibid, 2020). This is inevitably felt from within marginalized and neglected communities and impacts greatly on mental health outcomes.

In my work with Sam, I witnessed how these societal realities and attitudes impacted his sense of self through the symbolism of his artwork and my experiencing of the therapeutic relationship. I was able to reflect on ways in which my own experiences, feeling both similar to and different from Sam's, might impact my own feelings in the work, manifesting in the possibility of over-identification and difficult countertransference. This needed extended emotional and ethical exploration.

There was a clear distrust displayed by Sam and his family towards care services, which in many ways mirrored my own childhood experiences. This manifested in Sam seeming surprised when I returned each week, revealing his expectation of abandonment from those offering support. Our sessions always had a 'frantic' quality to them. This felt instigated by Sam to test me and my ability to survive the chaos. To help manage this, I adapted the session length in response to the difficult feelings. As our relationship developed and when Sam seemed ready, we eventually progressed to working together for a full 45-minute session each week.

Nevertheless, I experienced such intense emotions in our sessions as we attempted to build trust in the relationship that I was often left feeling a great sense of shame when the time was up, as if I had committed an act of betrayal by walking away from him after each session. For me, these strong feelings resonated with my own sense of shame growing up poor and feeling trapped in socio-economic locations, as well as eventually leaving to 'do well'. All of this needed to be safely contained and explored in regular supervision, to diminish any unhelpful acting out on my countertransference feelings. I drew parallels between how I felt tested by Sam and my own experiences growing up with the familiarity of family intervention by multiple services. My own childhood experience of multiple professionals working with my family, seemingly expecting immediate trust, informed my understanding of Sam's experience of me in the therapeutic relationship. This felt helpful to my managing and understanding of his difficult feelings. Important to my work with Sam was my reflecting on how the only power I had felt growing up was in exploring how hard I could make the professionals 'work' for me. Sam's chaos resonated a great deal with me; I felt I knew from personal experience the degree to which Sam needed me to 'work' for him. I was also able to reflect on how assumptions due to sameness in the therapeutic space, without robust exploration, can hinder making appropriate clinical decisions.

In these moments, I found the art-making process and materials could contain the mess and chaos Sam brought; mess and chaos that I came to realize could hook my own feelings in response to past traumas. I needed to untangle my own shame and separate it from the feelings I thought were Sam's alone. I took my own feelings to personal therapy, where I began the process of making my mask to contain and subvert past struggles.

In the following sections, I will describe Sam's art-making in the context of two paths of exploration. Both seemed to represent feelings of judgement, shame and being 'deserving' of care or power, and brought themes relevant to the challenges faced at the intersect of being working-class and neurodiverse, or having a learning disability diagnosis.

Levelling up: Pokémon or monsters

Providing Sam with drawing templates seemed to help him to feel less overwhelmed by the blank page and art materials.

Figure 5.2: Pokémon

He appeared to enjoy the Pokémon cartoon character templates, seeming to take comfort in and gain confidence from the familiarity of images from popular culture. When considering class issues in art therapy, Wood (1999) notes the class-related associations with areas of popular culture, and highlights the many meanings and value that can be derived from the use of popular artefacts or mass entertainments and icons. Sam would use such familiarities as a starting point for creative explorations. This felt important in relation to his learning disabilities and related anxieties. His Pokémon (Figure 5.2) would often 'level up' (transform) into monsters or dangerous dragons with the power to take over, kill and destroy. Their power always held negative associations and I sensed this represented

Sam's unconscious feelings related to the 'bad' and 'dangerous' parts of his own, family or community identity. I was reminded of the stereotypes of the working-class and poor, and the associated dangerous and feared outcomes of power asserted by the working-class or economically disadvantaged. My thoughts felt reinforced by Sam's references to prison in his art-play, with the Pokémon often being locked up, taken away and punished as a result of asserting their power. Often Sam would explore such narratives in a joking way that seemed to lack actual fun or humour and instead seemed to mask difficult feelings of hopelessness. In reviewing Sam's artwork, I was struck by how the finished paintings conceal the characters beneath with such generous use of paint. Yet there is a precision in the lack of merging of colours that feels unusual when working with feelings of chaos or mess. Sam's painting seems to show containment while simultaneously responding to a desire to cover up; maybe representing something of difference and separation. I noted my countertransference feelings of helplessness as these characters were transforming into monsters, gaining insight into Sam's possible feelings of loss of autonomy and lack of control.

During the sessions, I noticed how often I felt detached from the monsters' stories, as they experienced being punished and imprisoned. I could acknowledge the impact of my own experiences of class and economic marginalization and the potential of my protecting myself from what Sam needed to bring to therapy. This demonstrates the importance of therapists working through their own identity-related pain in personal therapy so as to be adequately prepared to bear similar trauma in our clients. In parallel to this avoidance on my part, evident in my countertransference as a lack of feeling in response to what I believed to be Sam's pain, I also found myself switching off from social or economic deprivation when depicted on television or in the media. I now recognize my current privilege in being able to do this; yet can also reflect on my avoidance of painful issues from my past.

Eggs and chips: Being fed

Towards the end of my work with Sam, he began to focus his art-making on the theme of food and eating. His creation of different art objects replicating food might have been a metaphor for the nutrition and symbolic feeding that I felt he had lacked and which the sessions were now providing.

Figure 5.3: Egg and Chips

Sam would describe the types of food he liked and he then created his favourite meal of egg and chips, using collage materials and glue (Figure 5.3). His favourite food choice embodied something nostalgic and powerful for me in the session – what felt like an indicator of British working-class identity. Sam's celebration of this meal felt bitter sweet to me as I reflected on my own journey. I felt Sam's choice of 'nutrition' indicated a lack of being properly 'fed', which in turn felt like a response possibly manifested in my own internalized classism. Nevertheless, we ended our work together with him making me his favourite meal, followed by him metaphorically 'feeding' me. There was a celebratory atmosphere, which I think we both enjoyed, and I was able to challenge my own judgements and prejudices relating to 'good enough' care or 'feeding'. I could see how art therapy had 'fed' Sam, by meeting, however briefly, some of his emotional needs through mirroring and containment. Sam had also been given, and taken, a space to safely, symbolically explore his sense of self as part of, and also separate from, his class, family and social location.

Discussion

In some ways, my work with Sam reflected my experience of growing up poor and working class in the UK. I had internalized the experience of having less and, as a result, feeling less, perpetuated by capitalist constructs. I also internalized a sense of this being a failing of mine and my family alone, a degrading assumption maintained by the rise in neoliberal attitudes towards class transition, economic mobility and social location (Kuri, 2017; Ryan, 2014).

Through supervision and personal therapy, I was able to work through and untangle my own heritage and experience, addressing my blinkered spots in relation to class and the denials I used to defend myself against the pain of class-related shame. This informed my clinical thinking, enabling me to see my client and his experiences as separate from my own; challenging enmeshment, yet also using the aspects of our identities and experiences that did intersect as ethical tools in my gaining greater understanding.

My own sense that Sam's relationship to his social location and class was one of feeling trapped and powerless informed my interpretation of his needing to 'level up'; gaining power and autonomy to become the persecutor rather than persecuted in the symbolic space, despite the symbolic punishments for asserting such power. His explorations of sense of self and identity – as being 'deserving' of power that may be seen as dangerous in his hands, as a working-class and neurodiverse individual – seemed to question and contain his anxieties, sadness and lack of trust. In considering the social and political context, it's important to note the role of violence in the lives of the oppressed. Some marginalized people may unconsciously identify with the aggressor (Freud, 1936) as Sam seemed to do when becoming the 'persecutor'. This is a common defence mechanism for individuals subjected to adverse childhood experiences. If not recognized and processed early, the symbolic identification may become a concrete acting out of the social violence experienced previously toward oneself. Exploring the way in which empowerment can be gained, without perpetuating cycles of violence and consequential punishment, is crucial within the symbolic realms and beyond.

I was also reminded in this work of the unconscious and conscious judgements we continually make, immersed as we are in our own cultural conditioning. Sam's 'food' and 'feeding' felt inadequate and unrefined to me, representing a lack of care and nourishment. I can acknowledge that without exploration of my own feelings of shame and grief, the symbolism representing the possibility to feed, nurture and celebrate closeness, regardless of economic disadvantage, could be overlooked. This work, taking place at the beginning of my career as an art therapist, helped me to acknowledge my own responses to working with clients who have similar lived experiences to me. Using therapy and supervision, I was able to gain insight into why I may make specific clinical decisions based on personal judgements; overcompensate or ignore, and ultimately deny what manifests in the therapeutic space for the client, that may cause me emotional pain. I believe that greater space for such considerations needs to be created in art therapy trainings and literature; considerations that ultimately relate to wider social and political contexts that are internalized and responded to by therapists, as well as clients. An intersectional framework challenges the potential within our profession for colluding with neoliberal ideology that locates issues of mental ill-health, trauma and oppression in individuals alone, neglecting societal concerns. In psychodynamic therapeutic work, we must consider conceptions such as transference and countertransference in the context of examining the complexities of intersecting identities, social locations and the traumatic experiences our clients bring, beyond the clients' individual and familial experience (Layton, 2006).

Conclusion

When training as an art therapist my personal experiences drew me towards intersectional consideration and the inclusion of issues such as race, class and gender in my clinical thinking. In all theoretical realms, I felt the need for social and political grounding, yet my explorations often felt discouraged by my personal therapist and supervisors. This lack of contextual thinking beyond the personal or family (Wood, 1999) felt implicit in my reading of art therapy literature and the focus in curriculum on my art therapy training. My questioning at this time, and my continuing evaluation of my practice and its positioning within the art therapy profession in the UK, surrounds this continual absence of political consideration. Watts, Gilfillan and Hills de Zárate (2017) highlight the need to facilitate a more comprehensive understanding of poverty and its impact on clients in art therapy. Whether it is through explicit funding cuts to services or insight into our own implicit, socially constructed biases as practitioners, political context is ever present. What the client and the therapist bring, both consciously and unconsciously, is influenced by a multitude of experiences, determined in part by intersecting identity markers and economic and social locations (Talwar, 2010).

I believe this lack of acknowledgement can lead to neoliberal attitudes towards practice, where at times art therapists work in ways that are class-blind (Ryan, 2014). This lack of contextual thinking often neglects to help clients fully understand the complexities of difficult feelings; inadvertently locating the origins of mental ill-health in the client alone. This can encourage feelings of self-blame and shame that in psychodynamic therapy contexts may well be explored but may not be challenged.

By using intersectional self-reflexivity and recounting personal and professional experiences, I have highlighted how social location defined specifically by class, personal marginalizations and privileges can impact on therapeutic encounters, as both client and therapist. I have reflected on my own struggles associated with class identity and how they have contributed to personal, emotional avoidance related to specific identity markers. I have noted that these denials, used to defend against feelings of shame, can impact negatively on my clinical work with clients who are similar to me. Currently, I do not face the hardships of my past or of the economically poor, working class. I have tried to shed the guilt and shame of having 'done well'. As Wood notes, 'Therapists need to be able to make relationships with clients which are not corrupted by their own guilt' (Wood, 1999, p.136).

My personal therapy and art practice offer me a space in which to explore these different parts of myself and find personal integration and healing. Through my clinical work I can utilize and promote intersectional perspectives that help me to continually self-reflect and challenge internalized classism, along with racism, misogyny, homophobia and transphobia. These are prejudices that as practitioners we are all capable of harbouring as we are immersed in social and political structures that constantly reinforce problematic beliefs and accommodate abuses of power from dominant group perspectives.

As a practitioner, I can see how neoliberal ideologies can permeate practice as they do society. This can leave individual art therapists, and the profession as a whole, ill-equipped in challenging personal and societal accountability and complicity in structures of oppression. As art therapists, we have an ethical obligation and responsibility to work with the enmeshments of the political, social and interpersonal. By working within intersectional frameworks, we can maintain an open and honest dialogue, facilitating evolution and ethical change for our profession and the clients that we support.

References

Collins, P. H. (1986). Learning from the outsider within: The sociological significance of black feminist thought. *Social Problems, 33*(6), 14–32.

Duggan, L. (2003). *The Twilight of Equality? Neoliberalism, Cultural Politics, and the Attack on Democracy*. London: Beacon Press.

Freud, A. (1936). *The Ego and Mechanisms of Defence*. London: Karnac Books.

Gipson, L. (2017). Challenging neoliberalism and multicultural love in art therapy. *Art Therapy, Journal of the American Art Therapy Association, 34*(3), 112–117.

Gipson, L. (2015) Is Cultural Competence Enough? Deepening Social Justice Pedagogy in Art Therapy. *Art Therapy, 32*(3), 142–145.

Gurney, P. (2010). The acc(id)ental tourist: Exploring the tribal areas between class and race. *Journal of Psycho-Social Studies, 4*(1), 47–56.

Hamrick, C. & Byma, C. (2017). Know history, know self: Art therapists' responsibility to dismantle White supremacy. *Art Therapy, Journal of the American Art Therapy Association, 34*(3), 106–111.

Kaiser, D. H. (2017). What do structural racism and oppression have to do with scholarship, research, and practice in art therapy? *Art Therapy, Journal of the American Art Therapy Association, 34*(4), 154–156.

Kelvin, P. & Jarrett, J.E. (1985). *Unemployment: Its Social Psychological Effects*. Cambridge: Cambridge University Press.

Kuri, E. (2017). Toward an ethical application of intersectionality in art therapy. *Art Therapy, Journal of the American Art Therapy Association, 34*(3), 118–122.

Layton, L. (2006). Attacks on Linking: The Unconscious Pull to Dissociate Individuals from Their Social Context. In L. Layton, N. Caro-Hollander & S. Gutwill (eds) *Psychoanalysis, Class and Politics: Encounters in the Clinical Setting*. London & New York, NY: Routledge.

Marmot, M., Allen, J., Boyce, T., Goldblatt, P. & Morrison, J. (2020). *Health Equity in England: The Marmot Review 10 Years On*. The Health Foundation. Accessed 28/08/20 at www.health.org.uk/publications/reports/the-marmot-review-10-years-on?gclid=EAIaIQobChMI-fq27se96wIVE-3tCh006Q3_EAAYASAAEgLgMfD_BwE.

McIntosh, P. (1989). White privilege: Unpacking the invisible knapsack. *Peace and Freedom*, July/August, 8–10.

Ryan, J. (2014). Class is in You: An Exploration of Some Social Class Issues in Psychotherapeutic Work. In F. Lowe (ed.) *Thinking Space – Promoting Thinking About Race, Culture, and Diversity in Psychotherapy and Beyond*. London: The Tavistock Clinic Series.

Sennet, R. & Cobb, J. (1972). *The Hidden Injuries of Class*. New York, NY: W. W. Norton.

Skaife, S. (1995). The dialectics of art therapy. *Inscape, 1*(1), 2–9.

Talwar, S. (2010). An intersectional framework for race, class, gender, and sexuality in art therapy. *Art Therapy, Journal of the American Art Therapy Association, 27*(1), 11–17.

Watts, P., Gilfillan, P. & Hills de Zárate, M. (2017). Art therapy and poverty: Examining practitioners' experiences of working with children and young people in areas of multiple deprivation in West Central Scotland. *International Journal of Art Therapy, 23*(4), 145–155.

Wood, C. (1999). Class Issues in Therapy. In J. Campbell, M. Liebmann, F. Brooks, J. Jones & C. Ward (eds) *Art Therapy, Race and Culture*. London: Jessica Kingsley Publishers.

Chapter 6

Snakey Crazy Lady and the Air Head Princess: Considering 'Colourblind' Intersectionality and Normative Unconscious Processes in Psychodynamic Art Therapy Practice

CORRINA EASTWOOD

Introduction

Identity markers have often been explored in isolation in art therapy literature and discourse, paralleling institutional and societal structures. An intersectional lens allows exploration of the many ways in which identity is formed and impacts on experience. Clarity surrounding a client's story should be gained from considering all aspects of intersecting identities and histories of trauma. This lens must also be applied to the therapeutic relationship, as the therapist engages in self-reflexivity as a key principle of intersectional thinking, considering their own identity, experiences, biases and motives when facilitating the work they do. In addition, a consideration of where the identity markers of therapist and client intersect, and the impact shared experience or difference has on the therapeutic alliance, is vital.

In this chapter, I will consider these principles in the context of a case study of psychodynamic art therapy spanning four years with a client named Lindy. I will explore how my response art-making (Fish, 2019) as portraiture drawing (Carr & Hancock, 2017) of Lindy influenced the work, and the impact it had on my use of transference and countertransference. I will reflect on the value I believe much of the work held for the client who had survived multiple abuses and traumas and was experiencing debilitating alcohol dependence. I will consider the importance I believe feminist therapy (Brown, 2010; Lerman & Porter, 1990; Veldhuis, 2001) and psycho-educational interventions had in contextualizing Lindy's experiences of abuse to address feelings of self-blame and shame. However, I will also reflect on how I often applied 'colourblind' intersectionality (Carbado, 2019) and failed to be meaningfully reflexive when examining blinkered spots in my clinical decision-making. I consider this in relation to normative unconscious processes (Layton, 2020) and how this may have detrimentally impacted on the work and my client's ability to feel truly 'seen'.

Lindy, which is a pseudonym, kindly gave consent for me to publish my drawings of her which she felt were unlikely to identify her.

Lindy and I

Lindy and I worked together in a homeless hostel in an inner-city borough in the UK. Our relationship began when hostel staff advised that I should not approach her to discuss art therapy, describing her as avoidant and in denial. I was informed that she did not engage with any professionals, was debilitatingly alcohol dependent and had late-stage cirrhosis of the liver. I was told that Lindy was a 42-year-old Black woman, diagnosed with borderline personality disorder. She had previously disclosed details of abuse perpetrated by her father in childhood, and partners in adulthood. She later told me that her parents were from Trinidad and had moved to England just before she was born. Her father had died a few years prior to our meeting. Lindy was described as a 'waste of time' by otherwise committed hostel staff. A clear communication that the frustration and sadness surrounding Lindy, her drinking and prognosis, had become too much to bear.

When we met, I was 33 years old. A White Romanichal woman from the Gypsy, Romani, Traveller (GRT) community who, at that time, had an ambivalent relationship to my intersecting identities and social locations. Coming from a community whose identity has historically been formed in response to societal and systemic racism, I had grown to manage feelings of shame by denying explorations of my race. I had internalized advice from my community to hide my ethnicity. My logic at this time, and during my art therapy training, was that you could not be Romani Gypsy and an art psychotherapist. I used my White privilege (McIntosh, 1989) and 'assimilated' accent to 'not be' Romani when I studied or practised. I was also often race blinkered when considering my clients. Retrospectively, I feel this was rarely challenged in training, supervision or by art therapy literature, although I can now reflect on the tenacity of denial, despite challenge. I believe this to have been at the expense of best and ethical practice. As I held lightly my personal feelings of otherness in relation to my profession, I began to more actively explore the 'norms' that the profession has privileged (Hocoy,

2007; Talwar, 2019) and examine the practice of art therapy in relation to issues of power and oppression (Kuri, 2017). Reflecting on this process, I can see the blinkered spots that impacted my work and may continue to do so, without ongoing acknowledgement.

During my first year working at the hostel, I made time to sit with Lindy in the TV room. In this in-between session time, there seemed to be space where we could build trust and connection. I balanced being myself without disclosing a great deal about myself, while offering Lindy relational space to fill. In my second year, Lindy asked for time in the therapy room and began attending sessions sporadically. I then took a four-month sabbatical to travel and it was agreed the position would be left open for me. I informed the residents and Lindy seemed the most interested in my plans. I felt acutely aware of our difference, and felt shame and guilt surrounding my privilege in having such opportunities.

In personal therapy, I explored what my therapist named 'survivor guilt' in relation to my family dynamic. As Romani Gypsy, travelling is part of my ethnic identity, yet has become less achievable in the UK for GRT communities due to societal pressures to assimilate and discriminatory law changes (Gov.UK, 2019). I reflected on painful feelings evoked by my work at the hostel relating to my 'transitioning' from a place of oppression to privilege, and the irony of my now socially sanctioned, 'middle-class' plans to travel. Layton's (2020) concept of 'normative unconscious processes' links the psychic and the social in a way that illuminates how hierarchically defined identity categories are unconsciously reproduced and impact on therapeutic work. In considering theories of identity and power, categories such as race and gender are often socially constructed in binary and hierarchical ways; what is White is defined as not-Black, and what is male, not-female. Such categories are constructed as different but also in binaries of superior or inferior. Talwar (2010) notes the historic binaries of art therapy practice as having reinforced the reductive paradigm of normal versus abnormal. Layton (2020) considers subjectivity as being formed in the negotiation of two binary kinds of relational experience, one in which parts of us are accepted, and one in which parts of us are not. A conceptualizing of this splitting enables consideration of what happens when 'norms permit certain identifications and encourage dis-identifications with what is socially considered undesirable' (Layton, 2020, p.177). Similarities can be drawn with object relations theories, yet here there is focus on what Layton (2020) describes as the 'BIG history'.

Retrospectively, I see that when working with Lindy, my clinical considerations were not explicitly contextualized within my personal experiences and intersecting identities, particularly regarding race and ethnicity.

Despite personal therapy facilitating self-reflexivity surrounding identity and a rising of consciousness regarding what had been evoked of my personal relationships by therapeutic relationships in my work, I was unable to use clinical supervision to do the reverse. Supervision, as an extension of my professional identity, remained a place of blinkered spots regarding my intersecting identities and the potential impact on my practice of normative unconscious processes (Layton, 2020) or unhelpful assumptions or biases. It remained a place where, consciously, I did not consider experiences defined by social location in relation to race, including the oppression of Romani women, privileges experienced when read as White, or the experiences of oppression of Black women.

Despite my considerations of gender in relation to social and political context (Eastwood, 2012), I applied what I now consider to be 'colourblind' intersectionality (Carbado, 2019). I was able to utilize what are important feminist therapeutic approaches, considering analysis of gender in relation to unconscious processes and trauma. Yet despite mention of race in my work with Lindy, what lacked was a dimension linking critical race theory of 'colourblindness' to intersectional considerations of social formations (Carbado, 2019) – a dimension that could challenge the way in which 'White' was not seen as an explicit racial marker but one that operated invisibly, as a default and normative category (Eastwood, 2021).

'We should avoid framing the intersection of race and gender to mean the intersection of nonwhiteness and gender' (Carbado, 2019, p.210).

I lacked the theoretical frameworks to support self-reflexivity that could consider both intrapsychic and relational dynamics that enforce splitting demanded by binary and hierarchical social constructions of identities. I could not consider the splits dictated by my own experiences of social location and of what would become experienced tenaciously as 'not-me'; a form of racism potentially marking my psyche in distinct ways that could impact on my work with clients such as Lindy.

It was on my return from sabbatical that Lindy began to commit to therapy. I was informed that she had become seriously physically unwell and refused to engage with any other services. As our regular sessions began, I suffered overwhelming feelings of boredom and despair, as I spent time with her drawing. On occasions, I felt as if I might pass out and irrationally feared we may not have enough oxygen in the room to breathe. It was in response to the holistic impact of such bodily centred countertransference (Carr & Hancock, 2017) that I intuitively decided to draw Lindy for the first time. These drawings would often be created with little conscious decision-making while I focused on Lindy, her words and the space between us.

Vignette 1: 'It looks like how I feel'

Lindy began by describing how unwell she felt. She commented, 'I know I'm like this but I'm not scared.' I responded that it felt to me that she was scared. I eventually took what felt like a risk and asked, 'Do you feel like you are dying, Lindy?' She responded, 'Yes I do.' I was aware how difficult it was for her to acknowledge that fear, and I wondered aloud about whether her current feelings were what she needed to listen to when considering engaging with services. She seemed to hear this, yet only responded to say that she was tired. I drew her as she worked on her own art, and she gazed at my drawing (Figure 6.1) when it was completed, eventually commenting sadly, 'I look awful.'

Figure 6.1: 'It looks like how I feel'

She seemed uncomfortable, possibly angry, and yet we looked together for what felt like a considerable amount of time. She finally commented, 'It's the truth though.' I responded that it was *my* drawing and that it may be about me, and my worry for her. I asked her if she would like to accompany my portraits with some words of her choice, which I would write on my drawings. This week she dictated, 'It looks like how I look here, right now. It looks like I feel, tired, ill, a bit worried. Weak, faint.'

Horay (2006) notes, in US art therapy literature on substance abuse, a focus on using art-making to confront client denial, while in the UK, grounding in psychoanalysis suggests an exploratory rather than confrontational process. Springham (1999) promotes the need to support ambivalence about recovery in art therapy, with the patient conceiving of both good and bad aspects of addiction. Lindy would often draw party balloons and champagne bottles illustrating celebration surrounding her drinking. She seemingly faced her denials in my drawings, an embodiment of my countertransference, while often maintaining ambivalence in her own, perhaps in order for therapy to be experienced less catastrophically (Springham, 1999).

When conceptualizing Jung's (1959) active imagination as a means of mobilizing the psyche through an image, Schaverien (2005) reflects on the distinction between much imaginative activity and active imagination that is mobilized through 'fantasy thinking' and guided by unconscious motives that emerge in 'visualization, dreams and pictorial images' (Schaverien, 2005, p.41). My portraits of Lindy, created in a way that did not feel wholly conscious, seemed to respond to something of the 'unthought known' with Lindy's inabilities to express her conflicts in words, resulting in articulation of the preverbal transference, evolving in my countertransference (Bollas, 1987). Davidson (1966) notes the possibilities of the transference itself being a type of active imagination. Departing from the understanding that it is the patient alone who experiences active imagination, Davidson suggests that the therapist in fact regard the whole of the patient's unconscious, enacted through the transference. 'Lowering of consciousness in order to be in touch with the patient's inner world is certainly an imaginative act and a creative way of understanding the images, which arise in the analyst, as unconscious communication from the patient' (Schaverien, 2005, p.44).

Vignette 2: 'Something abstract today'

Lindy attended this session having been drinking and I wondered aloud if we should continue. She responded that she wanted to stay. She then drew what she described as 'something abstract today' and spoke about drinking and how she believed it was not a problem for her health or relationships. She went on to speak fondly of her father, associating drinking with him. She spoke of him in an idealized way as I drew her, focusing on a mug of water she held as it felt like the only thing of her I could capture. On three occasions, she called me 'Dad'. I noted this aloud on each occasion and eventually she commented, 'I keep calling you Dad! What is that about?' In supervision, I reflected on becoming Lindy's father in the transference and my supervisor expressed objection to my not ending the session earlier, as Lindy had been drinking and was experiencing such strong transference feelings. She was concerned about risk. I also questioned my decision, but in relation to power dynamics in the therapeutic relationship, noting the importance of therapy not re-enacting power inequalities that exist in the client's life (Brown, 2010). I wondered about this in relation to Lindy's vulnerabilities when drinking and how they may have been abused.

However, what was not considered in supervision was an intersectional perspective, locating us within social and cultural experiences of difference (Talwar, 2010). In retrospect, if my supervisor and I had been able to consider Lindy and her father in wider contexts, then maybe we could have made important links between Lindy's experience of her father as both hero and abuser, and of my becoming him in the transference. I may have been able to interpret transference and countertransference in relation to power, but on much deeper psychic levels. 'The rupture in the social link abandons the subject to a dyadic realm of victimizer/victim, kill or be killed. The restoration of trust, however, requires that the therapist recognize his or her part in the BIG history' (Layton, 2020, p.176).

I never asked Lindy about her family's migration to the UK, but can now speculate that Lindy's parents might have been part of the Windrush generation that brought workers from Trinidad and other Islands as a response to post-war labour shortages. Reni Eddo-Lodge (2017) outlines the nature of systemic and societal racism experienced by those of this post-war settlement. Hall (1984) reflects on the photographic archives of those who came to what was considered home as part of the Commonwealth, yet were abused on arrival on multiple personal and systemic levels. Such photographic archives have brought alive for me the descriptions Lindy would often give of her father.

Had I been able to consider the entanglements of our social locations, a White woman working with a Black woman with our own personal histories of transgenerational and intergenerational transmissions of trauma that respond to binary and hierarchical societal conceptions of race; if I had been able to raise a consciousness in relation to my 'not-me' that defended against the hurt and humiliation of exposing shameful vulnerabilities that I feared could be used against me (Layton, 2020) in relation to my profession, my newly acquired 'White/middle-class' social location and my ethnicity; if I could have considered Lindy's father's likely experience of White post-war society in Britain and the ways in which intergenerational transmissions of trauma can manifest through re-enactments of abuses of power in families; if I could have connected this to Lindy's experiencing of her father as both sadistic abuser and caring saviour, then maybe I could have gained far greater insight into Lindy's potential experience of our work and my drawing of her. A deeper interpretation of the transference, and my becoming Lindy's father within it, and the countertransference that my images contained, might have been possible.

In considering the reading of racial fetishism, Mercer (1994) explores the way in which White people 'look' at Black people and considers concepts of 'fixity' and stereotypes of Black people as 'colonial fantasy'. As Bhabha suggests, 'An important feature of colonial discourse is its dependence on the concept of "fixity" in ideological constructions of otherness' (Bhabha, 1983, p.18).

I can now consider such ideas in relation to me and Lindy, our difference, my drawing her and the colonizing of image. At the time in supervision, I considered my drawing of Lindy in relation to 'fixing' her in time a response to my fears of losing her if she were to die. When reflecting on power dynamics in the therapeutic relationship, I can accept that both theories may be true and connected. That histories of colonization and White supremacy have often been embedded in enactments of care.

The following week, I asked Lindy if we could look at the previous week's drawings. She was keen to see them and said that she clearly remembered the images and attending the session. Yet on viewing the images, I could sense that they captured something she did not have a clear memory of. She commented on her image, a page of scribbles, as being 'not very good really' and that mine wasn't really of her at all! Her sadness felt palpable and important. Her feelings around my drawing her maybe illustrated the importance of me 'seeing' her accurately. I commented that I just couldn't capture her that week; that she seemed so fragmented. She responded, 'My drawing is like that too, it's just not finished.' I asked her if this might be what it is like when she drinks, for her and for others with her. That something of her feels hard to capture, something that she avoids, that feels unfinished and chaotic. She agreed but was keen to move on, mentioning that she wanted to stay positive. Despite Lindy's ambivalence and inability to tolerate exploration, in this session she seemed faced with an awareness of her powerlessness over addiction (Julliard, 1995) in both my drawing and her own; an awareness she stayed with fleetingly.

Vignette 3: 'I think we need to do this'

Lindy drew the image 'triangles' and then went on to say, 'So triangles, what do they mean to me? The Bermuda triangle, a place where you get lost, you come back years later and you can't remember anything!' I considered her drinking in relation to these comments and the amnesia that she often experienced as both suffering and relief. I also reflected on her avoidance of connecting with past trauma, all of which felt too invasive to name with her. Yet in manageable ways, she seemed to use art to symbolically explore the deeply defended against and forgotten. Being able to view the images she had created provided connections through what could feel like a void of forgotten space between sessions, like the Bermuda triangle. Her artworks, as well as my portraits, also bridged a void between us in the relationship. I felt this session that my portrait (Figure 6.2) depicted her as healthier than usual. She disagreed. Despite seeming uncomfortable, she looked curiously for a long while, stating, 'That's how you see it.' I found her expression hard to interpret; she seemed both elated and angry. She dictated, 'I do like my life and love my family and I am not ready to die. I have got too much to live for.'

Figure 6.2: 'I think we need to do this'

I then asked Lindy if she would like me to stop drawing her. She responded, 'No, I think we need to do this, I trust you.'

I took my anxiety to supervision and discussed my feeling that my portraits were important yet uncomfortable for Lindy to view. I wondered if this were due to my responding to uncomfortable truths of her lived experience, communicated through my art as a countertransference vehicle (Fish, 2019; Wadeson, 1986). I also considered Lindy's attachment history and if she had ever truly felt 'seen'. Did my portraits make her feel seen in ways so unfamiliar that they could also feel like an attack? Did my drawings represent a part of her that she could not, yet desperately needed to, see? I reflected on whether this is what Lindy had meant by 'I think we need to do this'.

Vignette 4: 'Both touching and not touching'

Lindy spoke of the difficulties that other residents faced in the hostel and what felt like injustice in relation to women surviving or reporting rape or assault. We discussed some of the social and political context for women, the cycles of abuse and self-abuse, and Lindy seemed to find this important and containing as well as informative. I sensed Lindy answering personal questions related to her experiences of abuse and exploring feelings of self-blame. Lindy often presented as child-like in our sessions, yet this exchange seemed to encourage a more empowered, adult self. Lindy then began to speak of a fantasy of 'being posh' and 'a professional' and she wondered aloud if one day she could be a therapist, mirroring the way I may often do this with her. As we drew together, I felt very aware of our difference, the power imbalance in the client–therapist relationship and of my perceived position as the 'posh' professional. I thought about her fantasies about my privilege, and about my actual privilege, and wondered how I might respond to questioning about whether I felt she could be a therapist, like me. I also reflected on my Whiteness in relation to Lindy being Black, and what this might mean in this context, most likely prompted by my reflecting on how few Black therapists I actually knew or trained alongside. I wanted to avoid not acknowledging the part my privilege may have played in my achievements, inadvertently communicating that they were based solely on my own merit. I felt anxious that if we didn't acknowledge our difference and my privileges, then the negative aspects of her reality would seem to be as a result of her own personal failures alone. 'If they come to believe that their failure to measure up is a result of personal limitations – a lack of talent, desire or effort – they internalise the oppression' (Weber, 1998, p.24).

This direction in the session, led by Lindy, seemed in response to considering the societal location to greater contextualize the trauma of women from feminist perspectives (Brown, 2010). This wider contextual thinking seemed to prompt in Lindy questions about our identities, which inevitably included race and class. I responded to these considerations by saying nothing; frozen by the awkwardness and fear of naming our differences surrounding race. In retrospect, I can see my difficulties in resolving a clinical dilemma; that in naming racial difference to avoid Lindy's internalizing oppression (Weber, 1998), I might reinforce hopelessness or oppression (Young, 1990).

I had utilized feminist therapy perspectives and consciousness raising (Joyce, 1997) as a psycho-educational tool in conjunction with psychodynamic thinking to explore intersectional considerations of trauma related to gender (Eastwood, 2012). Yet, I could not consider the intersect of gender and race that differed for Lindy and me, or my potential leanings towards White feminist perspectives (Carbado, 2019).

This application of 'colourblind' intersectionality (Carbado, 2019) was in part a response to my personal experiences of radicalized trauma, yet to be metabolized (Menakem, 2017), surrounding the naming or denying of race; the invisibility of Romani women (Corradi, 2018) and feeling othered in my profession and being a victim of hate crimes in my life. I can reflect on the impact of additional layers; of feeling de-skilled and unprepared by art therapy training and literature to work with such difference. Also, on my White fragility, resultant of a lack of emotional stamina for critical conversations about race (DiAngelo, 2011) and evoking in me fears of losing my newly acquired power as a 'White, middle-class' professional. Lindy asked to see my drawing of her (Figure 6.3), and consciously noticing it for the first time, I felt relieved. I felt I had depicted her as capable, vibrant and alive. Lindy added her words, 'Carry on laughing, stay happy... forget your troubles...go with the flow and enjoy life, because you never know when your number is up!' She showed me her drawing, saying it had turned out just as she had wanted, a colourful bunch of flowers 'both touching and not touching'.

Figure 6.3: 'Both touching and not touching'

At the time, I felt that Lindy and I had begun to 'both touch and not touch'. Something felt 'good enough', and in supervision I was able to reflect on the importance of where I felt we metaphorically touched. Yet in retrospect, I was unable to tolerate important missing dimensions to our work, which Lindy seemed to be trying to name and explore. 'Colourblindness thus survives and thrives not because of what it produces, but because of what it prevents: that is, exposure, analysis and remediation of the skewing of social opportunities and life chances by race' (Lipsitz, 2019, p.24).

Vignette 5: Snakey Crazy Lady and the Air Head Princess

I eventually stopped drawing Lindy; something of the unbearable and unspeakable had shifted and the need to contain my countertransference lifted. In our final session, Lindy spoke about being 'an alcoholic' and about knowing she needed help. Far from non-engagement with services, she now often had appointments that conflicted with our session times, including with addiction services. She drew 'Snakey Crazy Lady' and the 'Air Head Princess?' (Figure 6.4).

Figure 6.4: Snakey Crazy Lady and the Air Head Princess

She described the Disney princess as 'not having a clue' about the snakey lady's world and she described the snakey lady as crazy, but worldly. A question mark hung over the princess's identity; her face obscured with a scribble. We both felt very fondly toward the snakey lady, she was adventurous and fun. We laughed about these characters, which were so very different. Despite her air headedness, neither of us felt animosity towards the princess; there was just lots she didn't know. The following week, I was informed that Lindy had been accepted on to a creative writing course that conflicted with our session time. I began the process of ending with Lindy, and at this time I reflected on the snakey lady's single tear, with the princess so far behind. I did manage to meet with Lindy one final time, as I decided to leave my role at the hostel. During this meeting, she read me some of her stories in the TV room, and it felt as if we ended where we had begun.

In supervision, I considered what Lindy might have wished to communicate about our relationship through her drawing of these characters. Their lack of understanding of each other's identities, with the Disney princess seeming to be the epitome of unknowing White privilege. In retrospect, I can reflect on how Lindy may have taken back the power I had used in drawing her. Our entanglements felt to be represented in our portraits of each other, my countertransference embodied in my portraits of her, responding to her denials and transference 'thought unknown' (Bollas, 1987). Her possible representation of the binary constructions of identity typical of normative unconscious processes, the crazy ethnic lady and the White princess, representing her perceptions of me as the princess, and of herself and my 'not-me' (Layton, 2020) as the crazy lady; a 'not me' I had also been tenaciously defending. Layton (2020) describes 'enactments of distinction' as conscious and unconscious conflicted motivations to simultaneously contest and sustain norms. She does not define such resulting 'double binds' as clinical errors, yet believes them to be 'relational repetition compulsions in which psyches shaped by social inequalities of all kinds unconsciously reproduce the very psychosocial structures that caused psychic pain in the first place' (Layton, 2020, p.178). Rather than reflect on my work with Lindy as clinical error or success in binary ways, I will acknowledge the work's complexity, its abilities to hold and value ambiguity, and the ongoing ways in which I must inform my psychodynamic practice as an art therapist; integrating non-'colourblind' intersectional thinking, considering psychosocial structures and deepening self-reflexivity.

Conclusion

The British Association of Art Therapists workforce survey (2019) revealed that approximately 93 per cent of UK practitioners are White. In 2013, the charity Mind conducted a report (Mind, 2013) on improving access to therapy for Black, Asian and Minority Ethnic (BAME) clients. Only 10 per cent of BAME clients surveyed felt that therapy adequately took into consideration their cultural background. However, 75 per cent of therapists surveyed believed that they did indeed meet the cultural needs of BAME clients. Liebmann (1999, p.264) writes, 'The combination of therapist/client and white/black power imbalances means that often clients will not feel able to say if I am being racist. This awareness in itself is one small step towards redressing the balance.' I feel Lindy and I were able to forgive the airhead princess for all she didn't know; yet we *must* challenge an inability in the profession to acknowledge and respond to such client feedback without defensiveness (Eastwood, 2021). In considering the responsibility art therapists have to dismantle White supremacy, Hamrick and Byma (2017) suggest the first steps towards embracing critical consciousness are for White art therapists to unlearn socialized White fragility (DiAngelo, 2011), caused by White supremacist culture shielding White people from race-based stress. Intersectional self-reflexivity (Talwar, 2019) and racial cultural identity development (Doby-Copeland, 2013) can support explorations of self for therapists who aid ethical explorations of blinkered spots in practice and deepen understanding of 'other' and unconscious processes.

Art therapy trainings in the UK and beyond continue to under-address multicultural considerations in the curriculum and teach from Eurocentric (Awais & Yali, 2015; Gibson, 2015; Talwar, Iyer & Doby-Copeland, 2004) and dominant societal group perspectives that marginalize many voices. Incentives to greater understand othered communities should be incorporated into curriculum and assessment of registration renewal, to aid greater client understanding, but also understanding of marginalized peers and encourage greater diversity in the profession. Cultural variables that affect a client's use of marks, symbols and colour can be considered to greater inform our explorations of visual media as art therapists (Acton, 2001) and be learned by attending diverse cultural events (Doby-Copeland, 2013). Importantly, the role White art therapists can take in decolonizing the visual realm in art therapy practice must be considered (Eastwood, 2021). Intersectional thinking and theory can guide processes of self-reflexivity so all intersects of therapist and client identity can be considered on psychic and social levels, to achieve best and ethical practice.

Acknowledgements

I would like to thank Lindy for all she has taught me. I would also like to thank Kati Gray for her vital part in my big history.

References

Acton, D. (2001). The color blind therapist. *Journal of the American Art Therapy Association, 18*(2), 109–112.

Awais, Y. J. & Yali, A. M. (2015). Efforts in increasing racial and ethnic diversity in the fields of art therapy. *Journal of the American Art Therapy Association, 32*(3), 112–119.

Bhabha, H. K. (1983). The other question... *Screen International Journal, 24*(6), 18–36.

Bollas, C. (1987). *Shadow of the Object: Psychoanalysis of the Thought Unknown*. New York, NY: Columbia University Press.

British Association of Art Therapists (2019). Workforce survey *International Journal of Art Therapy, 24*(2), 1–2.

Brown, L. S. (2010). *Feminist Therapy*. Washington, DC: American Psychological Association.

Carbado, D. W. (2019). Colorblind Intersectionality. In K. Crenshaw, L. Harris, D. HoSang, N. Chaddock & B. Hinderliter (eds) *Antagonizing White Feminism: Intersectionality's Critique of Women's Studies and the Academy*. Washington, DC: Lexington Books.

Carr, S. & Hancock, S. (2017). Healing the inner child through portrait therapy. *International Journal of Art Therapy, 22*(1), 8–21.

Corradi, L. (2018). *Gypsy Feminism: Intersectional Politics, Alliances, Gender and Queer Activism*. Oxford: Routledge.

Davidson, D. (1966). Transference as a form of active imagination. *Journal of Analytical Psychology, 11*(2), 135–140.

DiAngelo, R. (2011). White fragility. *International Journal of Critical Pedagogy, 3*(3), 57–70.

Doby-Copeland, C. (2013). Practicing Multicultural Competent Art Therapy. In S. Prasad, P. Howie & J. Kristel (eds) *Using Art Therapy with Diverse Populations: Crossing Cultures and Abilities*. London: Jessica Kingsley Publishers.

Eastwood, C. (2012). Art therapy with women with borderline personality disorder: A feminist perspective. *International Journal of Art Therapy, 17*(3), 98–114.

Eastwood, C. (2021). White privilege and art therapy in the UK: Are we doing the work? *International Journal of Art Therapy*. https://doi.org/10.1080/17454832.2020.1856159.

Eddo-Lodge, R. (2017). *Why I'm No Longer Talking to White People About Race*. London: Bloomsbury.

Fish, B. J. (2019). Response art in art therapy: Historical and contemporary overview. *Journal of American Art Therapy Association, 36*(3), 122–132.

Gibson, L. R. (2015). Is cultural competence enough? Deepening social justice pedagogy in art therapy. *Journal of the American Art Therapy Association, 32*(3), 142–145.

Gov.UK (2019). *Government Consults on New Police Powers to Criminalise Unauthorised Encampments*. Accessed 23/07/20 at www.gov.uk/government/news/government-consults-on-new-police-powers-to-criminalise-unauthorised-encampments.

Hall, S. (1984). Reconstruction work. *American Psychological Association, 16*, 2–9.

Hamrick, C. & Byma, C. (2017). Know history, know self: Art therapists' responsibility to dismantle White supremacy. *Journal of the American Art Therapy Association, 34*(3), 106–111.

Hocoy, D. (2007). Art Therapy as a Tool for Social Change: A Conceptual Model. In K. Kaplan (ed.) *Art Therapy and Social Action*. London: Jessica Kingsley Publishers.

Horay, B. J. (2006). Moving toward gray: Art therapy and ambivalence in substance abuse treatment. *Journal of the American Art Therapy Association, 32*(1), 14–22.

Joyce, S. (1997). Feminist-Perspective Art Therapy: An Option for Women's Health. In S. Hogan (ed.) *Feminist Approaches to Art Therapy*. London & New York, NY: Routledge.

Julliard, K. (1995). Increasing chemically dependent patients' belief in step one through expressive therapy. *American Journal of Art Therapy, 33*(4), 110–119.

Jung, C. W. (1959). *The Archetypes and the Collective Unconscious*. New York, NY: Bollingen Foundation, Princeton University Press.

Kuri, E. (2017). Toward an ethical application of intersectionality in art therapy. *Art Therapy: Journal of the American Art Therapy Association, 34*(3), 118–122.

Layton, L. (2020). Intersectionality, Normative Unconscious Processes, and Racialized Enactments of Distinction. In M. Belkin & C. White (eds) *Intersectionality and Relational Psychoanalysis: New Perspectives on Race, Gender, and Sexuality*. New York, NY: Routledge.

Lerman, H. & Porter, N. (1990). *Feminist Ethics in Psychotherapy*. New York, NY: Springer Publishing Company.

Liebmann, M. (1999). Being White: Engaging with a Changing World. In J. Campbell, M. Liebmann, F. Brooks, J. Jones & C. Ward (eds) *Art Therapy, Race and Culture*. London: Jessica Kingsley Publishers.

Lipsitz, G. (2019). The Sounds of Silence: How Race Neutrality Preserves White Supremacy. In K. Crenshaw, L. Harris, D. HoSang & G. Lipsitz (eds) *Seeing Race Again*. Oakland, CA: University of California Press.

McIntosh, P. (1989). White privilege: Unpacking the invisible knapsack. *Peace and Freedom*, July/August, 8–10.

Menakem, R. (2017). *My Grandmother's Hands: Racialized Trauma and the Pathways to Mending Our Hearts and Bodies*. Las Vegas, NV: Central Recovery Press.

Mercer, K. (1994). *Welcome to the Jungle: New Positions in Black Cultural Studies*. London: Routledge.

Mind (2013). *We Still Need to Talk – A Report on Access to Talking Therapies*. Accessed 17/03/20 at www.mind.org.uk/media-a/4248/we-still-need-to-talk_report.pdf.

Schaverien, J. (2005). Art and active imagination: Reflections on transference and the image. *International Journal of Art Therapy, 10*(2), 39–52.

Springham, N. (1999). All Things Very Lovely: Art Therapy in a Drug and Alcohol Treatment Programme. In D. Waller & J. Mahoney (eds) *Treatment with Addiction: Current Issues for Arts Therapies*. New York, NY: Routledge.

Talwar, S. (2010). An intersectional framework for race, class, gender, and sexuality in art therapy. *Journal of the American Art Therapy Association, 27*(1), 11–17.

Talwar, S. (2019). *Art Therapy for Social Justice: Radical Intersections*. New York, NY: Routledge.

Talwar, S., Iyer, J. & Doby-Copeland, C. (2004). The invisible veil: Changing paradigms in the art therapy profession. *Art Therapy: Journal of the American Art Therapy Association, 21*(1), 44–48.

Veldhuis, C. B. (2001). The Trouble with Power. In E. Kaschak (ed.) *The Next Generation: Third Wave Feminist Psychotherapy*. New York, London, Oxford: The Haworth Press.

Wadeson, H. (1986). The influence of art making on the transference relationship. *Journal of the American Art Therapy Association, 3*(2), 81–88.

Weber, L. (1998). A conceptual framework for understanding race, class, gender and sexuality. *Psychology of Women Quarterly, 22*, 13–32.

Young, I. M. (1990). *Justice and the Politics of Difference*. Princeton, NJ: Princeton University Press.

Chapter 7

Consent and 'The-rapist': Positions of Power in Art Psychotherapy with a Sex Offender

JESSICA COLLIER

Introduction

The Office for National Statistics (2017) estimates that approximately 20 per cent of women and 4 per cent of men have experienced sexual assault since the age of 16. Given that the large majority, around 85 per cent (*The Guardian*, 2009), of art psychotherapists are female, we can extrapolate that a significant number of clinicians will have been subjected to these kinds of offences. In addition, there is some evidence of a high prevalence of sexual abuse history among adult male sex offenders (Jespersen, Lalumiere & Seto, 2009). This chapter explores the complexities of power and consent in the relationship between a female art therapist who has experienced sexual violence, and a convicted male offender who has been both the victim and perpetrator of sexual violence. Questions around unconscious re-enactments within the therapeutic relationship, as well as the perpetuation of toxic gender stereotyping, will bring to light the importance for both the therapist and the patient of acknowledging their own anger and potential for acting out unhelpful or retaliatory ways of communicating. The cultural response to rape and sexual assault will be considered through forensic psychoanalytic and intersectional theory, an exploration of depictions of gendered sexual violence in classical Western art, and the ways in which men are inculcated into believing their power and privilege is innate. A case study will consider the institutional response to the male sexual offender's relationships within the secure hospital and the female art psychotherapist he worked with. Finally, the ways in which the therapist might unconsciously exploit her authority in the therapeutic relationship will be considered in relation to the patient's observation that her staff badge could be read as 'the-rapist'. This comment is the basis for considering power and control between men and women, institutions and patients, perpetrators and victims, the complexity of these binary designations and the issue of consent.

Rape and sexual violence: A psychoanalytic approach

There is a rich literature of forensic psychotherapy, and increasingly arts psychotherapy, that has long sought to understand what drives men and women to perpetrate sexual violence (Collier, 2021; Gilligan, 2000; Liebmann & Hastilow, 2021; Welldon, 1988). While these writings are influenced by psychoanalytic theory – including attachment theory and object relations theory (Hyatt-Williams, 1998) – that foreground the understanding of unconscious actions as the primary focus, there has also been an emphasis on social influence. Forensic psychotherapy tends towards the perception of violence as a response to external cultural as well as internal conflicts. For example, Gilligan and Welldon emphasize the importance of humiliation and shame as the root of violence and sexual perversion. Indeed, Gilligan (2000) considers the feeling of being disrespected as intrinsic to the perpetration of violence. He proposes that we know inequality and discrimination cause violence, but suggests there is no political will to transform the status quo. Gilligan supposes that the class system supports racism, sexism and homophobia in a terrible hierarchy of shame when he states: 'The poor and members of minority racial and ethnic groups are regularly subjected to maximal degrees of shame, humiliation and feelings of inferiority.' He goes on: 'Nothing stimulates crime and violence more than the division of males and females into the roles of violence object and sex object, respectively... Nothing stimulates violence more powerfully and effectively than homophobia' (Gilligan, 2000, pp.188–189). Gilligan believes there is an epidemic of structural violence which depends on the upholding of the patriarchy and can only be challenged by reconfiguring what we mean by masculinity and femininity. He contends that the act of rape itself 'may tell us something about the patriarchal legacy and making of "manhood" which is at the heart of "civilisation" as we know it, with all its violence between men; its class structure and racial prejudice; and its asymmetrical treatment of women and men' (ibid, p.179).

Welldon's writing also highlights shame as the fundamental foundation of sexual perversion. She suggests that early sexual humiliation may manifest later in violence as a compulsive psychological defence, intended to alleviate overwhelming anxiety and fear of depression and annihilation. Welldon argues that perpetrating a sexual offence may transfigure feelings of shame into something closer to pride, excitement or even fame (Welldon,

2009). It should be noted that the term sexual perversion is used here to describe a particular concept of sexual violence, and does not denote any form of consensual sexual expression that may be considered 'perverse' by illiberal or intolerant opinion (Collier, 2020). Welldon also pioneered the psychoanalytic conception that violence perpetrated by women is different from violence perpetrated by men; the primary difference, put simply, being that male violence is directed externally, while female violence is directed internally, either against themselves or their children, who they may unconsciously experience as an extension of themselves. Importantly, Welldon notes that while men's stories of enacting violence are everywhere, nobody wants to hear about women's experiences of violence, either as victim or perpetrator. 'The aetiology of perversion, I believe, is intertwined with the politics of power... It is possible that this difference of response is caused by society's inability to see woman as a complete human being' (Welldon, 1988, p.104). This denial of the female experience of violence, the disinterest in hearing about it, is an observation corroborated in many testimonies, including those by mental health professionals who have themselves experienced sexual violence (Lee & Palmer, 2020).

Rape and sexual violence: An intersectional approach

Sexual violence is inextricably linked to social injustice. It is not an individual, isolated problem but is entrenched in systemic oppression and inequality (Crenshaw, 1994) and 'reproduces inequalities of gender, race/ethnicity, class, age, sexuality, ability status, citizenship status, and nationality' (Armstrong, Gleckman-Krut & Johnson, 2018, p.99). Patriarchal society normalizes toxic masculinity and stereotypical essentialist gender roles, which extol male violence and hypersexuality and rationalize, even eroticize, male sexual aggression as natural and evolutionary:

> Gender essentialist thinking makes men evaluate sex crimes more leniently...including rigid gender stereotypes that tightly circumscribe appropriate female norms and responsibilities, hypermasculine norms, societal excuse making for violence towards female partners...and government's low financial and political investment in the problem. (Fine, 2017, pp.189–191)

Key to an intersectional approach is the recognition that the complexity of multiple identities impacts lives differently. This is clearly manifest in the way rape is understood on a societal level and the way it is reported and prosecuted; rape victims are frequently failed. For example, victims of rape may choose not to report abuse due to community stigma or adverse relationships with the police in response to systemic racism. 'Victims of colour respond to rape differently or face different issues than White victims do... [V]ictims of colour are more likely than White victims to remain silent about their victimization...' (Maier, 2008, p.303). Black women, women of colour, LGBTQ+ individuals and people living in poverty come forward even less frequently to report sexual violence against them than their White, heterosexual, cisgendered peers because of the presumption of guilt their 'difference' may carry; and this includes homophobia and racism they may encounter from services that may be systemically discriminatory.

Fervour or force? The grey areas of consent

The feminist writer Margaret Atwood once famously asked a male friend why he thought men felt threatened by women and a group of female friends why they felt threatened by men. The man responded, 'They are afraid women will laugh at them', while the women responded, 'We're afraid of being killed' (Dickson, 1996). This difference in the experience of interpersonal threat is important because it adds nuance to how consent is interpreted. Many men I have worked with who have committed sexual assault or been convicted of rape have protested their innocence and insisted the sex was consensual, even as they have been found guilty. But Atwood's axiom suggests that many women may fear for their lives during unwanted sexual encounters and thus are not in a position to consent. Many women report 'spectatoring' when they feel sexually compromised, a kind of dissociation in which the sex act is watched as if by a third party. This is described in the short story *Cat Person* (Roupenian, 2017), in which a woman initiates sex, changes her mind during the encounter, but cannot find a way to stop it. If a woman believes she may be killed during a sexual assault, consent is not possible.

Victim blaming and institutional collusion

The concept of victim blaming is well known (Ryan, 1971) and is intrinsic to the patriarchal phenomenon of rape culture, alongside misogynistic sociological notions including slut-shaming, rape jokes and sexual objectification. In this milieu, victims are held responsible for their own assaults, and the trivialization of sexual violence permeates society, organizations and institutions where it is unconsciously introjected by women and men. In many instances, it is raped women who are deemed the problem; accused of bringing shame on their families, of falsely accusing the perpetrator – in reality men are more likely to be raped themselves than wrongly indicted (Shand-Baptiste, 2019) – or ruining the life opportunities of the men who have raped them. For example, in 2015, Brock Turner, a White, middle-class swimming scholar at Stanford University, sexually assaulted Chanel Miller, a Chinese-American, while she was unconscious. He was apprehended at the scene while assaulting her and was consequently found guilty in court. Nevertheless, Turner was given an unduly lenient sentence of six months and his father described prison as 'a steep price to pay for 20 minutes of action' (Hunt, 2016). The negation of sexual assault as 'action' is typical of attitudes to sexual violence and the nullifying of the victim's experience. Indeed, universities and workplaces in the United States and the UK are rife with sexual violence, victim blaming and institutional collusion. In a 2018 study, 70 per cent of female students and recent graduates surveyed had experienced sexual violence at university, rising to 73 per cent of students with a disability. Eight per cent reported having been raped, while 78 per cent agreed that certain people blame the victim for the sexual violence they experienced (Revolt Sexual Assault, 2018).

While these figures represent actual physical assault, the attitudes that perpetuate sexual violence are commonplace in environments where they remain unchallenged. I once had a reflective practice meeting with my work associates in which I stated that I felt dominated and undermined by the way a colleague behaved towards me. On hearing this, the facilitator declared I had a 'father complex' and stated that I could not tolerate men in positions of authority. The implication here was that my concerns held no validity. I left the position soon after this incident, feeling unsupported and not wanting to collude with such a misogynistic and defensive perspective. I am not alone in having experienced such attitudes. These assertions are common in the workplace and certain groups of women face them routinely. Black women are most likely to have their professional judgement or expertise questioned, while lesbians and women with disabilities may frequently be subject to demeaning remarks about themselves or others like them (Women in the Workplace, 2019). In the UK, nearly half of female managers identified their workplace as sexist (Oppenheim, 2019) and sexual harassment and microaggressions continue to harm women; 'No matter what form they come in, microaggressions can have a serious impact and create a toxic working environment' (Smith, 2019). This is relevant because institutional environments that are hostile to women perpetuate misogynistic attitudes, which include the continuance of sexual violence as acceptable and the denigration of women who complain; '...the problem becomes not the men who violated women, but the women who had the audacity to speak up and not keep it to themselves' (Gentile, 2018, p.719). The situation is more dangerous still in institutions such as the Criminal Justice System and the Health Service, in which marginalized women are routinely discriminated against as victims, perpetrators, staff and patients (Hinde, 2020; Lammy, 2017).

A visual history of sexual violence

Rape and sexual violence have been a central theme of Western art since ancient Greece. These myths and images, painted by the great 'masters' Botticelli, Caravaggio, Titian, Rubens, Poussin and many others, depict rape as 'heroic' and paint the victims of rape as compliant, mad or monstrous. Medusa, for example, is brutally raped by Poseidon when she refuses him. She is then blamed for breaking her oath of chastity by Athena, who punishes her by making her a monster, a Gorgon, who is so repulsive that anyone looking at her will be turned to stone. She is then re-brutalized by Perseus, who murders her in cold blood and cuts off her head to use as a weapon. In all these depictions of masculine strength and sexuality, the rapists and murderers are heroes and gods, valiant and celebrated. Rape is conceived as an act of virility and courage, feeding into the patriarchal idea that women are merely subjugated objects. This matters, because 'Images have power; they don't simply reflect reality, but can influence attitudes and this way affect actual events' (Wolfthal, 1999, p.25). The approbation of male virility and double standards are easily recognizable in modern rape culture, and although sexual violence is most commonly experienced by women, we most often see it from the male perspective.

During this period of classical painting, only Artemisia Gentileschi offers us a woman's experience of the shame, vulnerability and rage that may follow rape, in her painting *Judith Slaying Holofernes.* Gentileschi had herself been a victim of rape and had been tortured in court to prove the veracity of her story. However, while some feminist scholars see this formative experience of sexual violence as intrinsic to her identity as a woman artist and the very essence of difference in her work, others argue there is more to this woman than being a rape victim and the experience should not define her or her art. Griselda Pollock suggests that 'the feminine subject must be recognized as being implicated in a socio-symbolic formation that can never be grasped if we only construct either victims or heroines' (Pollock, 1990). Nevertheless, *Judith Slaying Holofernes* offers us a glimpse of how women might really feel when they are violated, and their desire for violent retribution. This image, painted in seventeenth-century Italy, feels very close to the revenge fantasy Michaela Coel reveals in her multilayered television series *I May Destroy You* (2020), exploring rape and consent and the experience of being a Black woman in modern-day London. But how do we make sense of Black women's experience of sexual violence as depicted in classical Western art? *The Rape of the Negro Girl* painted by Christiaen van Couwenbergh in 1632 does not portray a myth, nor does it attempt to create heroes from the men jostling and holding down the victim. Nonetheless, there is a look of fear on the woman's face and a smirking expression on the man looking out towards the viewer with impunity, which reminds us that slave owners, and their families and employees, were legally permitted to rape their slaves. This entrenched sense of entitlement and the breaking of the fourth wall have much in common with the gang rape of an unconscious woman by a group of male students in Steubenville, Ohio in 2012. The rape was filmed and posted on social media with commentary and jokes which included one of the boys laughing, 'She is so raped right now...dead body.' When the boys were apprehended it was the victim who was initially blamed. Responses on social media included, 'I have no sympathy for whores' (Horton, 2019), once again substantiating the continuing prevalence of victim blaming and rape culture.

Case study

This clinical material examines the way in which issues of power and consent change and transform, becoming multifaceted and ambivalent as the therapeutic relationship progresses, much like the situation described by Roupenian (2017): 'She was starting to think that she understood him – how sensitive he was, how easily he could be wounded – and that made her feel closer to him, and also powerful.' The complexity evoked by this publication increased further when, several years later, it emerged that the protagonists were in fact based on real people who recognized their lives in the story. As with art psychotherapy, this raises questions about who owns a story and the reliability of its narrators.

For some years, I worked on a medium secure unit in a modified therapeutic community. The 15 residents were men who had been given a diagnosis of severe personality disorder and had, almost without exception, perpetrated heinous acts of violence or sexual violence resulting in the injury or death of their victims. I facilitated a regular weekly art psychotherapy group on the unit, as well as taking part in many other clinical and social aspects of the therapeutic community. This collaborative ethos complicated the already intricate negotiation of boundaries and hierarchies and blurred the lines of all our identities, both as mental health professionals and as mental health patients. Thus, the men who were referred by the team to the art psychotherapy group witnessed me in a number of different contexts, and I them.

The men on the unit were predominantly White and working class, with high levels of underlying physical complications associated with poverty, such as diabetes. Throughout the rest of the hospital, located in a large ethnically diverse city, the patients were more mixed. Personality disorder is a predominantly White diagnosis (Hossain *et al.*, 2018), although this was never directly addressed as an outcome of complex unconscious racial bias. Nevertheless, the unit was envied and seen as 'special' by the rest of the hospital; perhaps symbolic of systemic White male privilege at work even in the most impoverished and vulnerable populations. Indeed, antisocial personality disorder itself seems to reflect traits that could be seen as expressing oppressor privilege; for example, feelings of entitlement, violation of the rights of others, a lack of guilt or remorse, blaming others when things go wrong, feeling misunderstood, and difficulty empathizing or seeing an alternative perspective (NHS, n.d.).

The art psychotherapy group was attended by five men who stayed for an average of two years. The group followed a typical pattern of making art, cleaning up and discussion. When Dean joined, the group consisted of two men who had murdered their mothers, one man who had assaulted an elderly woman, and one man who had murdered a male associate. All had experienced domestic violence in childhood and all were perpetrators of domestic violence in adulthood, a stark illustration of intergenerational trauma re-enacted and the veracity of the repetition compulsion (Freud, 1920). Dean was in his early thirties and had been convicted for violently raping an older woman. He struggled to take responsibility for this, insisting she had consented and had only changed her mind later. Dean couldn't manage the boundaries on the unit easily, but seemed committed to therapy and was initially tolerated by the staff and his peers.

As a child, Dean had been violently beaten by his father from an early age. He was neglected by his mother, who was assaulted by the father if she showed any kindness to Dean. He had been thrown out of the family home by his father aged 15, and had experienced drug addiction and homelessness, frequently perpetrating violence against women and sabotaging anything good in his life. This included work opportunities, housing and relationships. As Dean became more involved with the therapy, he disclosed that his father had also sexually abused him as a child. This final admission of humiliation triggered a change in Dean's behaviour on the unit. While he had always spoken in casually sexist terms, Dean now began to use overtly misogynistic language. He spoke about women stinking, called the female staff bitches and cunts, and repeatedly harassed them using sexualized and racist language and touching their clothes inappropriately. The community responses to this behaviour varied enormously and seemed to be influenced by age and ethnicity as well as gender. It seemed the young White women whom Dean targeted were given duties away from him and offered sympathy, while the Black women were expected to 'get on with it' and their experience was minimized, perpetuating the racist stereotype of the strong Black woman which continues to be pervasive and is especially apparent in healthcare settings. Meanwhile, the male staff and his peers almost unanimously wanted Dean to leave the community, mirroring his father throwing him out of the house. As is often the case with complex patients, Dean split the team into those who supported him and those who hated him (Main, 1957). I found myself supporting him, despite my conscious disgust at his behaviour, and wondered why this might be. Dean's disclosure had coincided with a significant change in the management team. The consultant, an experienced older woman who was able to challenge and support the men with authority, and with whom he had a good relationship, retired and was replaced with a much younger man. Dean began to imagine that the medication this man recommended was shrinking his penis; a rivalrous response perhaps to the new powerful male who had prescribed it.

Throughout his time in the art psychotherapy group, Dean had developed a way of working with pastels that revealed complex landscapes and weather patterns; often combining several different elements at once and suggesting reflection and transformation. Following the disclosure of sexual abuse however, Dean began working on an oil painting, the paint leaving a smelly, oily mess on his hands that he could not wash off. The colours were dark and foreboding (Figure 7.1).

As he worked on it, I found myself admiring his process and was shocked and dismayed when he started to get angry at his failure to control how the image was progressing, to the point where he ripped it off the wall each week, eventually tearing it into two. I found myself scared and anxious in the group, worried he might become violent, but also trying to control his rage, to convince him not to spoil his work and again wondering about my intense response.

I have been raped. This statement fills me with ambivalence. Like many women, my own experience of sexual violence left me feeling disoriented by a complex amalgam of feelings that included fear and compliance in the moment, followed by guilt, anger, shame and, most confusingly of all, responsibility. I didn't tell anyone. It didn't cross my mind to report it. At the time, street harassment was common and men regularly exposed themselves on public transport, followed me home or propositioned me. Men's sexualized behaviour towards women in public, now more widely perceived as part of rape culture, was completely normalized. I minimized the experience so as to carry on, but also, because society itself minimizes sexual violence against women. At the time I was raped, the law did not even recognize sexual violence within marriage, stating that a husband could not be guilty of raping his wife (Collier, 2021). In addition, as a lesbian, speaking out about sexual violence or gender inequality would inevitably be met with derision or suggestions that I was frustrated and just needed the right man to change my mind. In the 1980s, when I was coming of age and coming out, this kind of narrative was ubiquitous in the UK. Section 28 of the Local Government Act 1988 forbade teaching 'the acceptability of homosexuality as a pretended family relationship'. I was frequently verbally assaulted and threatened with violence. I was told I should have been aborted and described as 'an abomination'. I learned to stay quiet about my sexuality. When the law explicitly labels your intimate relationships as 'pretend' and legitimizes sexual violence as normal, fear, humiliation and internalized shame and misogyny are likely consequences.

Figure 7.1: Dean's oil painting

Given my own experiences, I began to realize that my response to Dean – my support of him, my attempts to influence his creative process and constrain his anger – might be connected to my own working through of having been raped and my complex feelings about gender. This man might have represented an opportunity, albeit unconsciously, for me to take control of and be the more powerful in the dyad between 'a rapist' and myself. I had encouraged his own disclosure of sexual violation – which had left him exposed, fearful, angry, humiliated and vulnerable – perhaps unconsciously aligning our mutual experiences of sexual violence and shame. My empathic feelings for Dean, who it must be remembered had been convicted of the violent rape of a woman only a little older than myself, began to make sense as an introjection (Klein, 1946). In a society that negates the great harm done personally and systemically by gendered violence, perhaps women can identify with men's vulnerability in a way that they cannot identify with their own, as this would be too painful. The cultural expectation that women are carers and nurturers of men can be understood perhaps as a broader societal manifestation of their attempts at survival through identification with the aggressor (Freud, 1937). I needed to recognize that my own internalized misogyny might play a part in my feelings of empathy for Dean and prioritizing his feelings and wellbeing above my own, as men are routinely prioritized in society. Certainly, when he or other residents on the unit insulted me, commenting on my appearance or assumed sexuality, I absorbed this, consciously only calling out sexism or homophobia when directed at others, for fear of the repercussions from the men, and from some of the staff, that might come with identifying myself as different and, therefore, vulnerable.

The power I held in my relationship with Dean, although complex, lay primarily in my position as the therapist. As Dean's release date approached and he was due to be returned to prison, he made the observation that my staff badge could be read as 'the-rapist'. While consciously I was a supporter of Dean, advocating for his extended stay on the unit, attempting to understand his racist and misogynistic abuse and encouraging his use of therapy, unconsciously, perhaps I was forcing on him my own interpretation of his experience as I understood it as a mirror to my own. By symbolically becoming 'the-rapist', perhaps I was able to vanquish my own feelings of powerlessness.

Dean did not finish his oil painting. Instead, having destroyed it, he started work on a much more modest scale. He made an evocative pencil drawing of an isolated hut, a depiction perhaps of the place where he felt he deserved to be, on his own, removed from society, in contrast to the bold, layered but filthy landscape he had previously explored. This was the final piece he made in the group and it too remained unfinished (Figure 7.2).

Figure 7.2: Hut

Conclusion

The ideas I have written about here did not surface while I was working with Dean, but have emerged retrospectively, once I had left the unit, knowing I had done all I could in my work there. What I did understand while working with Dean was the complexity of our relationship and the struggle for power in the dyad, within the therapy groups, the community, and ultimately within our patriarchal society; as a man and a woman. I knew I wanted to write about Dean because I had felt so emotionally connected to his spoiling of the good things in his life. In a small way, I recognized and identified with his manifestation of self-loathing and sabotage as the result of feeling neglected early in his life and disregarded by society. Before he left, I asked Dean to sign a declaration of consent for me to write about him. As he scrawled his signature, I realized just how little this man had consented to in his life. I comprehended the fundamental importance of acknowledging the position of power we hold as therapists and the infinite value of understanding our own process, even as we seek to support others in understanding theirs. I recognized that when our patients give us their consent to work together, we bring different ideas and experiences of what consent actually means. Our reflexivity is only as good as our desire to really understand our motivation to work in such a powerful position with vulnerable people. Indeed, I am thinking, even as I write, about why I am writing, and whether the content of this chapter is what Dean thought he had consented to.

Ultimately then, I come to the conclusion that we should not deny our own desire to wield the power that is inherent in working as a therapist. Otherwise, we run the risk that we are merely sublimating the same objective as 'the-rapist', no matter how unconscious and deeply hidden, to be in control. By believing that as therapists we are only good, empathic, compassionate, non-judgemental and enlightened is disingenuous and potentially dangerous. While the time-honoured concept of the wounded healer (Jung, 1961) is convincing and brings some succour to our difficult work, we should also recognize that those who are wounded and feel wronged may seek not only to heal others, but also to find retribution.

Acknowledgements

My thanks to Dean for giving me his consent to write about him. I have changed his name and some details.

References

Armstrong, E. A., Gleckman-Krut, M. & Johnson, L. (2018). Silence, power and inequality: An intersectional approach to sexual violence. *Annual Review of Sociology, 44*, 99–122. www.annualreviews.org/doi/full/10.1146/annurev-soc-073117-041410.

Coel, M. (2020). *I May Destroy You*. BBC & HBO.

Collier, J. (2020). Mark making or making a mark? Perversion and sublimation in the work of Estela Welldon, Martin Frishman, and Aubrey Beardsley. *The International Journal of Forensic Psychotherapy, 2*(1), 26–41.

Collier, J. (2021). Behind Closed Doors: Art Psychotherapy with Female Sexual Offenders. In M. Liebmann & S. Hastilow (eds) *Arts Therapies and Sexual Offending*. London: Jessica Kingsley Publishers.

Crenshaw, K. (1994). Mapping the Margins: Intersectionality, Identity Politics and Violence Against Women of Colour. In M. Albertson, *The Public Nature of Private Violence*. New York, NY: Routledge.

Dickson, M. (1996). *A Woman's Worst Nightmare*. www.pbs.org/kued/nosafeplace/articles/nightmare.html.

Fine, C. (2017). *Testosterone Rex: Unmaking the Myths of our Gendered Minds*. London: Icon Books.

Freud, A. (1937). *The Ego and the Mechanisms of Defence*. London: Hogarth Press.

Freud, S. (1920). Beyond the Pleasure Principle. In J. Strachey (ed.) *Standard Edition, 18*, 7–65. London: Hogarth Press.

Gentile, K. (2018). Give a woman an inch, she'll take a penis: The expanded version. *Contemporary Psychoanalysis, 54*(4), 709–723.

Gilligan, J. (1996, 2000). *Violence: Reflections on our Deadliest Epidemic*. London: Jessica Kingsley Publishers.

The Guardian (2009). Career by numbers: Art therapist. Sat 14 November. www.theguardian.com/money/2009/nov/14/art-therapist-career.

Hinde, N. (2020). Women of colour are paying with their lives for healthcare inequalities. *Huffington Post*, 6 March 2020. Available at www.huffingtonpost.co.uk.

Horton, A. (2019). Roll red roll: Behind the chilling documentary on high school rape. *The Guardian*, Tue 9 April. www.theguardian.com/film/2019/apr/09/roll-red-roll-behind-the-chilling-documentary-on-high-school.

Hossain, A., Malkov, M., Lee, T. & Bhui, K. (2018). Ethnic variation in personality disorder: evaluation of 6 years of hospital admissions. *BJPsych Bulletin, 42*(4), 157–161. https://doi.org/10.1192/bjb.2018.31.

Hunt, E. (2016). 20 minutes of action: Father defends Stanford student son convicted of sexual assault. *The Guardian,* Mon 6 June. www.theguardian.com/us-news/2016/jun/06/father-stanford-university-student-brock-turner-sexual-assault-statement.

Hyatt-Williams, A. (1998). *Cruelty, Violence and Murder: Understanding the Criminal Mind.* Northvale, NJ: Aronson.

Jespersen, A. F., Lalumiere, M. L. & Seto, M. (2009). Child abuse and neglect: Sexual abuse history among adult sex offenders and non-sex offenders: A meta-analysis. *Child Abuse and Neglect, 33*(2), 179–192. https://doi.org/10.1016/j.chiabu.2008.07.004.

Jung, C. G. (1961). *Memories, Dreams and Reflections.* London: Fontana.

Klein, M. (1946). Notes on some schizoid mechanisms. *International Journal of Psycho-Analysis, 27*, 99–110.

Lammy, D. (2017). *The Lammy Review: An Independent Review into the Treatment of, and Outcomes for, Black, Asian and Minority Ethnic Individuals in the Criminal Justice System.* London: Lammy Review.

Lee, D. & Palmer, E. (2020). *#Metoo – Counsellors and Psychotherapists Speak About Sexual Violence and Abuse.* Monmouth: PCCS Books.

Liebmann, M. & Hastilow, S. (eds) (2021). *Arts Therapies and Sexual Offending.* London: Jessica Kingsley Publishers.

Maier, S. L. (2008). Rape victim advocates' perception of the influence of race and ethnicity on victims' responses to rape. *Journal of Ethnicity in Criminal Justice, 6*(4), 303–334.

Main, T. F. (1957). The ailment. *Psychology and Psychotherapy: Theory, Research and Practice, 30*(3), 129–145.

NHS (National Health Service) (n.d.). Antisocial personality disorder. www.nhs.uk/conditions/antisocial-personality-disorder.

Office for National Statistics (2017). *Sexual Offences in England and Wales: Year Ending March 2017.* www.ons.gov.uk/peoplepopulationandcommunity/crimeandjustice/articles/sexualoffencesinenglandandwales/yearendingmarch2017#toc.

Oppenheim, M. (2019). Almost half of women managers say their workplace is sexist. *The Independent*, Thurs 20 June. www.independent.co.uk/news/uk/home-news/sexism-work-female-bosses-young-women-trust-pay-gender-gap-a8965681.html.

Pollock, G. (1990). Book review. *Art Bulletin: A Quarterly*, Sept 1990, LXXII, 3. www.collegeart.org/pdf/artbulletin/Art%20Bulletin%20Vol%2072%20Vol%203%20Pollock.pdf.

Revolt Sexual Assault (2018). *Students' Experience of Sexual Violence.* https://revoltsexualassault.com/wp-content/uploads/2018/03/Report-Sexual-Violence-at-University-Revolt-Sexual-Assault-The-Student-Room-March-2018.pdf.

Roupenian, K. (2017). Cat person. *The New Yorker.* www.newyorker.com/magazine/2017/12/11/cat-person.

Ryan, W. (1971). *Blaming the Victim.* New York, NY: Pantheon.

Shand-Baptiste, K. (2019). Men are 230 times more likely to be raped than wrongly called a rapist. *The Independent*, Wed 2 October. www.independent.co.uk/voices/gang-rape-trial-ayia-napa-false-accusation-sexual-assault-cyprus-israel-a9131796.html.

Smith, L. (2019). *Why Sexist Microaggressions Are Holding Women Back at Work.* https://uk.finance.yahoo.com/news/why-sexist-microaggressions-are-holding-women-back-at-work-073408356.html.

Welldon, E. (1988). *Mother, Madonna, Whore: The Idealization and Denigration of Motherhood.* London: Karnac.

Welldon, E. (2009). Dancing with death. *British Journal of Psychotherapy, 25*(2), 149–182.

Wolfthal, D. (1999). *Images of Rape: The 'Heroic' Tradition and its Alternatives.* Cambridge: Cambridge University Press.

Women in the Workplace (2019). https://wiw-report.s3.amazonaws.com/Women_in_the_Workplace_2019.pdf.

Chapter 8

Therapists Too: Disclosure and Solidarity at the Crossroads of Art Therapy, Survivorhood and Activism

SEJAL CHAD

Introduction

The #MeToo movement shone light on the devastatingly high prevalence of sexual violence globally.[1] It also offered an unprecedented opportunity for survivors to share their personal experiences publicly in a context where they were more likely to be believed, challenging long-standing denial, isolation and stigma. It has since led to increasing numbers of survivors speaking out about their experiences of sexual violence, and in doing so challenging long-standing socially sanctioned power dynamics in various communities and professional fields.

As a psychotherapist, art therapist and survivor, I have often wondered if such a movement might occur within my own profession and what its implications might be for clinical work and social change. While speaking out about personal experience has long been a component of feminist activism, and sharing experiences with the aim of reducing shame and increasing self-acceptance is also crucial to therapeutic practice, disclosures of sexual violence among therapists is still a relatively unexplored area. As shame is a common burden carried by survivors – and fear of additional shaming contributes to silence, denial and continuation of oppressive structures – it is imperative to now consider how we as therapists engage with shame held

1 The Council of Europe (n.d.) estimates that in Europe one in five children are the victims of some form of sexual violence. In March 2017, the Crime Survey for England and Wales estimated that 20 per cent of women and 4 per cent of men have experienced some type of sexual assault since the age of 16 (Office for National Statistics, 2017). The National Center for Transgender Equality in the US also estimates that 47 per cent of transgender people are sexually assaulted at some point in their lifetime (James *et al.*, 2016).

both by our clients and ourselves in relation to our histories and the social and political realities we inhabit.

This chapter explores how unexamined assumptions about the impact of therapist disclosure on clinical work may limit healing for survivor therapists, clients and society at large, and considers how we might become less complicit in societal silencing of this trauma. I will also discuss the potential of art therapies to shift barriers to disclosure for survivors, using vignettes from two groups to demonstrate art-making as a form of witnessing, disclosure and solidarity in groups where all members are survivors, including the facilitator/therapist.

My journey to this chapter

My awareness of the many aspects of sexual violence grew during my years of work at a respite centre for people in suicidal crisis. Previously, I had been involved in experimental arts and political publishing, and was used to utilizing various means of making sense of social and cultural phenomena. However, my understanding of the particular ways oppressive dynamics within the family and society intersected to affect people at the deepest level grew rapidly at this crisis centre.

Witnessing the vast majority of women I worked with disclosing experiences of sexual violence alerted me strongly to the links between sexual violence and mental health, and the overarching secrecy and stigma surrounding both. During this time, I also began training as an arts psychotherapist, and in placements continued to hear accounts of sexual violence as I expanded my repertoire of tools to safely and creatively work through the impact on clients.

While I had explored my own experiences as a survivor previously in personal therapy, the social dimension of the issue was still largely abstract for me. Growing up as a South Asian in the Middle East and also being an immigrant most of my adult life, I had likely internalized codes of silence and loyalty common to many immigrant communities, where risks of ostracization and insecurity function as major barriers to public disclosure.

Working with survivors in a state of crisis, and helping them to understand they were not to blame, involved exploration of social and power dynamics. The impact of secrecy and stigma became clearer for me, as many survivors expressed high levels of anxiety about others finding out about their struggles. Splits between functioning and non-functioning aspects of self also seemed particularly pronounced for survivors navigating ways to access support without destabilizing the good parts of their lives.

I have since considered whether I might have been engaging in forms of splitting myself, as a survivor with a responsibility for the wellbeing of others. Being exposed to the sheer scale of the issue, however, made it impossible for me to ignore its political aspect, and I experienced a growing desire to act beyond providing therapeutic support for my survivor clients. Not to be actively challenging the social forces enabling sexual violence felt like a shirking of my particular position as a psychotherapist, witness and survivor. Perhaps some of the feelings I was regularly experiencing in my work – powerlessness, rage, empathy, shame, despair, hope, numbness – needed wider channels to process than personal therapy and supervision alone, though I utilized both. The idea of becoming more vocal in ways that related to my own experiences and emerging values both excited and terrified me, and was met with conflicting opinions and advice from colleagues.

I found an opportunity to bring these identities and experiences together in 2015, when I joined the organizing team for Clear Lines Festival. The first four-day event of its kind, focused solely around sexual abuse and consent, it offered space for survivors and interested attendees to explore ideas and build solidarity within a creative environment. It was here I met survivor-activist and dramatherapist Kai Grygier and joined an organization they had co-founded called Survivors Collective, an open activist group for child sexual abuse survivors. One of the stand-out features of the group was that activism was encouraged at whatever level felt manageable to each participant, with a unique awareness and understanding of the difficulties survivors might face. The definition of activism was intentionally wide, including anything from self-care, disclosing to a family member, reporting abuse, creating guidelines for survivor needs, protesting legal treatment of survivors, and creating art.

This organization highlighted for me the enormous capacity for solidarity between survivors to reduce isolation, normalize feelings and coping strategies and actively participate in creating change in a context where legal justice remains an elusive prospect. It also made me aware of the enduring impact of abuse and the inevitability of fluctuating levels of engagement while trying to mobilize action around an issue that easily retriggers feelings of fear, shame and exhaustion, and which is often met with denial and minimization from institutions targeted for change.

I eventually became part of the Not the Only One project with Grygier, delivering training and workshops to universities about survivor needs in education. We also offer therapeutic support groups for survivor students, incorporating trauma psychoeducation, consciousness-raising, art and dramatherapy practices to help develop coping skills, confidence and community for participants. This was my first experience of working therapeutically with survivors while also being open about being a survivor myself. I will later draw on this work to consider issues around therapist disclosure in art therapy practice.

Sexual violence and the therapy profession: A contextual overview

Sexual abuse in the framework of psychotherapy and psychiatry has a complicated and controversial history, influenced by social and political forces. Many writers (e.g. Masson, 1992; Rush, 1980) have critiqued Freud's infamous retraction of his original assertion in 1896 that a high number of his patients had experienced child sexual abuse (1962) and linked this to a wider cultural denial of women and children's abuse and oppression. Freud faced serious social and professional ostracism after presenting his discoveries, writing at the time, 'I am as isolated as you could wish me to be: the word has been given out to abandon me, and a void is forming around me' (Masson, 1992, p.10). Later, he took on a position of full denial, claiming a need to 'recognize that these scenes [of child abuse]...had never taken place, and that they were only fantasies which my patients had made up' (1959, p.34). His amended views thrived among the medical society of the time and influenced a number of emerging psychoanalysts.

Freud's reversal and portrayal of survivors as liars or fantasists mirrors the denial, silencing and victim blaming common in wider society, and highlights the social risks of attempting to speak about the reality of sexual abuse. Rush (1980, p.82) suggests that Freud's decision may also have been influenced by concerns to preserve his self-image and identification with other men of his class, resulting in 'eventually gaslighting an age into ignoring...a very serious social problem'. This is a legacy the psychotherapy profession must continue to address.

The roots of psychotherapy seriously acknowledging sexual violence and its impact on women and children lay in the feminist movement from the mid-1970s (Herman, 2001), which led to research confirming that sexual violence was endemic and functioned as a form of gender oppression. One of the most extensive studies in the US showed that one in four women had been raped and one in three had been sexually abused as children (Russell, 1984). Feminist organizing led to the creation of rape crisis centres, often staffed by activists rather than professionals. The analysis of rape and child sexual abuse as linked with patriarchy and power gained ground and influenced the newly emerging feminist therapy movement. Many of the resulting ideas and models are now widely used therapeutically with survivors, such as groups, creative healing methods, and consideration of the psychosomatic effects of abuse. The benefits of 'speaking out' also emerged from these movements as medicalization of mental health issues of survivors was critiqued. Therapeutic understanding of the long-term impact of trauma was aided by feminist research and the work of grassroots survivor-activist organizations in collecting testimonies.

Feminist efforts to address sexual violence were often diluted by successful attempts by state and other institutions to shift focus away from challenging social and political power (Whittier, 2009). This has led to a continued tendency to individualize problems and solutions. The tendency to individualize is raised as problematic by some feminist therapists (Burstow, 2003) who critique the application of psychiatric diagnosis to trauma survivors as well as the common therapeutic goal for survivors to regain trust in a world where the risk of violence remains unchanged.

The ways in which training institutions engage with the topic of sexual violence warrants ongoing exploration and critique. Lee (2017) has written about the frustrating experiences of listening to conversations 'about' survivors in training institutions, and Smith and Mollis note a pervading sense of 'acceptable' and 'unacceptable' trauma:

> [T]here's still this idea that abuse and assault is something our clients experience and we don't. Even if we have actually experienced it, the process of training dissociates you from it because it's too difficult to confront that dual identity... [I]f we feel too much shame or doubt to be comfortable with owning 'unacceptable trauma' in the training process, what does this say about how we feel about our clients? (Smith & Mollis, 2020, p.90)

In the survivor workshops I co-facilitate, we regularly collate myths about survivors that members encounter. These include: being wounded, weak, unstable, dishonest, manipulative, gay, attention-seeking, motivated by money, provocative, promiscuous, vulnerable due to coming from a certain community, careless, naive, 'at fault'. I have encountered many of these myths in my own therapy, trainings and supervision, including once when I shared with my therapist my desire to become more involved in activism. Their response: 'That's really good. You could start helping people learn how not to get raped.'

Shame and disclosure

Sgroi (1989) suggests that unlike feelings of fear, anger and loss, shame functions for survivors as a form of contemporary denial. Even after acknowledging the reality of the abusive experience, attempting to avoid shame requires minimizing its significance. This provides conditions for perpetrators to continue abusing.

Finkelhor and Browne (1985) link shame and stigmatization, suggesting that victim blaming is a core aspect of stigmatization, and, accompanied by the need for secrecy, produces shame. Kaufman (1992) notes that while shame is initially produced interpersonally, it eventually becomes internally induced, with significant effects on individual and social identity:

> Our identity is that vital sense of who we are...embracing our worth, our adequacy, and our very dignity as human beings. All these can be obliterated through protracted shame, leaving us feeling naked, defeated...and intolerably alone... To feel shame is to feel seen in a painfully diminished sense. The self feels exposed both to itself and to anyone else present. It is this sudden, unexpected feeling of exposure and accompanying self-consciousness that characterizes the essential nature of the effect of shame. (ibid, pp.8–9)

Intrinsically, shame links the experience of exposure to feelings of powerlessness. Being shamed publicly creates deeper wounding than shame produced from private experiences, which might help add to our understanding of why disclosure of sexual violence is often avoided altogether. To disclose in the context of stigmatization is to risk further ostracization, and also involves being identified with pervasive myths about sexual violence victims.

At the same time, not feeling free to disclose is also linked with feelings of shame. Disclosing in some form is usually a requisite to seeking justice, support, intimacy, making sense of events and reclaiming agency and choice. Dolezal (2017) suggests that shame is not simply about impaired self-esteem but arises from embodied vulnerability in order to preserve the social bonds necessary for survival. As the need to both speak about and hide past experience to ensure belonging and safety is common to survivors, creating avenues for speaking which also increase belonging could be a helpful way to experience shame safely and begin to heal. Appropriate therapist response to client disclosure, and preparing clients to disclose to others only when they feel able to manage any potential responses, is also vital.

Herman asserts that:

> Sharing the traumatic experience with others is a precondition for the restitution of a sense of a meaningful world... Restoration of the breach between the traumatized person and the community depends, first, on public acknowledgement of the traumatic event, and second, on some form of community action. (2001, p.70)

What might this mean for therapists considering disclosing their experiences publicly? If community acknowledgement of traumatic experience is a necessary component of restoring meaning, what effects might the continued silence have for our sense of healing, meaning and relationships? And conversely, what effect might speaking out have on clinical work?

Therapist disclosure

In recent years, there has been increasing research and writing on therapist disclosure. While traditional psychoanalytic approaches (Freud, 1958) advocated a blank screen approach to avoid impeding transference and shifting focus from client to therapist, humanist approaches (Jourard, 1971) have explored ways therapist disclosure can improve therapeutic outcomes through increased genuineness and empathy. Feminist therapy approaches (Brown & Walker, 1990) have also advocated for self-disclosure as a means of furthering equality and transparency in the relationship.

Intersectional thinking provides a reminder that regardless of orientation, certain identifiers are always disclosed in face-to-face work, including race, gender, class and age. All of these affect the transference and power dynamics in the therapeutic relationship, influenced by structural inequalities, stereotypes and the client's history. Furthermore, therapists continuously disclose aspects about themselves non-verbally, including their emotional state through body language (Singer, 1977). When considering therapist disclosures that are more deliberately chosen, these can be roughly divided between disclosing thoughts and feelings in relation to client presentation, or disclosure of the therapist's personal life.

Some studies have shown particular types of disclosure are linked to improved clinical outcomes and therapeutic relationships. Levitt *et al.* (2015) found that disclosures that humanized the therapist or conveyed similarity between therapist and client were associated with reduced clinical symptoms. Disclosures of similarity have also been associated with a favourable impact on a client's perceptions of the therapist's 'realness' and sense of regard for the client (Henretty *et al.*, 2014). Rao and Mehra (2015) studied the therapeutic relationship between two people who were both victims of Hurricane Sandy and explored how disclosure relating to shared trauma facilitated healing and resilience for both therapist and client.

Despite this growing area of research, the topic of therapist disclosure remains contentious. Bottrill *et al.* (2010) found that contradictory theoretical approaches, lack of adequate training and unclear ethical guidelines led trainee therapists to feel anxious about disclosure decisions, and suggested trainees needed more support in working out their personal position. There is also variation around the use of self-disclosure among therapists, depending on the therapist's orientation, personal comfort, own experiences of therapy, and the norms of the clinical setting. Reasons therapists are hesitant to disclose include beliefs about boundary setting (Farber, 2006), fear of not being accepted by clients (Singer, 1977) and having become accustomed to being idealized (Renik, 1995). Some concerns outlined through research specifically around mental health professionals' disclosure of lived mental health experience (Zingaro, 2016) include: fear of overwhelming the client; the client feeling that the specificity of their own story is lost or diluted; the professional feeling overwhelmed and unsupported during or after disclosure; and the professional feeling stigmatized and losing a sense of their professional identity, instead risking being seen as only their experience and its stigmatizing associations.

Implications of disclosure for survivor therapists

In addition to these factors, many survivor therapists may hold beliefs that disclosing would negatively affect both the transference relationship and their professional identity due to prevailing myths about survivors. Goffman (1986) defines stigma as an attribute that is essentially discrediting, and suggests that the stigmatized person experiences both being *discredited* and being *discreditable* in opposition to what is considered normal. Decisions around disclosure may therefore be amplified for survivor therapists by considerations around the risk of stigmatization in relation to clients and peers.

The transference impact may be different in settings or contexts where the therapy is specifically for survivors (e.g. survivor organizations) and those where it is not (e.g. private practice). Jacoby (1984) argues that although therapists are commonly regarded as embodying the parent transference, it may also occur the other way around. The therapist may experience their client as an oppressive or abusive figure in the countertransference, which may be either projection based on their own relational history or in response to the client's transference and behaviour. Clients may have conscious and unconscious beliefs about survivors which could also affect the transference.

A potentially crucial factor in dealing with shame in the therapeutic context is the extent to which the therapist has recognized and worked with their own sense of shame. If the therapist is anxious about any kind of disclosure around sexual violence experience, it may be helpful to notice embodied reactions to client disclosure and be mindful of unconscious attempts to also protect the client from associated feelings through avoidance. If the client's notion of speaking out about their own sexual abuse is still associated with confirmation of myths and self-blame, this might influence the client's opinion of the disclosing therapist, but equally it may help them challenge their own beliefs about 'what a survivor is', particularly if they value other qualities in the therapist and experience other kinds of positive transference. Could widening the range of transference possibilities through disclosure experience also widen the range of affect that can be safely experienced by both the client and therapist?

Kohut (1984) proposed three types of transference that present in therapy: mirroring, idealizing and twinship/alter-ego. The last is associated with a sense of belonging and feeling like other human beings; a developmental need all children need to experience fully before feeling safe to tolerate difference. A met need for twinship transference is described as 'a source of genuine joy' (ibid, p.204), and 'repeated experiences of shared affect' a factor leading to internalization of safety and harmony (ibid, p.138). This may be a useful framework for considering the impact of shared similar lived experiences, identities and affect between client and therapist, particularly when the result has previously been isolation and shame. Twinship transference may also be helpful for considering the value of solidarity within and between marginalized groups for developing internalization of joy and safety.

As survivors have experienced boundary violations and betrayal of trust, it is important not to over-simplify or over-identify in the transference, and part of this involves good boundary setting (Sanderson, 2006). Negotiation of boundaries is also important for creating trust, safety and recognizing differences between therapist and client (Herman, 2001). One of the boundaries that needs to be made clear is that although survivor therapists may have similar experiences to the clients, the therapeutic relationship will always prioritize focus on the client's needs and recognize explicitly the power dynamics in the relationship and therapist responsibility to client.

Areas of study that may aid deeper understanding to facilitate decisions around survivor therapist disclosure include the impact of therapist disclosure on client transference, therapeutic alliance and clinical outcomes (for those seeking help for sexual violence issues and those seeking help for unrelated issues); the number of practising therapists who are survivors and their own disclosure decisions; the factors influencing these decisions; and what further support is needed.

Survivor disclosure as an art therapist and activist

Junge (2007) suggests that a good therapist must also be a social activist, one who considers the impact of cultural forces on a client's life, helps the client understand social inequalities, and engages in changing culture. Junge *et al.* also warn that 'all too often therapists heal what is already wounded, and do not attend to the milieu that wounds and re-wounds again and more deeply' (1993, p.149).

Support groups for and by survivors have been known to offer comradeship, understanding and recognition, though without a clinically trained leader they may have struggles with continuity, managing power issues or safety needs (Gil, 1990). The support group we ran offered a model where we attempted to create the benefits of survivor groups generally and meet safety and continuity needs with acknowledgement of power differentials through our distinct roles as facilitators.

One of the enduring effects of sexual violence is loss or fragmentation of identity (Herman, 2001), so rebuilding identity in these areas in conjunction with exploring subjective experience and social forces could offer a way to engage both in social change and personal and interpersonal healing. When survivors began speaking out publicly in the 1970s, they were influenced by the Black feminism movement to formulate their own identity. Self-defining as 'survivor' was considered an important aspect of taking back control, challenging shame and situating themselves as the experts of their own oppression and reality (Whittier, 2009). In our groups, we sought to offer a space where ambivalence around identity could be tolerated and worked with, without imposing definitions. Creative practices further offered ways of reconnecting with, mourning and integrating lost aspects of self.

My own process of deciding when and how to disclose personal material in the groups was simultaneously experimental, intuitive, cautious and spontaneous. A clear boundary I felt helpful to apply was to not disclose any material in a way that could be perceived as requiring emotional support from group members, and staying mindful about sharing what I had normalized for myself within a tolerable range of affect. Still, at the beginning I experienced migraines following sessions that seemed to be a somatic response to this type of personal exposure in my work. These subsided as I became more familiar with the practice, while utilizing support from my co-facilitator, therapist and supervisor.

Another helpful boundary I came to was disclosing shared experiences of impact rather than specifics of the trauma stories themselves. One reason #MeToo became so accessible was that it offered a choice to disclose as much or as little as each survivor chose. Similarly, in the group we tried to foster an environment where no one was pressurized to disclose details of their stories. Instead, commonalities of impact and needs became a meeting ground for survivors through discussion and arts practice.

Feedback from the Not the Only One group suggests that at the very least therapist disclosures were not harmful in this context. Eighty per cent of respondents said they felt that knowing the facilitators were survivors was very helpful to them. Other written feedback about survivor facilitators included: 'Nothing was too much or unexpected for them', 'I wouldn't have gone if it wasn't [facilitated by survivors]' and 'It's encouraging to have role models who were in your position and are now much better, to the point where they can facilitate a group. It gives me hope that I can one day be there too as they have done it.'

The use of image as therapist disclosure

Talwar (2019) contends that when arts practice links trauma, feelings, memory, affect and subjective formation to the social construction of identity, it can provoke analysis of power dynamics to challenge inequality and transform relationships. Similarly, Hogan (2012) advocates a form of 'social art therapy' that encompasses a consideration of structural inequality and art-making as a form of consciousness-raising. If, as Burstow (2003) attests, people who have experienced trauma see the world *more* accurately than those who haven't, art therapy with survivors might involve exploration of the meanings of what has been seen. Schaverien (1997) suggests word-image juxtapositions in art therapy can be seen as attempts to first communicate an experience with the self and then with an 'other', functioning as transactional objects from individual to community.

The images below were created by me and my co-facilitator Kai Grygier. I produced Figures 8.1 and 8.2 in a Survivors Collective session where the group discussed how different parts of the body carried trauma and the disparity between survivors' social and private selves.

Figure 8.1: It's in a lot of me

Figure 8.2: Haunted warrior

Grygier produced Figure 8.3 in response to participants in the university support group, when members were lamenting the difficulties of navigating social structures that were unsupportive to survivors.

Figure 8.3: The world is a lot

In both cases, the drawing and writing were deliberately produced in response to group discussion, which was particularly helpful with management of potential overwhelm evoked from the shame of exposure for us as facilitators. The need to manage affect is especially pronounced in art-making, which has the potential to reveal unexpected and unprocessed traumatic material in an uncontained way.

The inclusion in Figure 8.3 of a quote from the group discussion, reframed through Grygier's own creative response, shifts the individual survivor from being the problem, somehow 'too sensitive', to identifying the social structure the survivor inhabits. The facilitator chose to focus on the effect of the world – not 'I'm too much', but 'the world is a lot' – and to further include imagery of stars and flowers to evoke hope and community. This could be seen also as a disclosure of their own stance as a survivor, therapist and activist within a survivor group setting.

Art-making in the groups may have provided a form of attunement (Stern, 1985), whereby a feeling state is *recast* by another in a different form, creating resonance, connection and 'mutual recognition' (Wright, 2009, p.7). Attunement necessarily includes aspects of the attuning person's state of mind, but in such a way that it contributes to the person being attuned to feeling met and understood. The art-making may have functioned as a form of containment (Bion, 1962), whereby raw experience is processed, transformed and returned in a more manageable form.

As survivor therapists, we sought to create an environment in which witnessing (of individual and shared experience), disclosure (of personal impact and responses to others) and solidarity (being explicitly supportive and including self in shared experience and aims around the issue) could be fostered between all group members to reduce the individual burden survivors often carry. The phrase 'a lot' came up in both sets of images. This points to the intersection of the personal and political and the reality that survivors commonly experience carrying too much without support or community. It also evokes the reality that there are *a lot* of survivors in the world, and forming links and solidarity might reduce despair and isolation.

Professional implications

Throughout this chapter, I have attempted to convey the need for survivor therapist disclosure to be discussed more openly, and for more specialized research to add to our understanding of survivors practising as therapists as well as the impact of disclosure on client outcomes and the therapeutic relationship. The long overdue time may be here to start broadening the conversation so that therapists who are survivors have more professional support and opportunities to speak about our own experiences and contribute to social change.

It is important, however, to remain mindful that all survivors, including survivor therapists, need agency and choice around disclosure decisions. Just as there should be no pressure on the client to disclose abuse until they feel resourced to manage whatever responses in themselves or others it may evoke, the same care and respect must also be afforded to survivor therapists in light of the significant personal and professional risks we face.

One clear need is for all therapists to be able to explore their experiences of sexual violence within therapy and supervision, with therapists and supervisors remaining mindful of how we may perpetuate common myths through shame, victim blaming and avoidance. It is also important that when art therapists do wish to come out as survivors, the wider professional community is supportive and reflective of conditioned and unconscious assumptions that may be playing out around this intersection of identities or experiences. As a profession, we need to normalize the idea that therapists also have lived experiences that they share with their clients, whether they choose to disclose or not within or outside the therapeutic relationship. As survivor therapists feel more holistically supported to engage in healing, speaking and agency within personal and professional communities, we may also be able to more convincingly communicate to clients that these possibilities can be worked towards.

The art therapies offer particularly helpful ways of working with sexual violence, in their aiding of expressing, disclosing, witnessing and containing previously unspeakable material. As art therapists who openly identify as survivors, we may be able to facilitate safety and containment for clients while also practising and modelling a social art therapy (Hogan, 2012) where the effects of structural oppression are not individually pathologized, but viewed within the context of the collective and political.

As a profession, we have a fantastic opportunity to contribute to creating change and reducing stigma around an issue affecting such large numbers of people. All art therapists, regardless of whether we identify as survivors, can engage with this work. Herman (2001) attests that 'public truth-telling is the common denominator of all social action' (p.208). This does not mean having to necessarily disclose personal histories, it can also be read as an invitation to practise solidarity by educating ourselves around survivor needs, actively seeking to understand political and intersectional issues around sexual violence, advocating for more trainings on the issue, and speaking out and challenging myths when they come up among professional peers and clients in our practice.

References

Bion, W. R. (1962). *Learning from Experience*. London: Heinemann.

Bottrill, S., Pistrang, N., Barker, C. & Worrell, M. (2010). The use of therapist self-disclosure: Clinical psychology trainees' experiences. *Psychotherapy Research, 20*(2), 165–180. doi: 10.1080/10503300903170947.

Brown, L. S. & Walker, L. (1990). Feminist Therapy Perspectives on Self-Disclosure. In G. Stricker & M. Fischer (eds) *Self-Disclosure in the Therapeutic Relationship* (pp.135–154). New York, NY: Plenum Press.

Burstow, B. (2003). Toward a radical understanding of trauma and trauma work. *Violence Against Women, 9*(11), 1293–1317. doi:10.1177/1077801203255555.

Council of Europe (n.d.). Compass: Manual for Human Rights Education with Young People. Accessed 23/09/20 at www.coe.int/en/web/compass/children.

Dolezal, L. (2017). Shame, vulnerability and belonging: Reconsidering Sartre's account of shame. *Human Studies, 40*, 421–438. Accessed 23/09/20 at https://doi.org/10.1007/s10746-017-9427-7.

Farber, B. A. (2006). *Self-Disclosure in Psychotherapy*. London: Guildford.

Finkelhor, D. & Browne, A. (1985). The traumatic impact of child sexual abuse: A conceptualization. *American Journal of Orthopsychiatry, 55*, 530–541.

Freud, S. (1958). The Dynamics of Transference. In J. Strachey (ed.) *Standard Edition, 12*, 97–108. London: Hogarth Press. (Original work published in 1912.)

Freud, S. (1959). An Autobiographical Study. In J. Strachey (ed.) *Standard Edition, 20*, J., 33–34. London: Hogarth Press. (Original work published in 1925.)

Freud, S. (1962). The Aetiology of Hysteria. In J. Strachey (ed.) *Standard Edition, 3*, 187–222. London: Hogarth Press. (Original work published in 1896.)

Gil, E. (1990). *Treatment of Adult Survivors of Childhood Sexual Abuse*. Walnut Creek, CA: Launch.

Goffman, E. (1986). *Stigma: Notes on the Management of Spoiled Identity*. New York, NY: Simon and Schuster. (Original work published in 1963.)

Henretty, J. R., Berman, J. R., Currier, J. & Levitt, H. M. (2014). The impact of counsellor self-disclosure on clients: A meta-analytic review of experimental and quasi-experimental research. *Counselling Psychology Quarterly, 29*(1), 7–28. doi:10.1080/09515070.2015.1090396.

Herman, J. L. (2001). *Trauma and Recovery: From Domestic Abuse to Political Terror (Revised Edition)*. London: Rivers Oram Press Pandora List. (Original work published in 1992.)

Hogan, S. (2012). *Revisiting Feminist Approaches to Art Therapy*. London and New York, NY: Berghahn Books.

Jacoby, M. (1984). *The Analytic Encounter: Transference and Human Relationship*. Toronto: Inner City Books.

James, S. E., Herman, J. L., Rankin, S., Keisling, M., Mottet, L. & Anafi, M. (2016). *The Report of the 2015 U.S. Transgender Survey*. Washington, DC: National Center for Transgender Equality.

Jourard, S. M. (1971). *The Transparent Self*. New York, NY: Van Nostrand.

Junge, M. (2007). The Art Therapist as Social Activist. In F. F. Laplan (ed.) *Art Therapy and Social Action* (pp.40–55). London: Jessica Kingsley Publishers.

Junge, M. B., Alvarez, J. F., Kellogg, A. & Volker, C. (1993). The art therapist as social activist: Reflections and visions. *Art Therapy: Journal of the Art Therapy Association, 10*(3), 149–155.

Kaufman, G. (1992). *Shame: The Power of Caring (Third Edition)*. Rochester, VT: Schenkman. (Original work published in 1980.)

Kohut, H. (1984). (ed. A. Goldberg & P. Stepansky) *How Does Analysis Cure?* Chicago, IL: University of Chicago Press.

Lee, D. A. (2017). Shocking revelation! There are women survivors of sexual violence training as person-centred psychotherapists. *Psychotherapy and Politics International, 15*, e1396. Accessed 23/09/20 at https://doi.org/10.1002/ppi.1396.

Levitt, H. M., Minami, T., Greenspan, S. B., Puckett, J. A. *et al.* (2015). How therapist self-disclosure relates to alliance and outcomes: A naturalistic study. *Counselling Psychology Quarterly, 29*(1), 7–28. doi:10.1080/09515070.2015.1090396.

Masson, J. (1992). *The Assault on Truth: Freud and Child Sexual Abuse*. London: Fontana. (Original work published in 1984.)

Office for National Statistics (ONS). *Sexual Offences in England and Wales: Year Ending March 2017*. Accessed 23/09/20 at www.ons.gov.uk/peoplepopulationandcommunity/crimeandjustice/articles/sexualoffencesinenglandandwales/yearendingmarch2017#toc.

Rao, N. & Mehra, A. (2015). Hurricane Sandy: Shared trauma and therapist self-disclosure. *Psychiatry: Interpersonal and Biological Processes, 78*(1), 65–74.

Renik, O. (1995). The ideal of the anonymous analyst and the problem of self-disclosure. *Psychoanalytic Quarterly, 62*, 553–571.

Rush, F. (1980). *The Best Kept Secret: Sexual Abuse of Children*. Englewood Cliffs, NJ: Prentice-Hall.

Russell, D. E. H. (1984). *Sexual Exploitation: Rape, Child Sexual Abuse, and Sexual Harassment*. Beverly Hills, CA: Sage Publications.

Sanderson, S. (2006). *Counselling Adult Survivors of Child Sexual Abuse* (third edition). London: Jessica Kingsley Publishers. (Original work published in 1990.)

Schaverien, J. (1997). Transference and Transactional Objects in the Treatment of Psychosis. In J. Schaverien & K. Killick (eds) *Art Psychotherapy and Psychosis* (pp.13–38). Hove, East Sussex: Routledge.

Sgroi, S. M. (1989). Stages of Recovery for Adult Survivors. In S. M. Sgroi (ed.) *Vulnerable Populations: Vol. 2. Sexual Abuse Treatment for Children, Adult Survivors, and Persons with Mental Retardation* (pp.111–130). Lexington, MA: Lexington Books.

Singer, E. (1977). The Fiction of Analytic Anonymity. In K. A. Frank (ed.) *The Human Dimension in Psychoanalytic Practice* (pp.181–192). New York, NY: Grune and Stratton.

Smith, L. & Mollis, S. T. (2020). Therapists' Lived Experience in Counselling and Psychotherapy Training. In D. A. Lee & E. Palmer (eds) *#MeToo: Counsellors and Psychotherapists Speak about Sexual Violence and Abuse* (pp.83–99). Monmouth: PCCS Books.

Stern, D. (1985). *The Interpersonal World of the Infant*. New York, NY: Basic Books.

Talwar, S. K. (2019). Identity Matters: Questioning Trauma and Violence through Art, Performance, and Social Practice. In S. K. Talwar (ed.) *Art Therapy for Social Justice* (pp.38–65). New York, NY: Routledge.

Whittier, N. (2009). *The Politics of Child Sexual Abuse: Emotions, Social Movements and the State*. New York, NY: Oxford University Press.

Wright, K. (2009). *Mirroring and Attunement: Self-Realization in Psychoanalysis and Art*. Hove, East Sussex: Routledge.

Zingaro, L. (2016). *Speaking Out: Storytelling for Social Change*. New York, NY: Routledge. (Original work published in 2009.)

Chapter 9

Intersecting Identities in a War Zone: A Music Therapist's Perspectives on Working with a Group of Mental Health Professionals in the West Bank, Palestine

ELENI TSOLKA

Introduction

Music, like identity, is constructed and consists of various and different components that intersect to create a complete piece. As music therapists, we are trained to listen carefully to our client's voice and music in a way that includes and analyses these components to best understand and engage with them. Intersectionality, on the other hand, is a complex phenomenon that describes how different 'axes' of one's identity impact the way people are perceived and treated as individuals by other people in society, governments and institutions (Crenshaw, 1989). Thus, power relations and differentials in interactions among individuals or groups of people are phenomena that can be explored through the lens of intersectionality (Riggs & Das Nair, 2012). It is essential for music therapists to have some knowledge and understanding of their clients' culture and life experiences, as well as to consider the way that power, privilege and prejudice inform therapeutic practice and the therapeutic relationship. This requires practitioners to explore their own intersecting identities in depth, including their own prejudice and unconscious bias, and also to 'acknowledge histories of oppression and be accountable for legacies and privilege within local and global contexts' (Hernandez & McDowell, 2010, p.29).

In this chapter, I will describe how I attempted to engage in critical analysis of the dynamics of power, privilege and oppression when running a music therapy group for social workers in the West Bank, Palestine, in the context of a music therapy project. Both the therapist's and clients' identity categories, including gender, social class, language and ethnicity, were examined not only from a psychodynamic perspective but also from a social, cultural and political perspective. My effort to build a safe relationship and enhance the clients' personal understanding and growth is presented throughout this chapter using self-reflexive thinking, as well as examples of incidents from the therapy room. Specifically, this chapter includes an overview of the relevant theory and continues with a thorough description of the music therapy project, the socio-political situation in the West Bank, the dynamics of the music therapy group, as well as the author as a person and a therapist. It further explains the manner in which the intersecting identities of the clients and the therapist shaped the therapeutic relationship with an emphasis on gender, social class, language and ethnicity.

Intersectionality in the literature

Intersectionality theory 'grew out of a critique of models of inequality which framed social forces as operating in layered or additive ways' (Taylor, Hines & Casey, 2010, p.99). Various authors have defined intersectionality as a theory or a concept, a method and a heuristic tool, as well as 'crossroads' or 'axis' (Davis, 2008). Regardless of the terminology different authors use, intersectionality theory derives from the idea of a crossroads of 'privilege and oppression relative to ethnicity, sexual orientation, class, ability, nation of origin, religion, and gender as they stand in social context' (Hernandez & McDowell, 2010, p.31). It is, however, a dynamic process which 'is never done, nor exhausted by its prior articulations or movements' (Carbado *et al.*, 2013, p.304). It can be seen as a flexible theory that can be directed or moved to different places depending on what social phenomenon or concern is examined.

The origins of intersectionality were first highlighted in 1989 when Kimberlé Crenshaw published her article 'Demarginalizing the intersection of race and sex: A Black feminist critique of antidiscrimination doctrine, feminist theory and antiracist politics'. Subsequently, the expansion of studies concerning this term have made it enormously influential (Taylor, Hines & Casey, 2010). In the last 30 years, several different disciplines have assumed intersectionality aspects, including lawyers, political scientists, sociologists and social scientists (Carbado, 2019). 'Despite the fact that its incorporation into healthcare has been seen to be advantageous, its foray into psychology and therapeutics has been more recent' (Riggs & Das Nair, 2012, p.16). I would hypothesize that the reticence in taking this theory up has occurred because of a lack of training and specific guidelines in psychological therapies as a whole and art therapies in particular. In addition, psychodynamic theory may be used to perceive prejudice and racism as the consequence of internal psychological processes and not as the potential cause of discrimination or intolerance (Dalal, 2001).

In psychodynamic music therapy, it is vital that therapists acknowledge the heterogeneity of all clients and cultural groups and comprehend the complexity of their own privileged role as therapists, as well as the possibility that they may be members of social classes that are different from their clients' (Riggs & Das Nair, 2012). Furthermore, therapists have to consider the 'crossroads' of privilege and oppression in their clients' lives (Riggs, 2011). They must remain open to what they do not know. According to Collins (1998), intersectionality 'highlights how social groups are positioned within unjust power relations, but it does so in a way that introduces added complexity to formerly race, class, and gender-only approaches to social phenomena' (p.205). Practitioners, therefore, have to carefully examine the intersects of diverse identities as well as the personal, social and political experiences of the client experience through the prism of their own power, privilege and prejudice when in the therapy room.

The music therapy project in context

Essential to the discussion in this chapter is a description of the project itself, the situation in the Palestinian territories, the therapy group and the therapist as a European woman in an Arabic country. As a newly qualified music therapist, who trained in the UK, I was offered the chance to undertake an eight-week clinical music therapy project in the West Bank, Palestine. The project was a clinically based, information-gathering venture, with the aim of providing short-term music therapy interventions to children with disabilities and adults, as well as enriching the community's experience and understanding of music therapy. It was a collaboration between a UK-based charity, which is a long-term supporter of healthcare in Palestine, and the Bethlehem Arab Society of Rehabilitation (BASR) hospital, where the project took place.

Entering a different culture, a country under occupation, unable to speak the language as well as embarking on my first job after graduation, challenged the basic conceptualizations of my music therapy practice. Working in such circumstances meant that I had to work with diverse music, unknown and unfamiliar to me, and with an unfamiliar population. Nevertheless, I chose to accept this job for various reasons; conscious and unconscious. If I am honest, part of my decision-making was that I felt honoured to be offered this work by the course leader and I wanted to prove I deserved this opportunity. On further reflection, I wondered if I was unconsciously, and perhaps narcissistically, wishing to be the first therapist who could successfully establish this placement for other students. I envisaged myself as a pioneer, bringing active music therapy to this hospital and proving myself above prejudices and open to new challenges. I can now reflect on how such motivations need to be acknowledged and considered in relation to practice approach and power dynamics within therapeutic work.

The situation in the West Bank, Palestine

To understand the complexity of this project fully, it is crucial to discuss the political situation in Palestine. Since 1967, the majority of the West Bank has been under Israeli occupation. This means that this part of the world is ostensibly a war zone; where Israel military governs the civilian population. There are military checkpoints with fully armed soldiers between all Palestinian cities and extensive arrests appear to be routine. In addition to this, the Israeli government continues the construction of a security fence which entails the demolition of houses and communities. These conditions mean that freedom of movement for education, work or pleasure is dangerous and limited and there are high levels of unemployment. The consequences of this cruel reality are that many Palestinians experience poverty, social difficulties, emotional problems and mental health issues. Unfortunately, due to the restrictions and appalling conditions, there are very few mental health professionals, and limited emotional support is available. Thus, 'social workers working in this environment face daily challenges associated with stress and anxiety' (Coombes & Tombs-Katz, 2015, p.69). Observing and examining the devastating impact this political situation has on the lives of Indigenous people through the lens of intersectionality, one can recognize that Palestinians' lives and identities exist outside the accepted Western way of living and have multiple sources of oppression. As with all societies, clear inequalities exist between Palestinians. The almost 2 per cent of the population who embrace Christianity is often wealthier, has more power and has more material privilege in comparison to the Muslim majority of the population. It is also important to acknowledge that Palestinians are forced into a position where they must defend their homes, their children and even their own lives, which may result in the use of violence, in itself an aggressive act of oppression towards the entire population. Worse still, however, is the experience of Palestinian women: 'The problems that Palestinian women face...originate in the persistence of patriarchal gender relations, the Israeli military occupation and non-resolution of the national problem and the conservative nature of the main political forces' (Moghadam, 2005, p.67). Working in this region as a mental health professional presupposes thorough examination of how systems of inequality – and not just intersecting identities – affect clients' lives and the unconscious processes in and out of the therapy room (Boggan, Grzanka & Bain, 2018).

The music therapy group

During the project, I facilitated groups and individual music therapy sessions in the BASR hospital and different refugee camps around Bethlehem. I was mainly working with children with complex special needs. However, in addition to this, a group of social workers asked for a music therapy 'self-awareness' group to support them. This was their name for the group and, insightfully, they argued that the demands of their work were impacting detrimentally on their emotional wellbeing.

The group sessions took place every week for one hour in the psychosocial centre of the hospital and lasted for six weeks until the project was completed. The group consisted of seven people: five women and one man, aged from 28 to 40, and myself, the music therapist. Five of the group members identified as Muslim and one as Christian. Their native language was Arabic, but we used English during the group sessions. None of them had previous musical education. They listened primarily to popular Arabic music and some popular Western songs. Finally, close professional relationships existed between the members as they had worked together for some time. It was clear, therefore, that these various threads would come together to form an intricate and complex matrix of power, prejudice and privilege within the group.

The music therapist

Here it is important to address the main explicit cultural as well as physical differences between me and the other group members. These differences informed both my identity as a therapist and my thinking about the unconscious processes in the group.

I am a Greek citizen who completed my music therapy training in the UK, as no such programmes exist in Greece. Qualifying in the UK, where evidence-based music therapy trainings have been in place since 1968 (Bunt, 1994), has obviously influenced my practice. Hence, while I attempt to be thoughtful and sensitive to my own and my clients' feelings and behaviour, I am also able to draw clear boundaries and act within the UK Health and Care Professions Council (HCPC) guidelines. When the project took place, I was a newly qualified practitioner who had never visited an Arabic country or a country under occupation before. I had various assumptions and fantasies about working in such a place. The clinical focus had to be informed by the local external conflict and how this might influence the mental state of the clients (Quin & Rowland, 2016). I was also aware of the language barrier – I do not speak Arabic – and of working in a culture that was different from my own. Arabic music was another aspect I needed to discover. I was, additionally, the youngest person in the group and had only experienced life in 'free' countries, giving me a different perspective and understanding about the very meaning of 'freedom'. All of these layers had a significant effect and guided my clinical work with the group.

How intersecting identities shape the therapeutic relationship

Professional music therapists in the UK and worldwide must work in an ethical framework in order to promote and protect the interests of service users. According to these ethical principles, music therapists have to undertake personal therapy and supervision to help them become more aware of their own internal difficulties, emotions and biases. Self-reflexivity and a degree of self-awareness are central to this process. In the context of intersectionality, however, these terms have to incorporate a thorough examination of the assumptions and biases that derive from external factors, including one's social status (Talwar, 2010) and pre-existing thoughts, habits, beliefs, ways of thinking and desires that are deeply informed and unconsciously constructed by the social systems we are born into (Dalal, 2015; Hernandez & McDowell, 2010). Hadley and Norris (2015) believe that both the client and the therapist express their cultural, intersecting identities in the therapeutic relationship, influencing each other's and their own self-experience in terms of gender, race, ethnicity, education, age, religion, social class and so forth. Furthermore, Weber (1998) argues that 'race, class, gender, and sexuality are historically specific, socially constructed hierarchies of domination – they are power relationships...in which one group exerts control over another' (p.20).

I attempt to address here my own understanding of the group's intersections of privilege and oppression using these concepts and the social context in which they stand. My experience with the music therapy group in Palestine, which implicitly incorporated the local context – both the political situation and social differences – impacted my thinking on the principle that the therapist must take care of and provide appropriate support for the service users. I quickly recognized that to successfully build a safe therapeutic relationship I had to give sufficient weight to my own and my clients' differences when reflecting on the group's musical or verbal, conscious or unconscious, interactions. This could only happen once I comprehended that being a working-class, Christian, Greek woman who studied in the UK had a significantly different impact on the Palestinian clients than it did on my UK clients. Hence, despite my psychodynamic theoretical background, where prejudice may be considered the internal process of an individual manifesting as a mechanism of projection, I agree with Dalal (2015) that psychotherapists must admit that power relations and social contexts structure the psyche as well. An analysis of how gender, language, social class and ethnicity shaped the therapeutic landscape of this specific group, according to my own reflexive thinking, is presented below.

Gender

In most societies, certain socially constructed characteristics are attributed to males and females respectively. Current gender studies find problems with binary models of male/female and recognize gender in far more complex ways. There is not room here to explore these ideas extensively in this chapter. However, during my own experience in Palestine, concepts of differently gendered individuals, that is the possibility of the existence of genders beyond male or female, were not explicitly mentioned or discussed. In addition to potential ethno-religious constraints, it might be possible that in such a violent, unstable and politically volatile situation it is difficult for these explorations of true self outside normative gender binaries to become mainstream, eclipsed as they are by the difficulties of everyday survival. As in many countries around the globe, in Palestine it is widely believed that women and men have a fundamentally different biological and social function (Ellis, 2012), which leads to the assumption that men are stronger and dominant while women are perceived as sensitive and more passive. In addition, where there is armed conflict, there is a particular effect on gender equality. This is true in Palestine where 'the inability of the Palestinian Authority to implement a women's rights agenda' and 'constructions of masculinity and femininity have tended to "normalize" and "naturalize" violence against women' (Moghadam, 2005, p.63), resulting in a 'culture of hegemonic masculinity' (Moghadam, 2005, p.64).

Through social struggles and persistent demand for gender equality legislation, women in some Western societies have won equal rights and opportunities in education, employment, social life and other areas, at least in law if not in practice. Nevertheless, inequality still persists in many ways and basic human rights are perpetually infringed. Women continue to be financially disadvantaged and there remains a low percentage of female representation in government and industry. Misogyny is pervasive, even in 'advanced' countries like the UK, and domestic violence continues worldwide, with minimal prosecution and low conviction rates.

In the Middle East, inequalities between the genders are even sharper and females face significant prejudice. Although women officially legally have equal employment and education opportunities, 'social assumptions and cultural discourses perpetuate male power and disadvantage women' (Ellis, 2012, p.36), whose efforts towards equality continue. The traditional perspective is that a 'woman's role is to behave modestly at all times, to marry, to bear children and to put home and family ahead of all else' (Velloso, 1996, p.527). This 'may affect both women with higher levels of education and those without' (Velloso, 1996, p.527) whether they are conscious of their gendered discrimination or not.

Although I felt welcomed in the various working environments I inhabited and never experienced an explicit verbal act of prejudice regarding my gender, it was obvious that because I was a woman, I would have to adapt the way I presented and expressed myself. For example, I was advised not to wear clothes that left my skin uncovered. While this may seem insignificant in itself, it is important to recognize the complexities of gender equality in countries where women are expected to dress modestly in varying degrees, and also my inexperience of these expectations, and ability to truly reflect on their impact as everyday lived experience. Moreover, although my colleagues would accompany me on short trips in different cities or walks around Bethlehem, I noticed curious glances from men when walking on my own, as most married women would not go out socially without their husbands. Although I had read and made some assumptions about the role of women in Arab societies, I had never experienced how it feels to be a woman in such an explicitly segregated society before. This proved difficult for me to acknowledge, think about and accept on any deep level as it led to feelings of anger and frustration. Only later did I realize that I had unconsciously blocked my own feelings of rage and distress at this inequality, perceiving them as both a result of my own anger and the possibility of group transference. I also noted that while I would consider myself actively against prejudice and inequalities in my own country, I never consciously considered the position of the women in the Palestinian community and seemed to accept the social rules unquestioningly. Perhaps it was too overwhelming for me to consider these feelings in such a new and unknown environment, in addition to the inherent fear we may feel when asking questions that might be culturally sensitive. Again, this is a hugely complex area that cannot be explored here, but given the history of Western colonialization, it is a complicated matter to enter a completely different culture and impose an alternative perspective.

During the group sessions, I wondered how the only male member would feel in a music therapy group with five female members and a female therapist. On this occasion I was, ostensibly, the dominant, strong and knowledgeable leader of the group; a position that in Palestinian culture would likely be held by a man. This ambivalence came to consciousness in the group when the man asked permission for another male colleague – not a social worker – to participate. While I might normally question the desire in a group to invite another member, on this occasion I accepted the request unquestioningly, perhaps mirroring the subservient role expected of me as a woman. This second male attended the group on just one occasion. Nevertheless, after a few sessions, the male's dominant masculinity emerged in the music; his playing was louder and it seemed as if all the females in the group were following him. This included me, unconsciously seduced into a position where I too was following the man's lead, leaving me feeling passive and undervalued. Such is the pervasive nature of social conditioning that it was only in supervision and with much reflexive thinking that I was able to make the link between feeling impassive and worthless in this group, and the local traditional relationships between men and women – and indeed external and internal relationships between the powerful and the subjugated worldwide. I had unconsciously internalized the position women have in society and this was reflected in my music-making and position in the group. Having made this connection, I attempted to use the music to challenge this stereotype. I emulated the man's rhythm, but adapted it to a similar but slightly different pace. Initially, nobody seemed to follow; however, one by one, the women joined the new tempo, while the man found it extremely difficult to change his rhythm. He did eventually manage the new cadence for a short period, but unfortunately, there was not enough time to explore this fascinating ambiguity of the power dynamic in the group.

Social class and language

According to Das Nair and Hansen (2012) 'social class is intersubjectively produced as part and parcel of our daily lives' (p.138). Furthermore, the concept of social class is embedded and contributes to the power relations both at the level of individuals and at the level of communities (Weber, 1998). As music therapists, it is vital to be able to acknowledge our clients' connection with dominant hierarchies and be mindful of how this is reflected in the therapeutic relationship. In so doing, therapists also need to identify their own social class and consider the possible unconscious prejudice this may or may not bring into the therapy room. Specifically, my assumptions about my clients' social class, as well as their assumptions about mine, directly affected the relationships between us. My stereotypical belief that all Palestinians are oppressed, poor people living under occupation led me, unthinkingly, to feel sorry for them. Nevertheless, I expected a trust relationship to be built through personal interaction, ignoring the impact of such power dynamics. In reality, most of the group members came from what might be described as middle-class backgrounds and were well educated and financially independent. Although I considered myself a working-class immigrant in this context, I also felt in a privileged position. After the first session, I understood that the group's assumption about me was that I had a middle-class background and a privileged lifestyle, at least financially. The patronizing feeling of sympathy that I had held towards the group began to fade when negotiated through the filter of privilege and oppression. I was able to challenge the clients around their own privileged positions in the group and in society, instigating conversations and ideas that perhaps 'no one can be completely powerless or completely powerful as power is first and last a relational attribute' (Dalal, 2015, p.6).

Language directly influences the way one experiences the world (Elias, 1991) and I was aware that this would play a significant role in the group, where the members' native language was Arabic, mine was Greek and we were speaking English. According to Dalal (2015), language is connected with the concept of prejudice and exists as 'unreflected social norms' (p.10). Indeed, in this group, language significantly determined my power as the therapist, since I was fluent in English while others were not. This was an opportunity for me to understand the power dynamics and emotional synchronicity taking place in the group. I noticed that language, in this case Arabic, was used by the group whenever I challenged them, either musically or verbally. Although I am unsure if it ever explicitly reached the group's consciousness, I wondered if Arabic was used to avoid my challenges and also as a display of the power they themselves had to exclude the unwanted other – in this case the therapist who did not speak Arabic, who came from the UK and who could be perceived as the 'occupier' in an occupied country. This conception perfectly matches Dalal's (2015) description of subordinate groups who may sometimes passively accept what the dominant group dictates yet 'actively resist oppression and devaluation in numerous ways every day' (Weber, 1998, p.22).

Ethnicity

Ethnicity is a complex concept that has been given various definitions (Das Nair & Thomas, 2012). However, in this chapter I will consider ethnicity as my clients' nation of origin. As a Greek national, I immediately felt a warmth and closeness offered by the Palestinians. Historically, the relationship between Greece and Palestine has been politically close. Greece has been a supporter of Palestine's independent state and many Greeks express solidarity with the Palestinians. Christianity also constitutes a connection, as a significant number of faithful Greek Christians visit the area, which they consider to be the Holy Land. Moreover, Greeks and Palestinians have a number of customs, food and music in common, cultural connections that cannot be overestimated. On the other hand, I was coming from and was supported by a charity in the UK. I had trained and lived in the UK for several years and speak English fluently. Thus, although I'm not a British citizen, I could be perceived as a British person. This may have affected the way Palestinians encountered me. The UK played a pivotal role in the formation of the state of Israel and has been influential in the ongoing conflict between Palestine and Israel for many decades (Rodgers, 2018). As a result, the relationship between these countries is complicated. The UK can be considered responsible, at least in part, for the conditions Palestinians live under, while at the same time being a country that offers support in different ways.

This creates a complex combination of ethnicities that could not be overlooked and the realization of these elements was of great importance to understand the following incident. During the third session, the group developed a specific and very stable rhythm which did not allow the music to develop further, despite my musical and verbal efforts to transform it. At first, I construed this act as an internal difficulty, a defence mechanism that psychodynamic theory might identify as resistance to change. At the time, I gave scant consideration to the possibility that this might be an unconscious act connected with the external, socio-political situation. However, resistance can also be defined as the opposition to someone or something, especially a political or military opponent. This meaning appears to be central in the structuring of Palestinian identity, acknowledging the specific political circumstances in which these people grow up and make their lives. Occupation, as a major form of oppression, undoubtedly contributes to inferiority and feelings of worthlessness. However, it also constructs the need and will to resist and fight for survival and the privilege of freedom. This is how I finally interpreted the incident. The group's act of power, using a traditional rhythm which was dominant and which excluded the therapist, could perhaps also be seen as an oppressed group opposing the 'oppressor': an individual who represented the UK and who even attempted to impose Western rhythms on to the group. This understanding was deeply significant not only for me to comprehend, accept and attempt to contain the group's feelings of anger and sadness, but also for the group to connect with and begin unfolding these suppressed feelings in a safe space. Throughout my time with the group, I felt aware of an undercurrent of sadness and anger that manifested in complex and sometimes subtle ways. However, in one session, I felt these feelings so strongly that I expressed them by playing a powerful and sad melody on my violin. It was the first time I had played a solo in the sessions and the group all stopped to listen. They watched me play and some of them seemed to fight back tears. One of the group stated simply, 'Sadness.' Following this moving incident, the music became more playful and melodic and discussion about sadness and anger became both more conscious and more bearable for the whole group.

Conclusion

Intersectionality, and the way it affects and informs the therapeutic landscape, provides a framework for wide-ranging discussions between mental health professionals. Discussions about intersecting identities, as well as similarities and differences between therapists and clients relative to different levels of privilege, power and oppression, have recently begun in psychological therapies (Riggs & Das Nair, 2012). Reflective dialogue, thorough research and relevant didactic activities must be considered essential for equity and justice to be developed in clinical work. In many cases, White, middle-class clinicians, living in independent, democratic countries, fail to acknowledge the privileges and power these intersecting identities add to the already privileged positions they hold as therapists (Riggs & Das Nair, 2012). According to Crenshaw (1991), these identities do not have to be an additional difficulty to the work; on the contrary, they add to the complex interactions relevant to existing social conventions.

By writing this chapter, I aim to demonstrate that social and psychological worlds can be seen as two sides of the same coin (Foulkes, 1964). It is not enough for art therapists to simply acknowledge social issues and intersecting identities. They must explore, stay engaged with them and understand how oppression becomes internalized (Gipson, 2015), even when this feels challenging and exposing. Only through continuous dialogue, reflexive thinking, supervision and transformational learning can the dynamics of power, privilege, prejudice and oppression between clinicians and clients, as well as the musical interactions in music therapy settings, be observed and utilized in the clients' best interests. It is imperative that music therapists, art therapy practitioners in general and academics incorporate intersectionality into their practice, thinking and training.

References

Boggan, C. E., Grzanka, P. R. & Bain, C. (2018). Perspectives on queer music therapy: A qualitative analysis of music therapists' reactions to radically inclusive practice. *Journal of Music Therapy, 54*(4), 375–404.

Bunt, L. (1994). *Music Therapy: An Art Beyond Words*. Hove and New York, NY: Brunner & Routledge.

Carbado, D. W. (2019). Colorblind Intersectionality. In K. W. Crenshaw, L. C. Harris, D. M. HoSang & G. Lipsitz (eds) *Seeing Race Again: Countering Colorblindness Across the Disciplines*. Oakland, CA: University of California Press.

Carbado, D. W., Crenshaw, K. W., Mays, V. M. & Tomlinson, B. (2013). Intersectionality: Mapping the movements of a theory. *Du Bois Review Social Science Research on Race, 10*(2), 303–312.

Collins, P. H. (1998). *Fighting Words: Black Women and the Search for Justice*. Minneapolis, MN: University of Minnesota Press.

Coombes, E. & Tombs-Katz, M. (2015). Interactive therapeutic music skill-sharing in the West Bank: An evaluation report of project Beit Sahour. *Approaches: Music Therapy & Special Music Education, 9*(1), 67–79.

Crenshaw, K. (1989). Demarginalizing the intersection of race and sex: A Black feminist critique of antidiscrimination doctrine, feminist theory and antiracist politics. *University of Chicago Legal Forum, 1*(8), 139–176.

Crenshaw, K. (1991). Mapping the margins: Intersectionality, identity politics, and violence against women of colour. *Stanford Law Review, 43*(6), 1241–1299.

Dalal, F. (2001). Insides and outsides: A review of psychoanalytic renderings of difference, racism and prejudice. *Psychoanalytic Studies, 3*(1), 43–66.

Dalal, F. (2015). Prejudice as ideology: The creation of 'us' and 'them' groups in society (and psychoanalysis). *Psychotherapy and Politics International, 13*(3), 182–193.

Das Nair, R. & Hansen, S. (2012). Social Class. In R. Das Nair & C. Butler (eds) *Intersectionality, Sexuality and Psychological Therapies: Working with Lesbian, Gay and Bisexual Diversity*. Chichester: British Psychological Society/John Wiley & Sons.

Das Nair, R. & Thomas, S. (2012). Race and Ethnicity. In R. Das Nair & C. Butler (eds) *Intersectionality, Sexuality and Psychological Therapies: Working with Lesbian, Gay and Bisexual Diversity*. Chichester: British Psychological Society/John Wiley & Sons.

Davis, K. (2008). Intersectionality as buzzword: A sociology of science perspective on what makes a feminist theory successful. *Feminist Theory, 9*(1), 67–85.

Elias, N. (1991). *The Symbol Theory*. London: Sage Publications.

Ellis, S. J. (2012). Gender. In R. Das Nair & C. Butler (eds) *Intersectionality, Sexuality and Psychological Therapies: Working with Lesbian, Gay and Bisexual Diversity*. Chichester: British Psychological Society/John Wiley & Sons.

Foulkes, S. H. (1964). *Therapeutic Group Analysis*. London: George Allen & Unwin.

Gipson, L. R. (2015). Is cultural competence enough? Deepening social justice pedagogy in art therapy. *Art Therapy: Journal of the American Art Therapy Association, 32*(3), 142–145.

Hadley, S. & Norris, M. S. (2015). Music multicultural competency in music therapy: The first step. *Music Therapy Perspectives, 34*(2), 129–137.

Hernandez, P. & McDowell, T. (2010). Intersectionality, power and relational safety in context: Key concepts in clinical supervision. *Training and Education in Professional Psychology, 4*(1), 29–35.

Moghadam, V. E. (2005). Peacebuilding and reconstruction with women: Reflections on Afghanistan, Iraq and Palestine. *Society for International Development, 48*(3), 63–72.

Quin, A. & Rowland, C. (2016). Intercultural Skill-Sharing in Music Therapy. In D. Dokter & M. H. De Zarate (eds) *Intercultural Arts Therapies Research: Issues and Methodologies*. London: Routledge.

Riggs, D. W. (2011). Queering evidence-based practice. *Psychology and Sexuality, 2*(1), 87–98.

Riggs, D. W. & Das Nair, R. (2012). Intersecting Identities. In R. Das Nair & C. Butler (eds) *Intersectionality, Sexuality and Psychological Therapies: Working with Lesbian, Gay and Bisexual Diversity*. Chichester: British Psychological Society/John Wiley & Sons.

Rodgers, J. (2018). *Palestine and Britain: Forgotten legacy of World War I that devastated the Middle East*. The Conversation. https://theconversation.com/palestine-and-britain-forgotten-legacy-of-world-war-i-that-devastated-the-middle-east-106408.

Talwar, S. (2010). An intersectional framework for race, class, gender, and sexuality in art therapy. *Journal of the American Art Therapy Association, 27*(1), 11–17.

Taylor, Y., Hines, S. & Casey, M. E. (2010). *Theorizing Intersectionality and Sexuality*. London: Palgrave Macmillan.

Velloso, A. (1996). Women, society and education in Palestine. *International Review of Education, 42*(5), 524–530.

Weber, L. (1998). A conceptual framework for understanding race, class, gender, and sexuality. *Psychology of Women Quarterly, 22*(1), 13–32.

Chapter 10

Culturally Appropriate Art Therapy in the Sikh Community: Theory and Practice

JASPAL KAUR LOTAY, WITH CORRINA EASTWOOD

Introduction

This chapter will address art therapy in the context of the client's community and the possibility of entrepreneurship when responding to culture and religion within the South Asian, Punjabi and Sikh communities. The case study presented was a pilot, student-led placement, established in my final year on a UK-based MA art therapy programme. The aim was to challenge issues surrounding accessibility and stigma that are commonplace within South Asian and Sikh communities in relation to seeking mental health support.

I will consider intersectional values such as self-reflexivity and exploration of identity through a prism of markers and oppressions, to better understand and give voice to marginalized communities (Collins & Bilge, 2016). In acknowledging the origins of intersectionality, I will explore the benefits and challenges of working collaboratively with communities. I will consider what makes the South Asian community categorized as 'hard to reach', with a particular focus on the Sikh faith and culture. As a Sikh Punjabi woman, I will reflect on my own experiences of faith, culture and community while training as an art therapist, both from a personal perspective and within the wider political and historical context. I will consider the intersecting markers of faith, ethno-religion and culture, in relation to grief, loss and normative gender roles. I will also examine how personal insight informed the work while simultaneously creating barriers to clinical thinking, working as I was within my own community while utilizing Eurocentric clinical theory. It should be noted that some culturally specific ideas and ways of thinking are difficult to fully articulate in Western conceptualizations and some Punjabi words describe states of being or feeling that have no adequate English language equivalent.

Art therapy training, self-reflexivity and institutional resistance

The development of the pilot placement aimed to further art therapy training and practice beyond the typical established institutions, such as schools or NHS settings, and extend the possibilities of engaging with those who might be reluctant to seek support from medicalized Western approaches to mental health treatment. The pilot sought to create innovation and challenge existing ways in which art therapy is accessed by South Asian and Sikh communities, responding directly to their specific needs. This posed a challenge to the established concept of therapeutic 'holding' within existing institutional structures; structures supported by the theoretical norms taught in the existing art therapy curriculum (Talwar, 2010). While training, I struggled to find theoretical frameworks to support my developing practice from the intersects of my own cultural, religious and social locations, and felt a resistance from university that manifested in fear of change and fear of risk from my tutors. The primary focus on the mitigation of risk rightly prompted careful consideration of the safeguarding protocols embedded within my placement structure. These challenges felt specific to my personal experience, and at times it was difficult for me not to perceive them as 'criticisms'. As a first-generation Punjabi Sikh woman, a child of Indian/Kenyan migrants under the colonial British Raj, I have personal experience of marginalization from within and outside my community. The first generation of Sikhs to migrate to the UK faced racism and isolation, due to complex issues including language barriers. Some Sikh men turned to alcohol to cope with this exclusion, and domestic abuse affected many women settlers (British Sikh Report, 2018). This cultural legacy was felt within my family, and I have been affected personally by the silencing of women and children in relation to issues of domestic abuse, and by the silencing of all in relation to mental health issues due to fears of stigmatization.

As a Sikh Punjabi woman who has challenged oppressions and socially expected norms, both within and outside my community, I have felt isolated and marginalized in social and cultural locations. The concept of intersectionality helps me to reflect on the ways different social identities can shape one another to create layered forms of subjugation; I am not only open to judgement of my gender but that of the colour of my skin and how I practise my faith (Kuri, 2017). I can also use intersectional reflexivity to understand my community and the transgenerational traumas I have inherited, resulting from historical colonization, family migration and acts of prejudice I have experienced both personally and professionally. I can see the complex matrix of difficulties in a profession dominated by White, Eurocentric theoretical perspectives (Talwar, 2010). My race and cultural positioning starkly represented otherness during my training and embodied very different culturally specific ways of thinking, learning and knowing.

Talwar, Iyer and Doby-Copeland (2004) note that diversity in art therapy educational programmes must incorporate socio-political, cultural frameworks that consider diversity in many ways, including values, interactional styles and cultural expectations. I sometimes felt unconscious attacks from my peers during experiential groups, attacks that felt ethno-religion related, representing as I often did a difference that could, and should, have been ethically explored. However, the university seemed reticent to explore the unconscious prejudices or abuses of power related to dominant group perspectives that often felt present in the symbolic content of group art-making. My voicing of such feelings was often silenced. Hamrick and Byma write, 'Consciously or unconsciously white people are socialized to feel entitled to greater respect and power than that granted to people of colour' (2017, p.107). They further note the way in which the collective White psyche is privileged.

My experience of these insensitivities from the university often compromised my ability to respond robustly to important clinical considerations surrounding my practice. For example, I found myself unable to think reflectively when questioned about safeguarding policies and felt attacked by my White tutor and peers. I responded defensively, protecting my vulnerabilities against White people (Gibson, 2019), and I felt pressure to achieve higher outcomes to gain equal recognition. When asked to reflect on my countertransference, I recognized a parallel process to the 'difficult to reach' client group. I had made myself difficult to reach, defending myself, my clients and my community from outsider misunderstanding. Prasad (2000) asks us to view culture not as a 'thing' but as a process, and this feels important when considering reflexivity in training and group work. Being open to the 'process' of cultural difference in others feels important in relation to my experiences.

Before undertaking the training, I worked in mental health nursing in an area with a high South Asian demographic. I was witness to ways in which my community experienced otherness in relation to mental health services. This otherness also manifested in my often being the only minority in my staff team, as a brown woman. I was frequently asked by those I supported within my community why I would venture into mental health and not the physical medical professions, a more common choice within my community which holds greater social value. When nursing, I was often used as a Punjabi translator and found this further emphasized my otherness in relation to my colleagues. This increased the potential for questioning from clients from my community, including interrogation of my agenda and alliances. While translating I was also confronted with how often I could find no words to adequately convey psychiatric terminology, diagnosis or symptoms. This remains a challenge in my therapeutic work, not only in practical terms, but also in finding meaning and bridging the gaps that I have discovered between Eurocentric theoretical traditions in art therapy literature (Talwar, 2010), and my practising in intersectional ways that adapt to cultural difference (Talwar, 2019). Bhugra and Bhui (1997) comment on the help-seeking patterns of different communities and how these can be counter-productive when applied in conjunction with psychodynamic therapeutic approaches if there isn't a clear mutual understanding. Singh (2017) acknowledges the growing need for the joining of mental health services with faith-based organizations.

Seeing members of my community struggling to navigate mental health services was personally painful. This pain seemed to mirror my experiences on my training, of feeling misunderstood and different. Reflecting on these experiences, I can acknowledge my intersecting identities and viewpoints: the Western approaches to mental health intrinsic to my trainings; institutional norms and treatment approaches led by a Eurocentric theoretical tradition; my identity as Sikh; and, importantly, my relationship to my community and with God. During training, these parts of me often felt highly incongruent and I struggled to find theoretical frameworks to support and consider my own identity and how it might impact on my art therapy practice working with those who may be the same or different from me. Talwar, Iyer and Doby-Copeland (2004) note how psychotherapy practice has often failed to meet the needs of individuals who are culturally different, stating that various cultural barriers such as class-bound and culture-bound values hinder the formation of a good therapeutic relationship.

Despite the difficulties, in my final year of training I felt able and ready to offer a service to my community that would attempt to address the issues of resistance I had observed from my personal and professional positions.

Cultural resistance and the art therapy pilot placement

Sikhi is the fifth largest world religion and the UK has the third largest population of Sikhs in the world. There is a strong focus on community care (Basics of Sikhi, 2018) and, like many faiths, my faith practice surrounds a service to others. Paradoxically, offering practical support to the wider community is embedded in a culture of keeping difficulties related to mental health within the boundaries of familial units, for fear of stigma. The origins of mental ill-health-related stigma in the Sikh Punjabi community is multifaceted and complex, yet can in part be understood within a culture of shame surrounding a lack of gratitude for God's will. Mental illness has traditionally been attributed to 'spiritual imbalances' arising due to a person's *Haumai* (ego and self-centredness) or because of their *Karm* (past actions) (British Sikh Report, 2018). Both concepts are unfamiliar in Western approaches to mental ill-health and psychotherapeutic theory. Contextualizing such belief systems has been essential in developing my work, including sensitivities around mental states in general and normalizing the care of mental self (Ottemiller & Awais, 2016).

In relation to intercultural therapy practice, Watkins and Terrell (1988) note feelings of mistrust, reluctance to engage and cynicism about positive outcomes from ethnic minority clients when working with White therapists. An independent review of the Mental Health Act (Modernising the Mental Health Act Report, 2018) found that profound inequalities exist for Black, minority and ethnic (BME) patients, and a lack of diversity in the workforce was cited as contributing to widespread distrust in services. This highlighted the importance of the pilot as an opportunity to listen to voices from the Sikh community.

I approached this lack of familiarity and trust of therapy within my community in different practical ways: promoting better mental health at religious gatherings; using media, including television, to reach wider audiences; and by liaising closely with established Sikh charities. I prioritized understanding the broader circles and social contexts of individuals throughout the pilot, in order to consider the importance of culture in art therapy practice from intersectional perspectives. It soon became apparent that there was a desire within the community to engage with such a service, despite some trepidation, and the community appeared to value an ethos of establishing culturally relevant therapeutic resources. It felt important to robustly reflect on my own intersecting ethno-religious and gender-related identities during this time, as I began to engage with my community from new perspectives.

As this engagement progressed, presenting as both a Sikh Punjabi woman, as well as a trainee art psychotherapist, I noticed my anxieties decrease and I became less defensive on my training. I also considered my own potential biases regarding my community, reflecting on not having had a space to voice my difficult past experiences. These personal struggles had evoked unconscious feelings of resentment from me towards my community, while paradoxically fuelling my drive to advocate for and empower others. Such feelings linked strongly with my faith practice of service and I used personal therapy to address emotional entanglements in relation to power in the therapeutic relationship and my sense of service to God in my work.

I was also aware of the risks inherent in making assumptions about my sameness. I explored my wearing of the Sikh turban at university and in personal therapy. In supervision, I considered the risk of excluding people from the community who might not view themselves religiously or may feel judged, based on presumed commitments to faith through the wearing of religious attire. I wondered how clients might feel speaking openly about subjects such as this with someone from their own community who they might perceive as judgemental. I also wondered how secure clients might feel around issues of confidentiality.

Prasad (2013) details her therapeutic approach when wearing the traditional Indian Salwar and the difficulties she feels some clients have in relating to her because of this attire. As therapists, we duly consider our appearance and our clients' perception of us. Yet when clothing choices also represent ethno-religious identity, added dimensions informed by social and political contexts must also be considered. Prasad reflects on an adjustment period in practice, noticing her own difference and owning her own identity in and through the use of peer supervision. In doing so, she feels less defensive when speaking about her culture and attire and finds ways to encourage curiosity from her clients about her difference. It was helpful to use my university peers in similar ways. I was able to explore more consciously the mistrust that I had felt in the context of my own experience, and acknowledge the limitations of my training body and White peers to fully understand and address this. I also recognized the sense of powerlessness and frustration I felt in voicing such difference to residual colonial power and accepted that; 'Understanding oppression from a global perspective means understanding colonisation the world over' (Talwar *et al.*, 2004, p.46).

Following this process, I began to experience my peers as more supportive, reflective and open to important conversations around difference and vulnerabilities. Acknowledging such issues in supervisory settings enabled a transparency and confidence in me related to identity and was important in my therapeutic work with individuals, as well as in setting up the pilot and liaising with community members to identify appropriate client referrals. I recognized all the difficulties that I had encountered in my past, as I felt a strong resistance to initial conversations regarding mental health in Sikh faith and cultural settings. Entering a *Gurudwara* (place of assembly and worship) and speaking about the need in our community to access mental health services was at first met with disbelief. The mistrust towards Western approaches inherent in the 'language' of mental health and fear of stigmatization was significant. For me, these conversations felt radical, and mirrored early experiences within my community of not being heard.

McGann notes how therapists must be attuned towards identification with clients of similar cultural backgrounds and how this will ultimately 'influence unconscious identifications and defense mechanisms' (2008, p.206). The resistance I encountered often seemed related to tensions between religious and cultural explorations evoked when promoting art therapy to religious congregations. For example, I challenged strongly held patriarchal norms when naming gender inequalities and potential links with mental health issues for women. However, I found that linking feminist thought with mental health concerns could be more comfortably explored when I was able to frame discourse within a religious context, acknowledging the beauty of the Sikh faith and how it seeks to empower women, emphasizing how the *Gurbani* (Sikhi scripture) promotes equality between genders.

Service to others, honesty and discipline are central to the Sikh faith and enshrined in the Sikh concept of *Sewa*. *Sewa* is defined as voluntary selfless service to others in the community, but also humanity at large (British Sikh Report, 2018). This parallels the therapeutic aim to ease the pain and unburden the path of another. Psychodynamic and intersectional theoretical approaches that advocate the exploration of the therapist's motivation to 'help' are valuable. Yet these parallels also offer me great vocational comfort and professional guidance, as well as supporting my promotion of art therapy within my community. Sikhs have historically fought against oppression, and this ancestral devotion embodies the very fabric of a modern-day ethic, relating to the foundations of intersectional perspectives and giving voice to the marginalized.

Image and spirituality

Additional barriers to promoting art therapy in my community surrounded the use of art. Growing up, art had provided a channel for me to understand myself outside confusing and strained experiences. Talwar (2019) suggests that art-making can help us notice our own difficult experiences and determine what seems incongruous socially, culturally, politically and personally. I had used art-making in my past to explore my relationship to self and culture. In promoting the art therapy pilot, I found that the lack of cultural value placed on this aspect of my work again enacted uncomfortable past experiences. Addressing both personal pain and professional challenges, I gave presentations to religious congregations where I spoke about the adornment of *Sri Guru Granth Sahib Ji* (our Sikh Guru in scriptural form) and the depiction of Sikh history and religious messages in art. When considering art therapy and spirituality, Bell notes that the principle of spiritual care is to:

> create the opportunity and potential to transcend the physical and the psychological. This then connects those who are suffering with aspects of life that often find imaginative expression through the arts and humanities and where spirituality and religion bring unique perspectives to human affairs. (2011, p.217)

In running therapeutic workshops in Sikhi camps with young people, I noticed the resistance to thinking about feelings in Western ways, manifesting as disruption to the group process. Integrating aspects of Sikhi, such as facilitating the chanting of *Waheguru* (the vibration of God) as a way of collectively engaging and slowing the pace, helped to contain the group and created space to think.

Referrals for the pilot came from partnering with established charities. This included culturally specific risk assessment, such as reflecting on the specifics of stigma and shaming. Particular risks around the experiencing of racism were considered, alongside the impact of religious beliefs and religious guilt. More specific to South Asian communities in general is the attribution of mental ill-health to cultural beliefs such as spirit possession, despite these being in opposition to Sikh religious teachings (British Sikh Report, 2018). The impact of this on the individual, within families and communities, was considered seriously.

Despite the rigorous assessment process, I sometimes found myself unable to acknowledge the potential risk to myself when working in clients' homes. This difficulty may have been connected to the familiarity I felt within my community, hindering the objectivity of risk assessment. Wright and Andrew (2017) note the importance of alterations to usual therapeutic boundaries in managing safety when working in people's homes, including crisis team procedures, reflective space and supervision. They also suggest that working in a client's home may allow a fuller impression of social and environmental cues to be noted and addressed. This adds dimension to risk management but also to the importance of the psychosocial and contextualizing elements of intersectional therapeutic intervention. Additionally, I considered the potential gains when responding to client needs as early intervention, rather than when they reach crisis (Singh, 2017), and the lowered risk inherent in non-crisis work. The majority of Sikhs accessing services do so under section of the Mental Health Act and therefore at the point of crisis (British Sikh Report, 2018). This once again emphasizes the need for the service and the importance of early community intervention.

Faith in the face of loss

The art therapy work described here took place over a period of four months with a boy of eight and his sister aged six. I will refer to the siblings using the pseudonyms Sach and Diya respectively. The primary focus will be on my work with Sach, his explorations in therapy of cultural and gendered attitudes to the grieving process and his relationship with Diya. Sach's cultural and religious background, and the place where these identity markers met my own, prompted my need to acknowledge the role of faith in the face of loss and its intersect with cultural expectations related to normative gender identities.

Sach lived with his mother, father and younger sister. His mother was in the final stages of pregnancy with a third child. The family had been referred by a Sikh charity who were aware that Sach's father had been diagnosed with terminal cancer. Sadly, his father died over the course of the therapy. The family were disciples of the Sikh faith and Sach attended a faith-based school. He was seen as bright, academic, confident and social. However, he had recently become introverted, and at times aggressive. His aggression was often directed at Diya and included him excluding her from his room.

Vignette 1

Sach started the session by showing me his sketchpad, filled with religious art depicting historical battles. Learning about our history is an important part of practising our faith. Our tenth Guru, *Sri Guru Gobindh Singh Ji*, created the *Khalsa* (the pure) who were a sovereign army; they surrendered to the faith in order to stop oppression of the people of India. Sach was very interested in recounting such stories and reflecting on the bravery of Sikh men in battle. Following a period of listening and observing, I invited him to use the materials and he sat at the table to draw. Sach remarked that he abhorred the use of colours in his drawings and preferred monotone. I was struck by his adult-like presentation and I wondered about cultural expectations around masculinity and responsibility, as Sach moved towards the inevitable reality of becoming the sole male presence in his home.

Sach put pencil to paper and created a scene, each mark feeling purposeful. He drew a sniper gunning down a soldier using a parachute, as he verbally recounted more historical narratives (Figure 10.1).

Figure 10.1: Sniper and soldier

I noted how Sach's focus on battles and war felt very familiar to me as a Sikh, yet I also reflected on the symbolism of the imagery in wider cultural contexts; its potential to represent not only bravery but fear, anger and sadness. I was struck by my clinical thinking in relation to my sense of 'normal' from Sikh Punjabi perspectives and challenged this, considering the symbolism of vulnerability and inevitable death, depicted in the figure of the parachuting soldier.

> Visual art has the potential to present its audience with signs and symbols that invite the contemplation of existential themes, and it is the participation of the viewer and their receptivity that facilitates the connection with spirituality. In turn, the impact of this invocation of the spiritual can be a sustained process of reflection for the viewer, way beyond the encounter with the art object, carried along by memory and associated feeling. (Bell, 2011, p.220)

Sach spoke intermittently as he drew. He appeared comfortable with the silences, engrossed as he was in his image making. He added a hammerhead shark, saying it had been harpooned, again seeming to explore themes of power, victimization and vulnerability around death.

Vignette 2

Sach created an image that depicted a soldier slaying a dragon, alongside a dead soldier with an axe (Figure 10.2). He commented throughout on the valiance of the soldier. I observed that his drawings often depicted fallen soldiers, and Sach spoke of death, and the normality of death in warfare. Again, he began to speak of historical Sikh battles and how Sikhs had fought bravely without fear. His comments on fear resonated with me and I hoped to give permission for fearful feelings to be felt in the space. I asked what might have happened in battle, if the brave Sikh soldiers had been afraid of death? He replied that the overtly fearful would not succeed. I found Sach's composure striking as I spoke of the death and dying symbolized in his artwork and wondered about his understanding or denial surrounding his father's diagnosis. I further reflected on Sach's gender-related position within our culture and his family, along with wider societal gender norms that discourage expressions of vulnerability in men and boys. Case and Dalley (2014) note the nature of stereotypically 'masculine' imagery and how it may act as a defence against fragility and sensitivity.

Figure 10.2: Soldier, dragon and axe

Vignette 3

There was a break in our sessions following the death of Sach's father. The prioritizing of *Antam Sanskaar* (last rights including religious rituals) caused abrupt endings and uncertainties in our work. When we did meet, Sach surprised me by using colour. Moving away from his usual themes of warfare, killing and death, he instead drew a dragonfly and coloured its wings. I noticed his use of colour and he acknowledged this, then swiftly moved away from the observation, adding a sword beside the dragonfly (Figure 10.3).

Figure 10.3: Sword and dragonfly

I was struck by the symbolism indicating a need for protection and related this to my acknowledgement of the loss of his father and my offering of condolences. Bell (2011) writes of how the visualizing of experiences, memories and feelings through the process of creating drawings can provide a material means through which spirituality can be explored safely. I asked Sach how he was feeling now, and as he drew, he spoke of confusion surrounding where his father's soul may have gone. He spoke about knowing that the body is temporary, but questioned the destination of the soul. I asked him where he felt it might go, and Sach spoke in a detached way of a returning to God. I wondered if he had felt that this was a response expected of him from another Sikh disciple, and if our sameness created barriers in his explorations of feelings such as confusion or anger. He presented as very contained, and on leaving the session I noted my own countertransference feelings of detachment.

Sikhi is viewed as a way of life and contains much discipline and structured worship. The concept of *Chardi Khalla* relates to the resilience and fulfilment that praying and fully surrendering to God may bring as one moves into a state of oneness with God. The relinquishing of *Haumai* (I or ego or self-centredness) and trusting fully in God's will is seen as the way to true healing. I reflected on this in relation to Sach's presentation in our sessions. I also felt confusion, my countertransference perhaps giving insight into Sach's own confusion around his religious beliefs in relation to his loss and his possible desire to perform religious resilience and a surrendering to God's will. I too questioned religion, but in relation to the significance of our shared religious beliefs in the therapeutic space. How could I use my lived experience to offer Sach insightful support while allowing him space to question, to find his own path and feel angry?

Conceptions of Sikhi *Hukam* call us to accept the will of God, and I considered my clinical decision-making and ability to make space for angry feelings in the sessions for Sach, while honouring our religious practice. Bell (2011) suggests that when images, symbols and stories take hold of the imagination, and add spiritual dimension to meaning making, this provides potential to open a process of exploration, discovery and transformation into faith development. Sach's use of art, stories and symbols felt like an important way for him to consider his own spiritual explorations in the face of loss.

In offering child-centred therapeutic approaches, and art materials to communicate difficult and potentially stigmatized feelings, I aimed to facilitate a space for Sach where permission to be vocal about sadness or fear was granted, yet *Chardi Khalla* was also honoured and used to potentially heal. The acknowledgement of positive spirits to mentally contain remained of value in our sessions. I also held in mind the need to challenge the masking of pain, which may feel counter-productive to healing and the accessing of unconscious processes from a psychodynamic perspective.

Discussion: Religion, culture and gender

In writing the above clinical vignettes, I have questioned my decision to focus on my work with Sach rather than his sister Diya. Sibling rivalry inevitably became a theme in my work with the children and needs to be considered. A parallel process took place in my university when I recognized the rivalry I felt with my peers in seeking approval from the 'parent' tutor; an insight into the maternal transference evident when working with siblings. However, I also reflected on the inherent cultural attitudes around gender in my community and my potential unconscious prioritizing of the male child. Talwar (2019) writes as a Sikh woman noticing the significance of witnessing her father and brother tie their turbans every day. She comments on how history and politics were carried on their heads as part of cultural gendered experience. Sach often seemed to adopt a pseudo-adult role in our sessions, perhaps related to his strategies for coping with demands within patriarchal cultures to be the strong male (Case & Dalley, 2014). In further considering Sach's gender and the 'masculine' imagery he often created in art therapy, I noted his reluctance to use colour and to avoid 'mess'. This felt like a reluctance to surrender control or move towards developmental regression. Sach's relationship to his sister Diya was also significant. She had seemingly come to represent the 'feminine' vulnerable and fragile self, an identity that could not be tolerated by Sach. He defended against closeness to sensitivity or fear, not allowing Diya in his room, remaining the strong Sikh soldier who would not be defeated in his grief. Sach seemingly wanted to scapegoat Diya as a fallible vessel containing his unwanted feelings of weakness (Schaverien, 1999). In a joint session I held with both children, Sach was guided towards valuing and supporting Diya's perceived fragilities, representing as they did a complex part of him that he needed to accept and nurture.

Conclusion

Bell suggests that 'Meaning-making is diverse and multilayered. It draws on the complex psychosocial needs of the individual, and their socio-economic and cultural history and context' (2011, p.222). He goes on to contextualize meaning-making as the territory of belief, values, personhood and faith, where personal and collective identity reside. It has been a difficult and sometimes lonely journey, finding meaning and bridging the gaps between my own identities and the psychotherapy theories I have studied in university. Finding my own way of navigating systems not designed for me or my community has been a complex process, requiring much creativity, adaptation and research. Earley's (2002) study of the social evolution of consciousness over five eras of human history shows an ever-increasing distancing in the evolution of Western consciousness from participatory consciousness to a reflexive consciousness. Self-reflexivity in practice is a vital component in the use of psychodynamic concepts such as countertransference. However, failing to utilize intersectionality and not connecting aspects of identity, including the religious and spiritual self, can be harmful when working therapeutically. This is especially so if not contextualizing or challenging the fragmentary self worldviews that dominate Western thinking.

In creating theoretical and practice-based bridges, I have adapted important ideas that can support and complement each other when considered robustly. I am far more 'forgiving' in the practice of my faith. I consciously create space in my art therapy practice within my community for clients to voice their feelings of 'failure', sometimes by using my own faith-based struggles as an example of the fluidity of spiritual journey. Art-making stimulates the creative processes that are blocked by the sense of inferiority that logical processes can engender. It can revive and repair the soul (McNiff, 1992). The art in art therapy is well equipped to adapt to culturally specific use, if intersectional thinking is integrated into considerations of the visual realm.

This chapter has illustrated the way in which my own identities have impacted on my training and practice within my own community, using intersectional perspectives with a specific focus on sameness. I have shown the benefits of understanding difference and some barriers inherent in working with clients with whom you share identity markers. However, while religious affiliation is often a specific choice, spirituality can be felt as a fundamental aspect of a person that is universal across cultures and history (Cobb, 2001). Alongside art, spirituality may be a place where sameness and difference can be explored sensitively for and by all.

References

Basics of Sikhi (2018). Resources [online]. Accessed 17/06/18 at www.basicsofsikhi.com/resources.

Bell, B. (2011). Art therapy and spirituality. *Journal for the Study of Spirituality, 1*(2), 215–230.

Bhugra, D. & Bhui, K. (1997). Clinical management of patients across cultures. *Advances in Psychiatric Treatment, 3*(4), 233–239. http://citeseerx.ist.psu.edu/viewdoc/download?doi=10.1.1.622.2462&rep=rep1&type=pdf.

The British Sikh Report (2018). Accessed 29/05/20 at http://britishsikhreport.org/wp-content/uploads/2018/05/British-Sikh-Report-2018.pdf.

Case, C. & Dalley, T. (2014). *The Handbook of Art Therapy*. New York, NY: Routledge.

Cobb, M. (2001). *The Dying Soul: Spiritual Care at the End of Life*. Buckingham: Open University Press.

Collins, P. H. & Bilge, S. (2016). *Intersectionality*. Cambridge: Polity Press.

Earley, J. (2002). The social evolution of consciousness. *Journal of Humanistic Psychology, 42*(1), 107–132.

Gibson, L. (2019). Envisioning Black Women's Consciousness in Art. In S. Talwar (ed.) *Art Therapy for Social Justice: Radical Intersections*. New York, NY: Routledge.

Hamrick, C. & Byma, C. (2017). Know history, know self: Art therapists' responsibility to dismantle White supremacy. *Journal of the American Art Therapy Association, 34*(3), 106–111.

Kuri, E. (2017). Toward an ethical application of intersectionality in art therapy. *Art Therapy, 34*(3), 118–122.

McGann, E. (2008). Colour me beautiful. *Journal of Emotional Abuse, 6*(2–3), 197–217.

McNiff, S. (1992). *Art as Medicine: Creating a Therapy of the Imagination*. Boulder, CO: Shambhala Publications.

Modernising the Mental Health Act Report (2018). Accessed 29/05/20 at www.gov.uk/government/publications/modernising-the-mental-health-act-final-report-from-the-independent-review.

Ottemiller, D. D. & Awais, Y. A. (2016). A model for art therapists in community-based practice. *Art Therapy, 33*(3), 144–150.

Prasad, S. (2013). The Impact of Culture and the Setting on the Use and Choice of Materials. In S. Prasad, P. Howie & J. Kristel (eds) *Using Art Therapy with Diverse Populations: Crossing Cultures and Abilities*. London: Jessica Kingsley Publishers.

Prasad, V. (2000). *The Karma of Brown Folk*. Minneapolis, MN: University of Minnesota Press.

Schaverien, J. (1999). *The Revealing Image*. London: Jessica Kingsley Publishers.

Singh, B. (2017). Mental health in the Sikh community. Forum. Sikh Press Association, Imperial College, London.

Talwar, S. (2010). An intersectional framework for race, class, gender, and sexuality in art therapy. *Journal of the American Art Therapy Association, 27*(1), 11–17.

Talwar, S. (2019). *Art Therapy for Social Justice: Radical Intersections*. New York, NY: Routledge.

Talwar, S., Iyer, J. & Doby-Copeland, C. (2004). The invisible veil: Changing paradigms in the art therapy profession. *Art Therapy: Journal of the American Art Therapy Association, 21*(1), 44–48.

Watkins, C. E. & Terrell, F. (1988). Mistrust level and its effects on counseling expectations in Black client–White counselor relationships: An analogue study. *Journal of Counseling Psychology, 35*(2), 194–197.

Wright, T. & Andrew, T. (2017). Art therapy in a crisis resolution/home treatment team: Report on a pilot project. *International Journal of Art Therapy, 22*(4), 180–189.

Chapter 11

A Black Therapist Sees Herself: Exploring Sameness and Difference in the Dramatherapy Room

— KAIRO MAYNARD —

Introduction

This chapter will focus on the importance of seeing yourself within the therapy room, in order to explore self-identity and self-worth. 'Dramatherapists and trainees need to take responsibility for educating themselves about relevant identity development models, historical and current discriminatory practices at a societal level and global socio-political and intergenerational issues that may affect the psychological welfare of clients' (Dokter, 2016, p.6). Projection, embodiment and especially time are the most useful elements of this process. Time is a luxury in child and adolescent mental health services (CAMHS), as they usually are, focused on delivering a limited number of sessions. Using case vignettes of my work with Black and mixed-race teenage girls, I will explore the importance of acknowledging the intersections in the therapy room, while understanding that my lived experience and process may not be the same as the clients. Nor are we likely to be at the same developmental stage of understanding our identity and experiences. It is the role of the therapist to support clients to make meaning out of chaos, while refraining from pushing them down a path they are not yet ready to take. The explicit aims of the therapy described here could not be addressed until the girls were able to understand and begin to process their authentic-self first, which many found difficult. Nevertheless, dramatherapy can encourage clients to 'explore unfamiliar aspects of one's inner world, moving away from the repetitive and destructive patterns we might tend to adopt' (Ciemnyjewski & Brown, 2010, p.15).

I want to explore my own theories on the importance of sameness in the therapy room. It has been argued that it is not necessary to match therapist and client by race or ethnicity, and that in some cases this policy might hinder ethnic communities accessing healthcare services, as over time it can '[exempt] medical and healthcare professionals from engaging in thinking around race and cultural process in clinical encounters' (Krause, 2014, p.110). Despite this, I believe it is important to have equal representation in all fields, especially in the mental health sector where Black and ethnic communities are over-represented in sectioning, but under-represented in senior roles (McManus *et al.*, 2016; NHS Workforce Race Equality Standard, 2017).

Context

I work in an inner-London CAMHS, serving a multicultural community. Thus, it was inevitable that I would meet many young Black girls in the capacity of therapist, group facilitator, assessing clinician or just a friendly face in the waiting room. However, I am also aware of the inequalities around access to mental health services for Black communities. In a CAMHS-specific context, Black girls are less likely to access services compared to their white counterparts. This may be due to the lack of referrals from primary care services and the CAMHS threshold not meeting the requirements of those 'deemed as not suffering from a "serious enough" mental illness' (Lambeth Black Health and Wellbeing Commission, 2014, p.34). Nevertheless, we cannot view Black girls' experiences alone, but must take into account Black adults' experiences and the influence on children and young people's journey into CAMHS.

The Adult Psychiatry Morbidity (APM) survey found that Black people in the UK are the least likely to receive treatment or adequate care and support for common mental health disorders, despite being one of the highest groups to be diagnosed and hospitalized (Maynard, 2019; McManus *et al.*, 2016). It is also important to note that while mental health disorders can affect anyone at any time of their life, risk factors such as stress, poverty and lack of social support can make a person more susceptible. Taking into consideration the social positioning of Black people, it's unsurprising that they may be more prone to mental health disorders (Maynard, 2019). Indeed, due to a number of socio-cultural reasons, perpetuated by institutional racism, the APM survey found a disproportionate number of Black people in mental health institutions. Admissions are often via the courts and police rather than primary care services (Matthews-King, 2018), perhaps due to a lack of knowledge about mental health disorders and a lack of trust in health professionals among Black people.

Many people are unable to access the support they need (Matthews-King,

2018), but mental health support for young people has its own difficulties: services are stretched and the number of referrals steadily increasing. Since 2010, young people attending Accident and Emergency departments due to mental health concerns has tripled (Young Minds, 2020). There is no way of knowing how many young Black girls are included in this data, but I will look more closely at the pathway of one Black girl and her journey into CAMHS later in this chapter, showing a single example of a young person in need who was not actively self-harming or suicidal, but whose behaviour was deemed problematic. It is fortunate that her school were curious about what might be underlying this behaviour. I wonder how many other young Black people have followed a different path into pupil referral units and youth offending services due to the identification of 'challenging' behaviour itself not being challenged.

Stereotyping Black women and girls

Young Black girls are frequently described as 'angry or irritable people', rather than individuals who *feel* anger or irritation. The 'angry black girl/woman' stereotype – a label I am all too familiar with as a Black woman myself – is closely linked to the strong black woman (SBW) stereotype which emerged in the Victorian era. Both are equally damaging, as they focus on Black women being 'strong', devoid of feeling and unable or prohibited from expressing their wants and needs (Beauboeuf-Lafontant, 2009). If a Black woman uses her voice to express herself, she is often dubbed 'angry' rather than passionate, hurt or simply disagreeing. These stereotypes originate with enslaved Black women masking their emotions from their slave owner as a method of survival.

Slavery was an international trade, in which the UK was heavily involved. Black people were seen and treated as stock and cattle. There were slave ports all over the country, although the actual plantations were overseas. Thus, unlike America, it was easier for the British public to turn a blind eye to their own atrocities while profiting immensely. Generations after the abolition of slavery, we still see its effects today, not least in the economic disadvantage of Black communities. As Eddo-Lodge states, 'despite abolition, an Act of Parliament was not going to change the perception overnight of enslaved African people from quasi-animal to human' (2017, p.6). The SBW stereotype may be seen as promoting empowerment and independence, yet the negative impact it has weighs far greater by keeping Black women subordinate and silent, lest they are perceived as wild, crazed and angry.

Michelle

Michelle was a 15-year-old Black girl. She was referred to CAMHS by her school, following concerns around what they termed 'challenging' behaviour with low mood. She had been excluded many times in the previous academic year and had been sent to an additional provision unit twice for a break from her mainstream school.

As a therapist working in multicultural communities, it is important to be aware of socio-cultural factors in order to acknowledge the client's journey into CAMHS (Talwar, 2010). I have worked with many Black girls when first referred to CAMHS, but am focusing on Michelle in particular, because this was her second period with CAMHS. The first referral had also been due to perceived 'aggressive and challenging' behaviour. However, when I met Michelle for an initial assessment, I did not feel I was meeting a child who had an assumed 'conduct' disorder. This made me question the label 'challenging'. I believe that if a child is acting out, it is because they are trying to communicate something and have no other way of expressing themselves.

Assessment

Nevertheless, during the initial assessment the focus remained on her 'challenging' behaviour. Michelle and her mother explained her actions and the reasons for her exclusions. I was aware that this was the information-gathering stage, but I also wondered if Michelle could not or was not allowed to connect with her vulnerability. She initially presented as 'standoffish'. The only emotion spoken about was her anger. It was only once therapy began that we were able to explore who she actually was, compared to how she was perceived. I left the initial assessment feeling protective and heavy. I sensed that Michelle was holding a lot in and had a strong defence structure in place to keep others out. She spoke about giving up on school, as she felt they had given up on her. It seemed she had unconsciously created a 'false self' (Winnicott, 1937) by repressing the undesirable aspects of herself through a process of introjection – an unconscious defence mechanism used to protect the self from feeling vulnerable and neglected. I wondered how other people's perceptions of Michelle had shaped her own sense of self (Maynard, 2018).

Following the assessment, I felt the standard eight to twelve sessions of therapy would barely touch the surface of what Michelle presented. I was aware this decision might be influenced by the countertransference I had experienced leaving the assessment. Thus, it was important for me to acknowledge these uncomfortable, protective feelings while seeing 'the value of taking one's time, not rushing and crafting something deeper and – possibly – more enduring' (Briggs, 2019, p.17). I wanted to offer enough space to explore themes of identity, while balancing the high demand for the service. I felt that addressing her low mood would take time as her defences, perhaps intended to convey that she did not care about anything, were deeply entrenched. I negotiated an extended therapy plan with my supervisor and felt relieved that the work with Michelle would not be limited by time pressures. I was aware of how powerful the dominant beliefs of an individual or group – including negative stereotypes held by society, family members and therapists – can affect a client and become internalized. I felt a determination to change this 'false self' narrative, while being aware that my own agenda should not cloud the therapeutic process. I discussed the outcome of the assessment and the offer of extended sessions with Michelle and her mum. They appeared grateful and relieved, both agreeing that she should be given time to 'open up'.

During this conversation, I also considered my status in the room with Michelle and her mum. I was not just another Black woman; I was also in a position of privilege and power as her therapist. Clients trust me for my expertise, knowledge and looking after their care, thus at times I do become another authoritative figure in their life. I was acutely aware that I represented my profession and organization and felt as if I was holding a door open for Michelle and her mother to enter a healthcare institution that systematically fails the Black community.

Addressing difference

As therapists, we should aim to explore and address working with difference empathically. However, despite having previously researched the effects of racial and gender oppression on Black women (Maynard, 2018), I did not feel the priority in these sessions was to explain how society might have shaped Michelle's understanding of who she is, but rather use the sessions to mindfully arouse her curiosity and support her exploration of identity and society and the complex connections between the two. I was relieved that the proposed timeframe had not suggested to Michelle that there was something wrong with her that needed a longer time to 'fix'. I did not want to collude with pathologizing her experience. Additionally, I wanted to revisit my own question: *what would the world look like with one more Black girl who was sure of herself and had a safe space to explore her identity?*

When discussing an intersectional framework, we cannot do so without acknowledging Kimberlé Crenshaw's original formulation (Crenshaw, 1989). Intersectionality centres Black women in the analysis of race and gender in response to the exclusion of Black women's experiences in feminist and anti-racist theories and policies. Michelle's experiences at school were unique to her being a Black girl. Had a Black boy or white girl presented as similarly irritable, angry, apathetic, withdrawn or tearful, I wondered if they would receive the same multiple detentions, exclusions and a managed move to an alternative provision unit.

Further, Talwar states that as therapists looking to engage in a more intersectional framework, we must be mindful of 'how we present and represent the lives and stories of others' (2010, p.12). Madison (2005) also encourages us to question how we predict consequences or evaluate our own potential to do harm. It was important for me to acknowledge that just because I am a Black woman, I cannot speak for all Black girls and women, even if there are similarities in our socio-economic or cultural upbringings. Failing to recognize this may do more harm than good, before the therapy has even started.

For example, I was once working with a young mixed-race girl who commented that I 'speak posh'. This was different from her because she did not pronounce her 'Ts'. I could have defensively brushed off what she had said, or denounced the difference and focused on the similarities of our physical appearance. However, this would not have allowed her to explore herself. This particular young person presented with appearance anxiety and often questioned her identity – where she fitted in at school, home and wider society. Working from a position of power as her therapist, I felt it was important to acknowledge what she was saying rather than attempt to focus on the similarities in order to make myself feel more comfortable. Had I not done this, the much-needed discussion, which I felt ultimately addressed her anxieties about her appearance, would not have taken place.

I had similar experiences of sameness and difference as a trainee. I was about to start dramatherapy sessions with a teenage Black girl who was physically very similar to me. I felt mixed emotions about working with her individually. The challenges presented by professionals and her case notes caused me anxiety. However, I gradually realized that this was also my reason for wanting to work with her and, perhaps, why I experienced a protective transference. Greenson's view supports my own experience of transference, describing it as a 'new edition of an old object relationship' (1967, p.152). The physical similarities she shared with my younger self had, perhaps, activated the wounded healer archetype, causing me to feel protective and determined to create a meaningful therapeutic relationship. I have frequently recognized countertransference feelings of protectiveness, heaviness and a determination for change and am aware that, by engaging in therapy with these young Black and mixed-race girls, something is also re-activated for me. The wounded healer archetype suggests it is the client's 'wounds' that mirror and activate those of the therapist. These wounds could be identified as experiences of oppression; be it societal or personal, internal or external. Despite the privilege and power difference between therapist and client, it must be acknowledged that the alliance comes with similarities, especially if these are rooted in marginalization or oppression. A client once declared to me that she was happy to have a young Black woman therapist as she would not have to defend or explain things related to her existence. This may also be the case for those who fall into similar intersections of class, gender, sexuality, disability and so on.

Although I encountered the exploration of sameness and difference while training, this was not formally addressed in my studies. Dramatherapy can be considered a primarily white-led profession and I was in a minority while training. Despite being encouraged to pursue and explore this topic for my dissertation, there was no space on the course to look at race, culture and ethnicity. An intersectional therapy practice should be everybody's concern; however, it felt, as it often is in society, that talking about oppression is left up to the oppressed and marginalized communities. Intersectional themes should be embedded throughout therapy trainings, not offered as an additional module or seminar on its own. This sends the message that engaging in this work is optional, rather than an ethical and clinical necessity to support meaningful work with a range of communities.

Connecting with feeling

As a dramatherapist, I feel pressure to be active and creative at all times in the therapy room. This may be my own internal pressure – a wish to represent dramatherapy perfectly because it is less well known than the talking therapies. My own dramatherapy journey has enabled me to come to terms with my identity, and I feel excited for my clients embarking on this undertaking. I query where this excitement comes from, as I know that exploration of identity and oppression is a difficult and uncomfortable process. My driving force is my awareness of racial inequalities in wellbeing and the importance of giving space to marginalized clients who experience poorer outcomes in mental health services. As Fanon states, 'it is through the effort to recapture the self and to scrutinize the self...that men will be able to create the ideal conditions of existence for a human world' (1952, p.181). However, it is important to recognize that, despite my excitement, as a therapist I must meet the client where they are at – consciously at least – in order to understand their lived experience. We are encouraged to enter the imaginative world of the client and tailor the therapy to their needs.

Nevertheless, in order to understand how the multiple systems of the client affect their daily lives, it is necessary to be aware of the influences not just from their internal and external realities, but from our own.

This was important to consider when working with Michelle. Following the assessment period, she seemed to find it increasingly difficult to connect to or engage in the therapeutic process. We worked together using spectrograms and creating small worlds, but it seemed that Michelle found this too emotionally demanding. She often complained about being tired, and at times would shut down completely. An example perhaps that 'The ego seeks to protect itself from emotional conflict by dealing with it cognitively' (Walrond-Skinner, 2014, p.84). I wondered if Michelle was shutting down in order to regulate the sadness and anger she might be feeling (Thorn, 2011). I often left the sessions feeling frustrated at myself or confused as to why the therapy wasn't *working* with her. Consciously, I did not want to project my sense of failure onto Michelle and feed into the view of her being difficult to manage. Yet I was aware of the possibility that Michelle was projecting these feelings onto me; she was experiencing similar feelings of failure in school and may have been enacting this in the therapy. I reminded myself that Michelle regularly attended the sessions and had always been on time, thus demonstrating that she valued the space. I also questioned if Michelle was shutting down emotionally in order to defend herself against experiences being stimulated by exploring her feelings. It was possible the therapeutic process might have been similar to pastoral meetings she had attended in her education settings and that difficult incidents were being re-enacted.

Following this reflection, I decided to take a step back from our work around her low mood as it seemed clear that both Michelle and I were unable to engage in this theme just yet. I appeared to have a different picture of Michelle compared to how she was described at home and at school. I wondered if Michelle was using the sessions to be 'passive' and not 'assertive', loud or rude as she was often perceived outside our sessions (Thorn, 2011).

I had not witnessed Michelle experiencing overt racial or gender oppression. However, I was aware of the 'cultural messages, institutional policies and practices that [benefited] the dominant group' (Talwar, 2010, p.15), a group that Michelle and I were not part of. Working within an intersectional framework requires analysis of how not only racism but also sexism and the patriarchy are embedded in theories which claim to help the Black community (Crenshaw, 1989). As Fanon states, 'in the white world the man of colour encounters difficulty in the development of his bodily schema' (1952, p.83).

I wanted to support Michelle in a way that balanced the similarities and differences of our experiences as a Black woman and girl. I hoped that in this process the authentic therapeutic relationship would develop. Caughey states that, when examining culture, we must look at how the individual manages their cultural conditioning, 'especially those whose subjective experiences and identities have been marginalized' (2006, p.8). Knowing how society treats Black women, I was aware that Michelle was still a child and wanted her to independently create her own idea of who she was (Alexander, 1996; Kincaid, 1969).

Transformation

It was in session six that I noticed a shift in Michelle. During our check-in, she chose a picture of a shadowed figure and the word card 'confused'. She explained that she was not getting on well at school and everything felt *very difficult*. We had encountered themes of confusion in earlier sessions and I wondered if this was something she was still feeling in the therapy. I was aware that Michelle was having difficulty in school. Although things had improved immensely since the previous year, she was still struggling. The feelings of difficulty and failure seemed to influence Michelle's self-esteem and perception of self, both of which were being processed in the therapy. She often stated she didn't know why she was sad or angry and I wondered if this was a defence mechanism to stop her from failing therapy and mirrored her perception that she was failing school. It was important for me to be aware that I might also represent the authoritative figures she felt unsupported by at school, and her anger might also be directed at me. Despite sceptical comments from members of my team on Michelle's engagement in the therapy, we continued; 'I resisted the temptation to believe that her story was fixed and unchangeable' (Holmwood, 2005, p.19).

We had developed a positive therapeutic relationship at this point, and I wanted Michelle to stay with the confused feelings, as I felt it was a huge influence on the transference experienced in the therapy room (Carter, 1995). I told her that I also felt confused and unsure how to move forward and acknowledged that everything was *very hard* work in the therapy room and in school. I hoped that being honest and transparent with Michelle would allow her to further express her feelings about what she needed. Although her defences were not completely down, Michelle started to explore the different parts of her identity and perceptions. By staying with this theme through projective and embodiment work, Michelle seemed closer to discovering her authentic self (Rogers, 1995).

Following this, I had a conversation in which her school referred to Michelle as being rude and having an attitude. I had heard both these descriptions about her already. However, in this instance, when she was found crying and inconsolable at school, she was described as scary.

This remark reminded me how Black girls' and women's emotions are perceived and how schools themselves exist within an education system and society where institutional racism and sexism are inherent. As with the stereotypes described previously, Michelle's sadness and tears seemed 'too much' for the school to manage. I was filled with anger after this conversation, a direct 'response to racist attitudes and to the actions and presumptions that arise out of those attitudes' (Lorde, 1981, p.22). I was holding a young Black girl who often presented as shut down and unable to express her feelings, yet when she did, she was seen as scary and intolerable. Michelle, as with Black women and girls everywhere, was in a double bind. It is not until cultural awareness and an intersectional framework are introduced into all systems that interact with marginalized communities that they will truly benefit (Crenshaw, 1989).

I have briefly acknowledged that as Michelle was a child, I did not want to impose my worldviews on her. However, this is a luxury not often afforded to Black girls. Adultification bias is a 'stereotype in which adults view Black girls as less innocent and more adult-like than their white peers' (Blake & Epstein, 2019, p.1). This stereotype does not take into account individual contexts and is not based on maturity. Moreover, it is an assumption assigned to all Black girls. As with the 'angry Black girl' stereotype, which lays the foundation for adultification bias, this is a form of racialized gender oppression, linked to harsher and more punitive treatment in society, particularly at school. It was no surprise to me that this view of Michelle led her to be sent to an alternative provision twice in one academic year. On one hand the school appeared supportive, but on the other it seemed unable to understand or contain Michelle's feelings. I wondered if she sensed this and introjected a similar view of herself as challenging; not only did she give up on school, she had given up on herself. This example is one I am all too familiar with and resembles the pupil referral unit to prison 'pipeline' that mostly affects children and young people from disadvantaged backgrounds by criminalizing their challenging and disruptive behaviour. Catherine West MP acknowledges this as being a societal issue, writing in *The Guardian* that 'often excluded children bounce around the system while falling further away from mainstream education' (West, 2019). Michelle was able to return to mainstream school, though this is not the case for many others.

Working towards an authentic self

As the sessions continued, Michelle gradually started to open up to an alternative perspective, recognizing that her story was not fixed and unchangeable. It became apparent that her low mood was very closely linked with her inability to hold herself in any regard, which was unsurprising considering her school experiences. Rogers (1995) suggests that part of the process of 'becoming' is in being supported to gradually drop the mask that has been adopted. This work cannot be done until the client themselves understands the need for the mask. At this point, it was still not possible to explicitly know what Michelle was shielding herself from. Despite being in a safe and containing therapy space, the process continued to be difficult. Ferguson states that we cannot ask a 'who am I?' (2016, p.155) question, without first questioning what others think of us. Michelle could describe what her friends and family thought of her, but she was unable to come up with any ideas for herself. I wondered how she could drop the mask she had unconsciously adopted, if she did not know she was wearing it.

Further, Frankel states that adolescents hold parts of the self in 'abeyance', 'yearn to be made visible' and 'must be granted the opportunity to reveal themselves in a genuine relationship' (1998, p.4). Adolescence must also be approached as a 'process' rather than a fixed 'state' that encompasses 'a dynamic field of emotions, anxieties, defences and relating to others' (Briggs, 2019, p.42). This I understood, having worked with young people for many years. However, it was important to also acknowledge the socio-cultural interactions that influenced Michelle's perception of herself (Talwar, 2010). This relates to the mask that Fanon (1952) describes when exploring blackness; Michelle was not just a Black girl, she was also a Black girl in relation to white society.

As the sessions continued, Michelle shared more about her identity and how she felt about herself. She held many negative thoughts on her physical appearance, including her body shape, eyes and hair. The politics surrounding Black women's hair is more frequently in the media nowadays. Afro hair is often policed, as it does not fit the Eurocentric beauty ideal, often being perceived as wild, ugly and undesirable (Adjaye, 2015; Olumide, 2016). I was angry that Michelle felt so negatively towards herself. As we explored this through image making, Michelle commented negatively about her hair, comparing it to mine. This felt like the right moment in the session to acknowledge this negativity and the impact of colourism. I was aware that I was lighter skinned than Michelle, and despite both wearing our hair in protective styles, there was still enough difference between us for Michelle to comment on it. This comparison reminded me of the earlier example, in which the young girl commented on the difference in our speech. There was simultaneously a sameness in being Black *and* there was a difference – I was another (Krause, 2014).

Jones (1978) found that Black clients frequently discussed race and tested their therapists' commitment to them in order to grow more trust.

Additionally, Carter reports that if the therapist denies race or racial issues in the therapy space the client may 'leave treatment with minimal therapeutic gain' (1995, p.130). It is important to note here that there may be some contradiction in my comments about discussing the impact of race with Michelle. The therapeutic relationship is one of complexity and contradiction, in which we must find balance within these discussions. As with any therapeutic work, the client must be at the centre. Thus, we explored the issues of colourism and experiences of being Black without my consciously imposing my own experience on her, while at the same time not denying my experiences if useful for the therapy process.

I cannot say if Michelle was able to completely remove and understand her negative self-image or the mask she wore by the end of therapy, but her low mood presentation had improved drastically. Additionally, I felt I had offered enough of an alternative perspective on what it means to be a Black girl for her to continue on the journey to embracing her full self.

Summary

In this chapter, I have explored my thought process on the need for sameness, while acknowledging difference in the therapy room, particularly with adolescents who are in an evolving state of development. I have focused on one client, but Michelle's experience can be applied to many other Black girls with and without access to CAMHS.

My own experience of being a Black woman therapist may differ from that of my colleagues of similar and different racial and cultural backgrounds. As therapists, we must approach themes of difference, prejudice, oppression and power with an open curiosity, a willingness to learn, reflect and listen to our clients' wants and needs. We are just one 'cog' in a system which enacts power and oppression on marginalized members of society. It is only by acknowledging and exploring this that we can hope to achieve our aim of creating an authentic therapeutic relationship and empowering our clients to recognize themselves and create positive, meaningful change.

References

Adjaye, N. A. (2015). *Melanin Monologues: A Black British Perspective*. London: The Wordsmith Workshop Limited.

Alexander, C. E. (1996). *The Art of Being Black*. Oxford: Oxford University Press.

Beauboeuf-Lafontant, T. (2009). *Behind the Mask of the Strong Black Woman: Voice and the Embodiment of a Costly Performance*. Philadelphia, PA: Temple University Press.

Blake, J. J. & Epstein, R. (2019). *Listening to Black Women and Girls: Lived Experiences of Adultification Bias Report*. Washington, DC: Georgetown Law Center on Poverty and Inequality.

Briggs, S. (2019). *Time Limited Adolescent Psychodynamic Psychotherapy: A Developmentally Focused Psychotherapy for Young People*. London: Routledge.

Carter, R. T. (1995). *The Influence of Race and Racial Identity in Psychotherapy: Towards a Racially Inclusive Model*. New York, NY: John Wiley and Sons.

Caughey, J. L. (2006). *Negotiating Cultures and Identity: Life History Issues, Methods and Readings*. Lincoln, NE: University of Nebraska Press.

Ciemnyjewski, J. W. & Brown, T. (2010). A question of identity and belonging: The self between familiar and unfamiliar, foreign spaces. *Dramatherapy, 32*(1), 14–16. doi:10.1080/21571430.2010.11675763.

Crenshaw, K. (1989). Demarginalizing the intersection of race and sex: A Black feminist critique of antidiscrimination doctrine, feminist theory and antiracist politics. *University of Chicago Legal Forum, 1*(8), 139–167.

Department of Health (2014). Closing the Gap: Priorities for Essential Change in Mental Health. Version 2.

Dokter, D. (2016). Intercultural Good Practice Guidelines. In S. Bilodeau, J. Bleuer, M. Carr, D. Dokter & N. Sajnanai (eds) *British Association of Dramatherapists. Intercultural Good Practice Guidelines*. Accessed at http://badth.org.uk/sites/default/files/content/pdf/badth_intercultural_good_practice_for_conference_2016_v2.pdf.

Eddo-Lodge, R. (2017). *Why I'm No Longer Talking to White People About Race*. London: Bloomsbury.

Fanon, F. (1952). *Black Skin, White Masks*. Paris: Editions de Seuil.

Ferguson, S. J. (2016). *Race, Gender, Sexuality and Social Class: Dimensions of Inequality and Identity* (second edition). Thousand Oaks, CA: Sage Publications.

Frankel, R. (1998). *The Adolescent Psyche: Jungian and Winnicottian Perspectives*. London: Routledge.

Greenson, R. R. (1967). *The Technique and Practice of Psychoanalysis (Volume 1)*. Madison, CT: International Universities Press.

Holmwood, C. (2005). A tale of tales. *Dramatherapy, 27*(1), 19–23.

Jones, E. E. (1978). Effects of race on psychotherapy process and outcome: An exploratory investigation. *Psychotherapy: Theory, Research and Practice, 15*(3), 226–236.

Kincaid, M. (1969). Identity & therapy in the Black community. *Journal of Counselling and Development, 47*(9), 884–890.

Krause, I-B. (2014). The Complexity of Cultural Competence. In F. Lowe (ed.) *Thinking Space: Promoting Thinking About Race, Culture and Diversity in Psychotherapy and Beyond*. London: Routledge.

Lambeth Black Health and Wellbeing Commission (2014). *From Surviving to Thriving*. London: Lambeth Council.

Lorde, A. (1981). Uses of Anger: Women Responding to Racism. In A. Lorde, *The Master's Tools Will Never Dismantle the Master's House*. New York, NY: Penguin Random House.

Madison, D. S. (2005). *Critical Ethnography: Methods, Ethics and Performance*. London: Sage Publications.

Matthews-King, A. (2018). Mental Health Act 'needs major reform' as black patients four times as likely as whites to be sectioned. Accessed at www.independent.co.uk/news/health/mental-health-act-detained-sectioned-ethnic-minority-bme-report-nhs-a8669246.html.

Maynard, K. (2018). To be Black. To be a Woman. Can dramatherapy help Black women to discover their true self despite racial and gender oppression? *Dramatherapy, 39*(1). https://doi.org/10.1080/02630672.2018.1432668.

Maynard, K. (2019). As a black therapist, I want to see action come out of mental health awareness discussions. Accessed at www.mentalhealthtoday.co.uk/innovations/race.

McManus, S., Bebbington, P., Jenkins, R. & Brugha, T. (eds) (2016). *Mental Health and Wellbeing in England: Adult Psychiatric Morbidity Survey 2014*. Leeds: NHS Digital.

NHS Workforce Race Equality Standard Report (2017). Data Analysis Report for NHS Trusts. Accessed at www.england.nhs.uk/publication/workforce-race -equality-standard-data-reporting-march-2017.

Olumide, Y. M. (2016). *The Vanishing Black African Woman. Volume Two: A Compendium of the Global Skin-Lightening Practice*. Cameroon: Langaa RPCIG.

Rogers, C. (1995). *On Becoming a Person*. New York, NY: Houghton Mifflin Company.
Talwar, S. (2010). An intersectional framework for race, class, gender, and sexuality in art therapy. *Art Therapy: Journal of the American Art Therapy Association, 27*(1), 11–17.
Thorn, R. (2011). Sugar and Spice and All Things Nice: A Black Woman's Anger in a Forensic Setting. In D. Dokter, P. Holloway & H. Seebohm (eds) *Dramatherapy and Destructiveness*. London: Routledge.
Walrond-Skinner, S. (2014). *The Dictionary of Psychotherapy*. New York, NY: Routledge, Taylor and Francis.
West, C. (2019). Rising youth crime reflects wider societal problems. *The Guardian*. Accessed at www.theguardian.com/society/2019/apr/03/rising-youth-reflects-wider-societal-problems.
Winnicott, D. (1937). *The Child and the Outside Self*. London: Tavistock.
Young Minds (2020). Accessed at https://youngminds.org.uk.

Chapter 12

'Men Just Hit You': Sexism and Internalized Misogyny in Art Psychotherapy with Female Offenders

— JESSICA COLLIER —

Introduction

Women incarcerated in prison in England frequently detail accounts of brutality at the hands of their male co-defendants, partners and family members. Speaking of their lives in the art psychotherapy room, they regularly describe intimate relationships in which male-to-female violence and abuse are expected, tolerated and considered acceptable. Even women who identify as lesbian may expect dysfunctional heteronormative hierarchies in their relationships, in which corporeal and emotional domination is an integral aspect of the power balance between the two partners. Despite this experience of gendered violence, during their sessions, female prisoners of all backgrounds habitually declare their hatred of women, citing 'bitchiness' as distinctly more painful than being physically assaulted, beaten or controlled. 'Men just hit you and it's over' is a common refrain from women who have experienced years of violence and degradation from the men in their lives when challenged about their feelings. This alacrity on the part of some women in prison to justify physical abuse is particularly disturbing given the association between the experience of domestic violence and female offenders presenting with acquired brain injury (Motz, Dennis & Aiyegbusi, 2020).

This chapter will look at the cultural and political influences that manifest in women's internalized misogyny and sexism. It will also examine the collusion of professionals and organizations working in forensic institutions in perpetuating outdated myths about what women should expect from their relationships and how they are seen in a society where roles for females remain limited and culturally appraised. This is further complicated by the fact that women in prison have transgressed their normative and stereotypical position in society through violent or unlawful acts (Collier, 2019, 2021). This transgression of stereotype leads to marked differences in their life outcomes when they are released from prison compared to men (Prison Reform Trust, n.d.) and highlights the intrinsic notion and influence of intergenerational trauma. The pattern of repetition is obvious in all but the most anomalous of prisoners' family histories and was starkly and painfully illustrated when I worked with a woman who was born in prison, to a woman whose own mother was incarcerated in the same prison. Three generations simultaneously oppressed and detained by a society unable to acknowledge the ways in which women are routinely and systemically subjugated. Savneet Talwar stipulates, 'As art therapists we need to consider how representations of race, ethnicity, class, gender, sexuality, disability and religion bring into the present the intergenerational trauma of the past' (Talwar, 2015, p.101). The concepts of internalized, externalized and systemic misogyny and sexism will be considered through an intersectional lens and further elucidated through images that address misogyny in the visual arts and through an art psychotherapy vignette, illustrating how women learn over generations from their families, their partners and their culture how to hate themselves.

The prison context: An intersectional analysis

The criminal justice system and the prison institution itself are concrete manifestations of a historical wish to control, castigate and oppress already disadvantaged members of society (Foucault, 1977). Women in the criminal justice system are 'doubly damned' (Lloyd, 1995) in this regard as they must navigate an oppressive structure designed by and for males while, in most instances, maintaining their female identity. 'As prisoners they must negotiate discourses of punishment and responsibility, while as women they are subject to notions of femininity... [P]ower, in prison, is constantly negotiated on the level of identity' (Bosworth, 1999, p.3). Indeed, the ways in which disadvantage is concentrated in prison 'constitute nearly perfect examples of the consequences of the multiple subjugation and the compounding impact of various stigmatising identities' (Richie, 2004, p.438). Poverty, substance dependency and poor mental health are frequently cited as reasons for criminal activity, and there is no doubt that these are important and valid underlying explanations for offending behaviour. Nevertheless, we must recognize that poverty, substance dependency and poor mental health do not afflict populations indiscriminately, and are mostly based on enduring socio-economic policies that favour and advantage certain groups over others. Any serious attempt at a thorough understanding of criminal behaviour must look at the manifold layers of power, privilege and prejudice which influence society and consequently lead to tens of thousands of individuals being, literally, removed from society, penalized and marginalized in such a profoundly severe way that reintegration or recovery is all but impossible.

In England, nowhere is this disadvantage and societal assault more apparent than in the female prison estate. It is the case that many women who find themselves in the criminal justice system have themselves been victims of sexual and violent crimes (Motz, Dennis & Aiyegbusi, 2020). For women, being a victim of domestic violence signifies a substantial risk of ending up in prison themselves as a consequence of the violence done to them (Crenshaw, 2013). The abuses experienced by women frequently far exceed the seriousness of the offences with which they are charged and convicted. The Prison Reform Trust estimates that over half of women in prison have experienced emotional, physical or sexual abuse as a child, while the charity Women in Prison suggests that well over three-quarters of all adult women in prison have experienced domestic violence or sexual abuse. The disproportionately high number of Black, Gypsy, Roma and Traveller and Foreign National women who are incarcerated will also have experienced the additional damage and trauma of racism and social exclusion within the context of society in general, but specifically in the criminal justice system (Joseph, 2006; Lammy, 2017). For example, many Foreign National prisoners are serving long sentences for smuggling drugs, an offence which gives the woman the nomenclature 'drug mule'. The mule has been used as a metaphor for the oppressive treatment of Black women extensively, notably in Zora Neale Hurston's classic novel *Their Eyes Were Watching God* (1937). Hurston 'speaks to a form of mistreatment and betrayal of the mule, and thus through this metaphor she speaks to how Black women are represented and treated by those both within and outside their racial group' (Jordon-Zachary & Alexander-Floyd, 2018, p.xiv). The metaphor clearly describes the lack of choice and opportunity which characterizes the triple disadvantage of poverty, sexism and racism (Cox & Sacks-Jones, 2017). 'Most of the smugglers are women, and many are single parents struggling to raise three or four children and finance them through school. Others are coerced by threats of violence to act as couriers' (Hyland, 2002). The disparate number of Black women in prison can be seen as a direct manifestation of deeply embedded disadvantage and enduring prejudice at the intersection of race, gender and class. '"Disproportionality" lies in the centuries-old abuse of the black body... [T]he picture seen today reflects that history and its generational re-enactment' (Aiyegbusi, 2020, p.55).

Defining sexism and misogyny: Internal, external and systemic

A simple definition of sexism is 'prejudice or discrimination based on sex *especially* discrimination against women', and misogyny is 'a hatred of women' (Merriam-Webster, 2020). While women from diverse backgrounds are at particular disadvantage, it is obvious that 'the female prison population...contains some of the most disadvantaged, damaged and vulnerable people in our society' (Motz *et al.*, 2020, p.5). In most cases, women in prison are being penalized and criminalized based on their own experiences of discrimination, abuse and poverty. It is likely then that the discrimination and hatred impelled onto these women by society, simply for being female, will be suppressed, leading to multiple mental health issues including personality disorders, low self-esteem, depression, eating disorders, substance misuse and post-traumatic stress disorder (Eastwood, 2012).

Experiencing sexist events is clearly related to psychological distress and this is further intensified when internalized misogyny is also taken into account (Szymanski *et al.*, 2009). In the female prison population, we see this demonstrated in unconscious survival strategies which may include identification with the aggressor (Freud, 1937; Ferenczi, 1949; Collier, 2018) and the use of the 'moral defence' (Fairbairn, 1952), a psychological defence in which 'victims of abuse, neglect or crime' – a status most female offenders hold – 'direct their anger at themselves rather than the aggressor' (Snider, 2018, p.771). This defence mechanism is used by many women, not only those who make up the prison population. As we are routinely told that women are empowered and have parity with men, we come to believe that when things go wrong – when we are raped, or ignored, or beaten up, or assaulted – it is *our own fault*. This taking on of responsibility gives the temporary illusion that we might be able to change and control the situation and make the immediate circumstances more tolerable. In the long term, however, this misconception distorts reality and leads to poor mental health and internalized sexism and misogyny. The problem is not an individual one, but is built into society. 'By deluding themselves that the problem is internal to individual women, rather than externally built into the culture, women can end up perpetuating the very systems of oppression that cause the harm' (Snider, 2018, p.771).

If patriarchal society is built on a foundation of sexism and misogyny, which is systematically internalized by those it oppresses, then why is this so? The family remains a profound 'ideological site of social control for women' (Barton, 2016, p.2) and motherhood continues to be idealized; the expectation of motherhood is so profound that the nouns woman and mother are often used interchangeably (Collier, 2021). Women continue to provide almost all unpaid childcare, and they 'frequently face gendered double standards in that the sacrifices they sometimes make for their children, leaving them with relatives, working long hours...are perceived negatively in women when the same behaviours in men would be considered heroic' (Crenshaw, 2013, p.26). Unlike men therefore, when women are imprisoned, there are tragic and cumulative consequences on society that result from children being made homeless. Approximately 17,000 children enter the care system each year due to their mother being sent to prison and so the cycle of intergenerational distress continues (Joint Committee on Human Rights, 2019).

The ongoing cultural expectation that women should remain primarily responsible for the nurturing of others, and particularly that womanhood and motherhood are analogous, can be considered through the concept of 'womb envy' (Horney, 1926). Male domination has long been seen through an evolutionary lens – that due to biology, male strength and power has prevailed. These biological arguments are quite easily contested (Fine, 2011). However, they continue to be regarded as fact, and women remain subjugated as a consequence. The analytic concept of 'womb envy' proposes that the narcissistic injury men experience because they cannot give birth results in over-compensation for their 'lack'. This manifests in a need to take control of or disparage what they cannot have; that is, whatever is regarded as female. When we envy what we cannot have we are left with feelings of inferiority; feelings that are transformed into pride by degrading and debasing what we wish we had. 'Devaluation of an envied object is a typical defence manoeuvre, for as long as an object is devalued it does not need to be envied' (Bayne, 2011, p.153). Nothing is more shaming for a heterosexual man in a patriarchal society than to be compared to a woman. In prison, such is the intensity of the internalized misogyny, the women do not even want to be compared with one another.

It's in their natures: Internalized and institutional collusion with gender myths

While 'womb envy' may be a single analytical way of thinking about society's unconscious desire to oppress women, the ways in which this actually happens are many and varied and are influenced by how the world is viewed. In a patriarchy, it is men who decide what is on the agenda and what kind of behaviour is considered 'normal'. The damaging stereotypes and archetypes that have been created over the years are difficult to challenge in society, especially in prison; a system which is designed to undermine those within it. The institution itself colludes with and enacts the very same prejudices and misuses of power that created the criminal behaviour in the first place (Collier, 2015). Support given to women by prison staff can be very good. There are many officers and healthcare staff who care deeply about the prisoners' welfare. However, the women are often under the control of male staff, or female staff working within a patriarchal context, which can cause damage if the officers are not alive and sensitive to the women's emotional distress and disturbing histories. This system of control amplifies the male gaze (Mulvey, 1975; Eastwood, 2012), quite literally if on 'constant observations' – a method of keeping suicidal prisoners safe by watching them through a hatch in the door 24 hours a day. Moreover, if an officer asks a woman to do something she does not want to do and she disobeys their order, she is likely to receive a negative report, which will look bad on her record and potentially mean the withdrawal of phone credit, association, even the opportunity for parole. Of course, the failure of the prisoner to report bad or abusive staff, male or female, leads once again to the oppressed colluding with the oppressor. Likewise, if staff use common misogynistic language, or make sexual innuendoes, the women, who are likely to have been previously sexually traumatized, may fear retaliation if they report them, and instead may internalize and normalize the language and behaviour so as to survive it. This is a double bind all women are familiar with. In Emma Jane's shocking paper exploring online misogyny (Jane, 2014), she describes the way in which women are seen by men, and thus by society, through a double lens of desire and disgust: 'targets were hypersexualized as "sluts"' and then 'derogated for being "sluts" who did not pass muster because they were too ugly, too fat...too old, too lesbian and so on' (ibid, p.560). The hostility of the language that she studied, language that is common parlance in prison, 'provides critical insight into the degree to which misogynistic views are still held by many in the community' (ibid, p.567). Given prison's status as a microcosm of societal power hierarchies, it is important to note that sexual misconduct is not uncommon (Grierson, 2019), and more routine bullying, discrimination, partiality, even banal incompetence by staff and fellow prisoners can leave women feeling neglected and betrayed. Often the women's complaints cannot be attended to or are disbelieved, mirroring previous trauma.

> Institutional betrayal is an additional component of trauma for most survivors of sexual misconduct... Even in the best case, when an institution responds appropriately and responsibly, the fact that one was rendered unsafe and victimized within a supposedly 'safe' institutional setting is itself a betrayal. (Gentile, 2018, p.716)

The art of misogyny

There is a wealth of writing about sexism and misogyny in the art world. Obvious manifestations of this include the negating of work made by females by art critics – the late *Evening Standard* reviewer Brian Sewell once stated that 'Only men are capable of aesthetic greatness' (Johnson, 2008) – and the resistance by major galleries, until very recently, to purchase or exhibit work made by women or people of colour. While teaching on an art psychotherapy master's programme, I was shocked to find this kind of sexist attitude to aesthetic process was held unapologetically by a course tutor, whose only comment after co-facilitating a large group of mostly female students was the derogatory statement that the experience had been boring, 'like a women's knitting circle'. The archaic sexist argument that only men have the imagination and intelligence to *give birth* to worthwhile artistic creations returns us to the concept of womb envy. Melanie Klein suggested that womb envy manifested in 'painters and writers, who feel they give birth to their works like a woman in labour after a long pregnancy' (Klein, 1937, p.32). Regardless, from 1985, this prejudice and the privilege it afforded White male artists to dominate cultural spaces was challenged by the anonymous feminist collective, the Guerrilla Girls. The Guerrilla Girls define their activism as 'an intersectional feminism that fights discrimination and supports human rights for all people and all genders'.[1] Their campaigns focus on publishing data exposing the sexist and racist bias shown by collectors, galleries and critics. It is disseminated on posters and stickers, many of which, paradoxically, are now in the permanent collection of the Tate Modern. Their activism is ethical, bold and witty.

Nevertheless, the racism, sexism and misogyny that female artists encounter is unequivocal, not just in the way they are treated by the establishment, but in the artworks themselves. Nan Goldin's work *Nan one month after being battered* shows the artist with bruises and a bloodshot eye having been beaten by her boyfriend. While this image is not explicitly intended to raise awareness of misogyny, it does portray the effects of being subjected to gendered violence. As we will note in the vignette below, this piece may also reveal aesthetically the violent internalized misogyny felt by women who depend on men as their carers and partners, and conform to the expectations of society.

If *Nan* shows us the gendered violence within an intimate relationship, the violence done to women by men unknown to them is evident in the audience response to female performance artists, who run the risk of assault when executing their work. During a notorious performance of her

1 www.guerrillagirls.com

piece 'Rhythm 0' in Naples in 1974, performance artist Marina Abramovic instructed her audience to utilize any one of 72 objects on her body. While initially visitors were respectful, by the end of the performance, Abramovic had been doused in water, physically assaulted, her throat had been cut and a loaded gun pointed at her. Again, the artist did not conceive or recognize this piece as a comment on misogyny, and understands the work herself as a reflection on the human fear of suffering. Nevertheless, Abramovic writes in her autobiography:

> Ultimately I think the reason I wasn't raped was that the wives were there...there was this strong Madonna/whore dichotomy in attitudes toward women... They put me on the table, spread my legs, stuck the kitchen knife in the table next to my crotch... He put the pistol toward my neck and touched the trigger. (Abramovic, 2016, p.69)

To me, this performance seems to encapsulate the hatred men feel towards women and the danger women may be in when societal boundaries of acceptable behaviour are reconfigured.

Violence done to women and people of colour by society is the explicit subject of Kara Walker's work, whose art explores race, gender, sexuality, identity, violence and subjugation through the subversion of race and gender stereotypes. Speaking about her 2002 exhibition, 'Kara Walker: For the Benefit of All the Races of Mankind; An Exhibition of Artifacts, Remnants, and Effluvia excavated from the Black Heart of a Negress', she commented that 'out of this subservient condition...I must escape, go wild, be free, after which I have to confront the questions: How free? How wild? How much further must I go to escape all I've internalized?' (Als, 2007).

Clinical vignette

The vignette below does not seek to proclaim art psychotherapy as a process of eliminating internalized sexism and misogyny, although I believe that a consistent, compassionate therapeutic relationship and imaginative communication can reveal new perspectives and different ways of relating and being that can be life changing for both people involved. Rather, it seeks to demonstrate how art psychotherapy can be used to recognize and understand that emotional, psychological and behavioural patterns that are detrimental to women's lives can be acknowledged as societal issues of prejudice and oppression as well as a demonstration of unconscious internal distress. The misogyny and sexism that women internalize, and in so doing collude in their own abuse and oppression, can be seen clearly in this example. It is imperative that we as therapists understand damaging and apparently self-sabotaging behaviour as a response to systemic pressures that we ourselves may inadvertently collude with as we unconsciously enact our own anger, envy and bias. Shelby has given consent for me to write about our work together and I thank her for her generosity. All names and some details have been changed.

Shelby

Shelby was a working-class White woman in her thirties and had been in and out of prison on a number of occasions, mostly due to affray and robbery in the context of alcohol and heroin addiction. Shelby's early life had been dominated by her father's extreme violence towards her mother. When she was around 12 years old, her mother found a new partner and left Shelby's abusive father. Shelby was angry with her mother for 'breaking up the family' and refused to stay in the house with her, choosing instead to live with her father, who she felt was blameless and the innocent victim of her mother's promiscuous behaviour. Although she was only entering adolescence, her father treated Shelby as if she was his adult partner, taking her to the pub, showing her off to his friends and expecting her to look after the house in the role of the subservient 'housewife'. She escaped this situation when she was in her middle teens by moving in with an older man who was an alcoholic and who quickly became violent. Her mother, with whom she had never reconciled, died prematurely the same week Shelby had her first child. She soon found herself with an abusive partner and two children. Shelby had mirrored her mother's experience; intergenerational trauma unconsciously re-enacted. This was exacerbated when the violence at home became too much and she moved in with a different man, who was a heroin addict. Shelby now had an alcohol problem and a spiralling heroin addiction. She was seen as an embarrassment to the wider family, while her aging father – whose new female partner was looking after Shelby's children – was seen as a kind and responsible grandfather, a hero, his own violence and abuse relegated in view of this new paternal role.

During this time, Shelby, desperate for heroin, broke into an old man's home and stole his money and alcohol, striking him down as she left. This action was seen by the court as a despicable act of violence perpetrated by an unthinking and immoral drug addict. From a sociological perspective, this would seem to be criminal activity based, as described earlier, on poverty, substance dependency and poor mental health. However, thought about from a psychodynamic perspective, this could be seen as a manifestation of the suppressed hatred Shelby felt for her father, mirrored in her unconscious choice of a victim, who was an old White man like her dad. In our art psychotherapy sessions, her rage and loathing of her father seemed to reveal itself in a 'reaction formation' (Freud, 1937). Shelby echoed the ingrained narrative that her father was a good and loving man; her conscious feelings for him expressed in direct contrast to the way she actually seemed to feel. Indeed, so conditioned was Shelby into considering herself inferior, and an embarrassment to her 'perfect' father, that she struggled to think about or reflect on her own identity. Instead, she seemed saturated and preoccupied with the narrative that she was a useless mother, an addict and a slag; that she deserved the beatings and the insults. That it was *her own fault*. She also continued to disparage her late mother, blaming her for the situation she was in and describing her as a slut who had chosen a man over her family. Her rage made it impossible to process the anger she may have felt at her premature death, leaving her unable to grieve or mourn (Freud, 1917; Collier, 2019).

Initially in the sessions, Shelby drew stereotypically female images: bunches of flowers, teddy bears and love hearts. Slowly, however, as she described the way she had been used as a substitute wife, she began to see her father differently. Her images became subverted: flowers surrounded by barbed wire, a teddy bear with a noose (Figure 12.1).

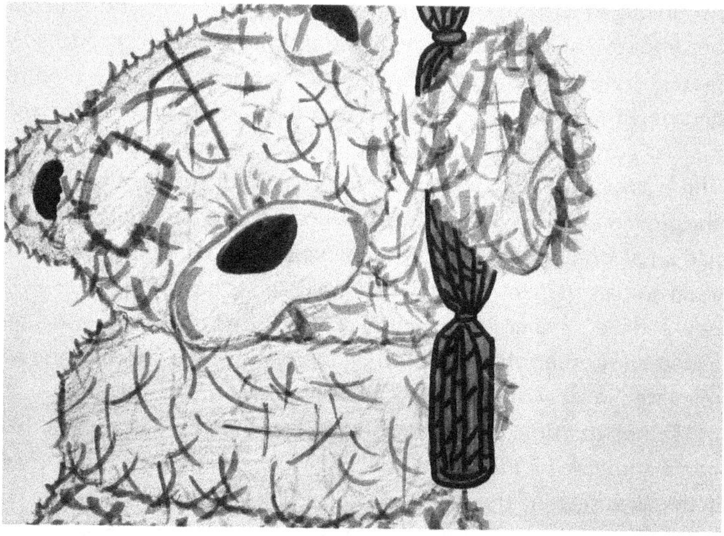

Figure 12.1: Teddy bear and noose

She drew her father with horns, and described the disparaging and belittling voices in her head, rendered in pencil as frightening, distorted portraits of him. Eventually, as Shelby disclosed more about her relationship with her father, including his sexual advances and insulting comments when she rejected him, she too began to see the familial, misogynistic pattern of abuse. She drew a self-portrait, battered and scarred, but staring defiantly at the viewer; unapologetic, acknowledging the violence done to her, like Nan Goldin, by a man she loved but who was abusive (Figure 12.2).

Figure 12.2: Self-portrait

Shelby began to see that her idea to live in her father's house on her release would need to be reconsidered. While trying to make sense of this, she spent several weeks on an image of a staircase, moving forward and upward to a door not yet open. However, outside the sessions, her licence conditions demanded that Shelby have an address to be released to, and her father's house was assessed by the probation service as the most appropriate. Society's idealization of the family, whatever destructive dynamics may be happening therein, reaffirmed Shelby's previous assertion that her father was good and she needed to be protected by him. The hard work done in art psychotherapy, the awakening of her own identity and the recognition that she had been caught in a cycle of intergenerational abuse was suppressed by a system which colluded with the stereotype of a woman within the context of (pseudo) wife and mother; back in the abusive family dynamic that had arrogated her identity. Shelby was put in a double bind by an authority perpetuating unconscious gender stereotyping: accept the licence conditions and move back with her abusive father or stay in prison. Given these limited choices, Shelby's offence, stealing from and beating an old man in his family home, was perhaps the only way she could enact her rage towards her father; 'showing' her anger instead of 'knowing' it (Orrell, 2020).

This sabotaging of complex progress by the institution is commonplace. For me as an art psychotherapist, and as an individual, making sense of my resulting feelings of hopelessness and disappointment is exhausting. However, as I come to understand my own emotional response, either as an introjection emanating from my relationship with the prisoner, or as explicit frustration at a cruel and unthinking system, I am left wondering how best to work decently with such a paucity of containment and psychological security within our criminal justice system in particular, but also in a society where the welfare of prisoners has so little political sway. Nevertheless, despite what may happen once the women are through the gate, providing the opportunity for them to be thought about and listened to is itself a worthwhile objective.

Conclusion

This chapter has examined the landscape of sexism and misogyny in which we live, and recognized the additional disadvantages experienced by women who are seen as 'other', either through their gender alone or through their race, class, sexuality or many other aspects of identity. It has proposed some hypotheses for why women are hated, and why this hatred is internalized, thus becoming more prevalent as women themselves collude in the idealization of family and motherhood and the cultural castigation of strong or 'unfeminine' women. Szymanski and colleagues suggest that in working towards a feminist psychology that includes social justice, we must encourage our clients in 'recognizing the potentially negative impact of sexism in their lives, help them see their problems in a contextual light in order to reduce shame and victim blame, and teach them skills for dealing with and confronting oppressions' (Szymanski *et al.*, 2009, p.107). This is not to suggest that art psychotherapy sessions must include lessons in feminist discourse; but rather that we reflect on our own internalized sexism and misogyny when we 'wit(h)ness' the stories our clients bring us (Pollock, 2010; Collier, 2015), challenge misogynist perceptions and recognize when we ourselves collude with the sexist status quo.

While researching this chapter, I came across a local police force social media page requesting help from the public in locating a woman wanted for robbery. A picture of the woman accompanied the appeal. Beneath her image was a torrent of abusive comments, seemingly from men and women who knew her, and also from strangers who had never met her. Comments included an image of a witch, crude discussion about her looks, 'jokes' about masturbating over her picture and other sexualized vilifications about heroin users. Eventually, someone commented, 'She needs help, not judgement.' For marginalized women, whose identity is shaped by misogynistic abuse and sexist systemic and societal expectations of femininity, nothing could be clearer than this.

Acknowledgements

Thanks always to Janetka Platun.

References

Abramovic, M. (2016). *Walk through Walls*. London: Penguin-Fig Tree.

Aiyegbusi, A. (2020). Caught in the Racist Gaze? The Vulnerability of Black Women to Forensic Mental Health and Criminal Justice Settings. In A. Motz, M. Dennis & A. Aiyegbusi (eds) *Invisible Trauma Women, Difference and the Criminal Justice System*. London: Routledge.

Als, H. (2007). The shadow act: Kara Walker's vision. *The New Yorker*. www.newyorker.com/magazine/2007/10/08/the-shadow-act.

Barton, A. (2016). *Fragile Moralities and Dangerous Sexualities: Two Centuries of Semi-Penal Institutionalization for Women*. London: Routledge. (Originally published 2005.)

Bayne, E. (2011). Womb envy: The cause of misogyny and even male achievement? *Women's Studies International Forum, 34*(2), 151–160.

Bosworth, M. (1999). *Engendering Resistance: Agency and Power in Women's Prisons*. Farnham: Ashgate Publishing. (Revised edition 2016, London: Routledge.)

Collier, J. (2015). 3 man unlock: Out of sight out of mind: Art psychotherapy with a woman with severe personality disorder in prison. *Psychoanalytic Psychotherapy, 29*(3), 243–261.

Collier, J. (2018). Trauma, Art and the 'Borderspace': Working with Unconscious Re-Enactments. In J. Collier & P. Stewart (eds) *The End of the Sentence: The Future of Psychotherapy with Female Offenders*. London: Routledge.

Collier, J. (2019). Cover Stories: Art Psychotherapy with Mothers in Prison who Have Killed or Harmed Their Children. In A. Foster (ed.) *Mothers Accused and Abused: Breaking Cycles of Neglect*. London: Routledge.

Collier, J. (2021). Behind Closed Doors: Art Psychotherapy with Female Sexual Offenders. In S. Hastilow & M. Liebmann (eds) *Arts Therapies and Sexual Offending*. London: Jessica Kingsley Publishers.

Cox, J. & Sacks-Jones, K. (2017). Double disadvantage: The experiences of Black, Asian and Minority Ethnic women in the criminal justice system. Agenda: Alliance for women and girls at risk.

Crenshaw, K. (2013). From private violence to mass incarceration: Thinking intersectionally about women, race and social control. *Journal of Scholarly Perspectives, 9*(1), 23–37.

Eastwood, C. (2012). Art therapy with women with borderline personality disorder: A feminist perspective. *International Journal of Art Psychotherapy, 17*(3), 98–114.

Fairbairn, W. D. R. (1952). *Psychoanalytic Studies of the Personality*. London: Tavistock.

Ferenczi, S. (1949). Confusion of the tongues between the adults and the child. *International Journal of Psychoanalysis, 30*(1), 225–230.

Fine, C. (2011). *Delusions of Gender: The Real Science Behind Sex Differences*. London: Icon Books.

Foucault, M. (1977). *Discipline and Punish: The Birth of the Prison*. New York, NY: Pantheon Books.

Freud, A. (1937). *The Ego and the Mechanisms of Defence*. London: Hogarth Press and Institute of Psycho-Analysis. (Routledge 1992.)

Freud, S. (1917). Mourning and Melancholia. In *Collected Papers Vol IV* (pp.152–170). London: Hogarth Press and the Institute of Psychoanalysis.

Gentile, K. (2018). Give a woman an inch, she'll take a penis: The expanded version. *Contemporary Psychoanalysis, 54*(4), 709–723. doi:10.1080/00107530.2018.1521696.

Grierson, J. (2019). More than 2,500 prison staff disciplined in five years, MoJ figures show. *The Guardian*. Monday 29 April 2019. www.theguardian.com/society/2019/apr/29/more-than-2500-prison-staff-disciplined-in-five-years-moj-figures-show.

Horney, K. (1926). The flight from womanhood: The masculinity-complex in women as viewed by men and women. *International Journal of Psychoanalysis, 7*, 324–339.

Hurston, Z. N. (1937). *Their Eyes Were Watching God*. Reprint 2020, London: Virago Modern Classics.

Hyland, J. (2002). *Britain: Behind the row over Jamaican 'drug mules'*. World Socialist Website: International Committee of the Fourth International.

Jane, E. A. (2014). 'Back to the kitchen, cunt': Speaking the unspeakable about online misogyny. *Continuum; Journal of Media and Cultural Studies, 28*(4), 558–570.

Johnson, A. (2008). 'There's never been a great woman artist.' So says the critic Brian Sewell, and the art market seems to agree, with men's work commanding millions more at auction. *The Independent*. Sunday 6 July, 2008. www.independent.co.uk/arts-entertainment/art/features/theres-never-been-a-great-woman-artist-860865.html.

Joint Committee on Human Rights (2019). *The Right to Family Life: Children Whose Mothers are in Prison*. UK Parliament. https://publications.parliament.uk/pa/jt201719/jtselect/jtrights/1610/full-report.html.

Jordan-Zachary, J. S. & Alexander-Floyd, N. G. (eds) (2018). *Black Women in Politics: Demanding Citizenship, Challenging Power, and Seeking Justice*. Albany, NY: State University of New York Press.

Joseph, J. (2006). Drug offences, gender, ethnicity and nationality: Women in prison in England and Wales. *The Prison Journal, 86*(1), 140–157.

Klein, M. (1937/1953). *Love, Hate and Reparation*. London: The Hogarth Press.

Lammy, D. (2017). *The Lammy Review: An Independent Review into the Treatment of, and Outcomes for, Black, Asian and Minority Ethnic Individuals in the Criminal Justice System*. London: Lammy Review.

Lloyd, A. (1995). *Doubly Deviant, Doubly Damned: Society's Treatment of Violent Women*. London: Penguin.

Merriam-Webster (2020). Misogyny. www.merriam-webster.com/dictionary/misogyny.

Motz, A., Dennis, M. & Aiyegbusi, A. (2020). *Invisible Trauma Women, Difference and the Criminal Justice System*. London: Routledge.

Mulvey, L. (1975). Visual pleasure and narrative cinema. *Screen, 16*(3), 6–18. https://doi.org/10.1093/screen/16.3.6.

Orrell, K. (2020). Tabula rasa: The attempt to forget what cannot be remembered. *International Journal of Forensic Psychotherapy, 2*(1), 52–62.

Pollock, G. (2010). Aesthetic wit(h)nessing in the era of trauma. *EurAmerica: Journal of European and American Studies, 40*(4), 829–886.

Prison Reform Trust (n.d.). England and Wales Factsheet. www.prisonreformtrust.org.uk/Portals/0/Why%20Women%20England%20and%20Wales.pdf.

Richie, B. (2004). Feminist ethnographies of women in prison. *Feminist Studies, 30*(2), 438–450.

Snider, N. (2018). Why didn't she just walk away? Silence, complicity and the subtle force of toxic femininity. *Contemporary Psychoanalysis, 54*(4), 763–777.

Szymanski, D. M., Gupta, A., Carr, E. R. & Stewart, D. (2009). Internalized misogyny as a moderator of the link between sexist events and women's psychological distress. *Sex Roles, 61*(1–2), 101–109. doi:10.1007/s11199-009-9611-y.

Talwar, S. (2015). Culture, diversity and identity: From margins to center. *Art Therapy: Journal of the American Art Therapy Association, 32*(3), 100–103.

Chapter 13

Disabled and LGBTQ+: A Music Therapy Perspective

— NAOMI ROWE —

Introduction

This chapter will address the intersection between being disabled and LGBTQ+ (lesbian, gay, bisexual, transgender, queer and others), encompassing those with physical disabilities, mental illnesses, learning difficulties and neurodiverse people within its definition of disability. As well as looking at the evidence base, it is also informed by my experiences as a disabled, LGBTQ+ music therapist. On qualifying, I began work as a full-time employed music therapist working in special education. When this became untenable due to my health conditions, I moved to freelance work and incorporated my years of LGBTQ+ activism. I now work with children in education settings and adults in private practice, the majority of whom are LGBTQ+ and neurodiverse.

My training as a psychodynamic music therapist did not include LGBTQ+ awareness, although this is now included on the majority of courses in some capacity (Coombes, 2019). I will address the many specific issues that cause LGBTQ+ people to seek mental health support. While there is some research into music therapists' attitudes towards inclusive practice (Boggan, Grzanka & Bain, 2018), there is no UK-wide analysis of attitudes towards the LGBTQ+ community within the art therapies. We can assume, therefore, that many art therapists do have some gaps in their knowledge of LGBTQ+ issues. This chapter examines detrimental conscious and unconscious attitudes LGBTQ+ clients may face within healthcare settings, and explores the challenges this may evoke in art therapists.

Research

Research within this intersection shows that LGBTQ+ people suffer from significantly worse mental, physical and sexual health outcomes than their cisgender, heterosexual peers (Hunt & Fish, 2008; Guasp, 2015). Gay people also tend to have poorer health outcomes than their heterosexual counterparts. Worse still are the outcomes experienced by bi people, followed by trans people, who are the group most at risk (Colledge, Hickson & Reid, 2015). This relates to the 'double discrimination' (Crenshaw, 1989) that bisexual and transgender people face from both the straight and gay worlds. Transgender people also face less understanding and positive mainstream attention than lesbian, gay and bi (LGB) individuals, and higher rates of violence (Bachman & Gooch, 2018). These statistics follow the intersectional principle that the more marginalized a person, the more minority stress they experience.

Within the LGBTQ+ disabled intersection, there are high rates of specific congruencies, including musculoskeletal and chronic pain issues for LBT+ women (Hunt & Fish, 2008), high rates of congruence between being transgender and neurodiverse (Heylens *et al.*, 2018) and an emerging connection between neurodiversity and diverse sexuality (Hillier *et al.*, 2020). The research in this area is predominantly focused on identifying trends; however, if we are to understand the complexity fully, it is important to propose some theories as to why these intersections are more common.

LGBTQ+ and neurodiversity

Many neurodiverse individuals grow up in a world surrounded by infinite unwritten rules they cannot access (Deweerdt, 2020b). Social norms are something to be learned and performed, and in most cases, it is up to the neurodiverse person to adapt their way of being to the world around them. It is possible that, for neurodiverse people, the concepts of gender norms are difficult to internalize (Brown, 2016). The concept of 'performing' as an assigned gender until a realization of actual gender is made is reported as commonplace within the trans-neurodiverse experience (Wenn, 2019). For many, this is part of a difficult, lifelong process of distinguishing the internal self from the 'masked', performative self (Russo, 2018). Neurodiverse people may already see themselves as outsiders, that their true self is not typical, and so may be more able than neurotypical people to recognize gender diversity within themselves.

LBT+ women and chronic pain

Some scientists currently theorize that fibromyalgia (chronic pain syndrome), a common chronic pain condition, is a physical manifestation of trauma (Gupta & Silman, 2004). There is certainly an overlap in conditions such as post-traumatic stress disorder (PTSD), depression, fibromyalgia and myalgic encephalomyelitis (ME). Extending the focus of Crenshaw's original proposition of intersectionality theory (1989) to encompass the LGBTQ+ community, we can recognize that LBT+ women face discrimination at the intersect of homophobia and sexism, and this may cause the kind of stress that can lead to health issues. In addition, as a minority group, bi women are at high risk of experiencing domestic violence, second only to disabled women (Bradley & Potter, 2017). Speaking as a bi disabled woman aware of this statistic, I would suggest this group may have additional difficulties with sharing their experiences, particularly with a male therapist or a therapist who may, unconsciously, represent a past abuser.

From a psychodynamic perspective, we can predict that a therapist may evoke past relationships, representing a parent or other significant figure (Wigram, Pedersen & Bonde, 2002). We can then acknowledge these associations and work with them, even using them to confront difficult issues in the safe therapeutic space. An intersectional approach recognizes that the therapist may not just represent a specific person or relationship, but may embody the privilege and power that a minority client has not accessed. In order to successfully merge these approaches, we must acknowledge both the person and the privilege the therapist may represent. This could be enough, in some cases, to form a therapeutic alliance with a multiple minority and socially aware client. We must also accept that some clients may need to see a therapist who has occupied a similar place in society to themselves (Talwar, 2010).

LGBTQ+ people and trauma

When looking at the poor health outcomes of those at the intersect of the LGBTQ+ and disability communities, it is vital to explore the role of trauma in what it means to be LGBTQ+. This community often report that their sexuality and/or gender is pathologized as the cause of their mental distress by uninformed mental health professionals (Somerville, 2014).

Bullying, experiencing anti-LGBTQ+ rhetoric from family, friends and in their place of worship and a lack of representation or normalization of their identities all contribute to trauma and the internalized homophobia/transphobia that is felt across the LGBTQ+ community and within it (Ghassemlou, 2018). Though we have undoubtedly made progress in our society in regards to LGBTQ+ acceptance, Western society is still a default heteronormative one. Furthermore, the default is to be able bodied, neurotypical, white, middle class and so on, based on individual circumstances and culture. Unfortunately, it is common that identifying as LGBTQ+ can lead to familial rejection (Albert Kennedy Trust, 2015). For a disabled LGBTQ+ person, this lack of care and financial support can be even more devastating, manifesting in the kind of complexity that art therapists are often called on to work with.

Acute medical-related trauma

Intersex is an LGBTQ+ identity that refers to the 1 per cent of the population whose biology does not fit within the sex binary. Intersex babies and children with ambiguous genitalia may be surgically 'corrected'; referred to in the community as intersex genital mutilation (IGM). Intersex adults often report high levels of medical trauma, sexual issues and an elevated rate of seeking transition-related healthcare (Creighton, 2001; Sainty, 2016).

LGBTQ+ people are also more at risk of acute medical trauma if they have undergone conversion therapy. Conversion therapy – the attempt to change someone's sexuality or gender within a heteronormative medical model – is an extreme manifestation of a cultural desire to 'fix' LGBTQ+ people, and many former clients report suicidal ideation and trauma (Drescher, Schroeder & Shidlo, 2001). This draws parallels to applied behavioural analysis (ABA), a type of therapy designed for autistic children and adults. Those who have been through the process often report enduring psychological damage (Devita-Raeburn, 2016). ABA is intended to make autistic children appear 'normal' and rejects the neurodiversity model which asserts that autism and other neurodiversities are conditions to be cured or masked. Ole Ivar Lovaas, the founder of ABA, was also involved in the Feminine Boy Project, where he developed interventions to change young people's gender identity and presentation (Gibson & Douglas, 2018).

These examples highlight the possibility that LGBTQ+ clients may experience multiple acute traumas when their intersecting identities are 'treated' or 'fixed' to better fit within heteronormative and neurotypical medical models. Other specific issues affecting people within this intersect are explored below.

Safe spaces

Many disabled people have difficulty navigating LGBTQ+ venues and do not experience them as safe spaces. In LGBTQ+ activism circles, a safe space is defined as being a place that is physically safe, allows freedom of expression and freedom from intrusive questions, societal expectations and being 'outed'. This mirrors the concept of therapeutic safe space, particularly the desire for freedom of expression and psychological safety. Currently, LGBTQ+ social spaces are often limited to clubs and bars (Desmond, 2019), making them inaccessible for individuals with social anxiety or in recovery from addiction, those with sensory processing issues or histories of trauma. In addition, there are issues with physical access, including day spaces and Pride festivals, communicating to disabled LGBTQ+ people that they are not welcomed by their own community and adding to their potential isolation.

Hypermasculinity, queer men and sexuality

Gay, bi and trans (GBT+) men face pressure to look and present in a hypermasculine and physically fit way. Thus, GBT+ disabled men are at particular risk of ostracization from mainstream gay culture, based on their looks (Arana, 2019). Hypersexualization can also be damaging to asexual men and any GBT+ man facing issues around sexuality, such as impotence or abuse-related trauma. This culture has led to high levels of eating disorders and drug abuse in GBT+ men (Guasp, 2015). The desexualization of disabled bodies and hypersexualization of LGBTQ+ identities illuminate an unfortunate reality that disabled LGBTQ+ people face (Martino, 2017).

Authentic gender presentations

Neurodiverse trans people may have to adjust to bodily changes that may trigger strong sensory discomfort, such as hair growth and weight changes (Cooper & Jackson, 2019), as medical transition can strain the physical and mental health of the transitioning person, even when able bodied and neurotypical. Genderqueer and transmasculine people may also flatten their chests with specialist underwear, known as binding. Many chronic pain conditions experienced by those assigned female at birth may cause pain in the upper body that can prevent binding altogether, and binding itself may cause physical problems. In addition, gender confirmation surgeries are usually major procedures requiring general anaesthetic and, therefore, unreachable for many trans people with existing medical conditions.

Visually and hearing impaired

Being visually impaired and trans may also make presenting authentically and 'passing' more difficult, an aspect of identity that can be vital to a trans person's mental health and physical safety (Anderson *et al.*, 2020). Deaf or hard of hearing transgender individuals may also have trouble accessing speech therapy and struggle to adjust to a new tone and timbre of voice.

In all these cases, disability is not a linear cause of bad mental health, but a complex obstacle to wellbeing, psychological contentment and the driver of anxiety in the form of gender dysphoria, the mental distress caused by a mismatch between the body and gender identity.

LGBTQ+ and the institution

LGBTQ+ people suffer detrimental attitudes within health and social care settings, with 24 per cent of person-facing staff reporting hearing negative attitudes from colleagues regarding LGBTQ+ patients (Somerville, 2014). Thus, trans patients are disproportionately affected by distress in medical settings: from issues such as single gender wards, misgendering during medical appointments, difficulties in accessing medical records and achieving appropriate care across modalities, as well as the conflation of their medical issues with their gender identity – a phenomenon known as 'trans broken arm syndrome' (Payton, 2015).

Older LGBTQ+ people outside the clinical population are already at high risk of loneliness (Kuyper & Fokkema, 2010) due to difficulty finding peers, relationships and acceptance within their own generation. This may be exacerbated by institutions that do not recognize LGBTQ+ relationships. Even after death, trans people may be buried under the wrong name and gender. Biological families may keep partners from funerals, in an attempt to keep the deceased 'closeted' (Bristowe, Marshall & Harding, 2016), a practice that illustrates the difficulties LGBTQ+ palliative patients and mourners may face.

For adults and adolescents with learning difficulties, there is an equal occurrence of being LGBTQ+ as that of the general population (Martino, 2017), and this includes those living in residential care. LGBTQ+ identities are often seen as 'difficult to know' or a phase, so an LGBTQ + person with a learning difficulty may be particularly vulnerable to misconception and adverse treatment.

LGBTQ+ and education

Currently, a child is defined as trans if they are 'persistent, insistent and consistent' about stating their identity (Meier & Harris, 2015). Some transgender people report knowing they were trans from the moment they had an understanding of gender itself, and transgender children are as sure of their gender identity as their cisgender peers. Yet damaging misconceptions about coming out as trans before puberty continue. The transition process for a prepubescent child is largely social. Pre-teens may use puberty blockers to prevent them experiencing the wrong puberty and the associated trauma, an intervention which is reversible. Forcing a transgender child to stay closeted and live as their assigned gender can be extremely psychologically damaging, and parents have reported these children expressing suicidal thoughts before being allowed to live authentically. Nevertheless, believing that these interventions are non-reversible, and consequently detrimental if the child changes their mind, is a common misconception. LGBTQ+ young people are also coming out more frequently at secondary school, a common place of work for many art therapists. A recent study showed having just one supportive adult in the life of an LGBTQ+ teenager can reduce their chances of attempting suicide by 40 per cent (Trevor Project, 2019). While there is progress, the rights of trans children to access healthcare remain contentious and are being discussed in the UK Parliament at the time of writing (Parson, 2020).

Adaptations to art therapies clinical practice

Music

In my experience, many LGBTQ+ clients may initially resist improvisation. To support them in finding their way, I may use small models and art materials and encourage the use of simple, percussive instruments that can provide additional sensory benefit. Clients of all ages are drawn to the ocean drum, a circular drum with a clear lid and metal beads inside. Adults are also drawn to the kalimba, a smoothed-out coconut shell with flat metal keys that are triggered with your thumbs. One client in my neurodiverse trans group described our work as 'musical stimming', a way of being free with the instruments without the pressure to make 'correct' tonal music. 'Stimming' is a term for the calming movements or vocal noises some autistic people make, often with their hands, in order to self-regulate (Deweerdt, 2020a). Making sounds, without pressure or expectation to create 'proper' music, is a key theme in music therapy. Another client described taking piano lessons age two, and insisting on having the 'correct recipe' (sheet music). This client refused to use the keyboard for this reason, but was happy strumming the cello or using the ocean drum. The use of simple instruments, and an initial discussion with the client about the value of working musically, seems to benefit this particular client group.

Therapeutic alliance

Becoming an art therapist requires serious financial investment. Economic privilege may be one of the complex reasons why the profession is dominated by white, middle-class practitioners (Talwar, 2010). However, a client may not be eager to form an alliance with a therapist who looks like other medical professionals and may represent a field that has harmed them in the past and does not share a lived experience. I reflected earlier on the importance of exploring the client's conscious or unconscious associations regarding who the therapist may symbolically represent and the resulting transference, in a psychodynamic and politically informed framework. Also vital is the acknowledgement of the client's current lived experience, in relation to societal prejudices, disability and LGBTQ+ intersects, as well as possible histories of rejection from parental and authority figures.

It is not assumed by activists that everyone working therapeutically will be well informed about struggles of all marginalized communities. However, the process of understanding issues of difference and validating an LGBTQ+ client's identity, even if they self-identify using language that feels unfamiliar, demonstrates the same willingness, respect and empathy that is expected in ethical practice with all clients, including those who are non-verbal or from differing cultural backgrounds.

Pronouns

When requesting gender identity in referral or on equality forms, an inclusive option is to leave an open question, as opposed to offering multiple choices. This ensures that non-binary people are not excluded from data and prohibits unnecessary distress for the client. An option for 'transgender' may also cause distress or offence. Transgender is an adjective, a description of how your gender relates to your sex/gender assigned at birth, and is not a separate category. On my own private practice referral forms, I ask for the client's pronouns and do not ask them to define gender. I introduce myself noting my own pronouns and use these on my email signature, normalizing the experiences for the client and perhaps providing additional reassurance. I also ask the client how I should refer to them, in recognition that many people do not identify by their legal name. This may be particularly validating for trans clients.

Self-diagnosis

Before we begin therapy, I ask potential clients to state any relevant diagnoses and conditions they may suspect they have, but are not diagnosed with.

The delays in treatment available in the NHS are widely known, including delays in diagnosis and appropriate care. For adults and young people seeking diagnosis and care for chronic pain issues, years can pass between first talking to a doctor about symptoms and finally receiving an appropriate diagnosis. The clinical vignette below discusses a client, November, with undiagnosed neurodiversity and Ehlers Danlos syndrome (EDS). This client expressed great appreciation at being able to list their self-diagnoses. They found it empowering.

EDS is a disorder of collagen categorized by hypermobility, chronic pain and a range of medical issues throughout the body. A UK study suggested an average of 19 years for diagnosis (Gillies, 2017). A leading expert in EDS, Professor Rodney Grahame (2015), stated: 'No other condition in the history of modern medicine has been neglected in such a way as Ehlers-Danlos syndrome.' EDS, along with a number of other chronic pain and musculoskeletal issues, disproportionately affects people assigned female at birth (Hunt & Fish, 2008). The combination of invisible symptoms such as pain, and the unconscious bias against women and LGBTQ+ people in the medical field, may have led to this neglect and lack of appropriate diagnoses.

For autism, the adult pathway to diagnosis can take years, with an average wait time of 30 weeks (Gov.UK, 2018). Receiving proper gender care under a gender identity clinic can take up to three years, a situation recently referred to as 'waiting list hell' (BBC, 2020). Thus, LGBTQ+ disabled clients may spend years waiting for lifesaving, or life-changing, care. As art therapists, enquiring about self-diagnoses recognizes this experience and trusts that some clients are the experts on their own bodies and minds, providing validation and reassurance that may have been missing in previous experiences with health professionals. The recognition of undiagnosed conditions is also grounded in person-centred therapeutic practice and the therapist as advocate. Person-centred therapy allows us to work with the client's assumptions about themselves and promote a shared understanding of truth. Where we may be working with fantasy or delusion, there is a case for assessing this and guiding the client to explore different perspectives. Nevertheless, in the case of a client's lived experience of undiagnosed health conditions or neurodiversity, we can combine the concepts of person-centred practice and client advocacy in a way that can be beneficial to the therapeutic process.

Clinical vignette 1: Working with medicalized trauma

November was looking for support in addressing childhood issues and becoming a more successful and self-empowered adult. They self-referred via the Pink Therapy Registry, an independent group for gender, sex and relationship diverse (GSRD) therapists. November wanted to discuss their childhood experiences of living with a neglectful father and a loving, but mentally ill, mother. They expressed being unable to eat the food their father and their school provided, due to what they described as sensory issues. At weekends, however, they would go straight to the supermarket with their mother and eat excessively. This began what November described as a lifelong pattern of disordered eating and an 'all or nothing' approach to satisfying their needs. November brought this to therapy with the aim of managing and understanding this unhealthy behaviour pattern.

November has experienced the fatphobic practice of being told to lose weight before receiving appropriate medical investigation, despite a long and complex history of disordered eating. This practice can be deadly (Royal College of Surgeons, 2016), yet it is one that many LGBTQ+ and disabled people report facing, as both groups are at an elevated risk of high weight due to stress and poverty (Colledge *et al.*, 2015). November had not sought a referral to a gender identity clinic, as they felt their weight would prevent them from being given access to the hormones and the gender-confirming surgery they desired. November is transmasculine, but unable to bind due to suspected Ehlers Danlos syndrome diagnosed in other family members. This client expressed frequently looking to the medical professions for support and answers, but being sent home either without support, or with potentially dangerous and unhelpful advice. November reported that they were rejected from an NHS mental health service due to their disordered eating. They were told they were 'too complex' and beyond the scope of the service. This discussion was in the context of them trying to address their high levels of anxiety around medical appointments, anxiety that had led to hospitalizations in the past. During therapy, I suggested that the medical neglect might mirror the neglect they experienced growing up. November grew more aware over time that this treatment was abusive and this helped them rationalize their medical anxiety and contextualize some of its root causes.

November was able to make a GP appointment and received a rheumatology referral following this intervention. While preparing for the appointment, November discussed the fear of being sent away with only advice to lose weight. Although they felt they would be able to discuss their mobility issues with a medical professional, sharing mental health issues with a new person seemed more difficult. I reassured November, and provided them with a letter describing their clinical history of disordered eating, recommending that weight loss should not form the primary aspect of their treatment plan. This allowed me to advocate for my client, using my clinical knowledge and privileged status, and support them in an anxiety-provoking situation outside therapy.

Clinical vignette 2: Working creatively

When I first worked with November, they were reluctant to improvise and so we discussed how the music could be used to support them. November feared 'getting it wrong', a common theme in improvisational music therapy. The communal trauma or sense of 'wrongness' that many LGBTQ+ disabled people share can lead to adults striving for perfection, turning their inability to achieve this inward in destructive ways. November is from a therapeutic art background, and described how they were struggling to make art in their free time, due to a lack of confidence in their ability to make 'good' art – similar to their fear of making the 'wrong' music. I recognized a need to depressurize the creative process, so we tried ways of creating art without a sense of permanency, responding to November's current struggles with art-making. I provided November with large heart-shaped glitter, which they arranged into a human-like figure that moved through various poses (Figure 13.1).

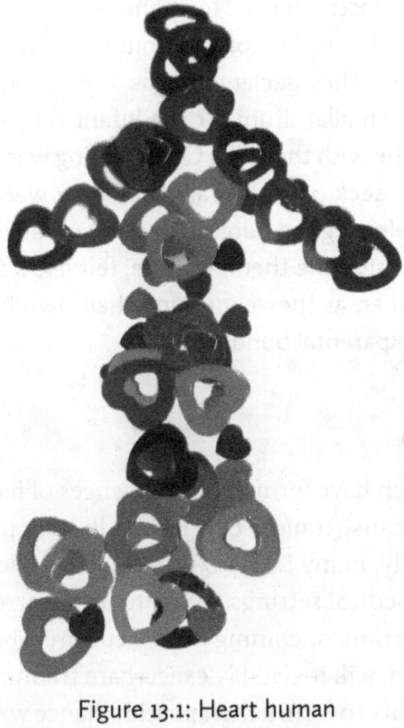

Figure 13.1: Heart human

November chose to take only a 'mental picture' of the resulting piece and permitted that I dismantle it post-session. They have since been creating digital art that shares the same ephemeral and incomplete qualities. Although trained as a music therapist, I believe allowing clients to work imaginatively in any way they choose enables acclimatization to non-verbal, creative methods of communication.

Sometime after this, November expressed a desire to be loud with the instruments and to fill the space in a safe way. This was a significant moment in their therapy, as they realized the lack of ownership over space they had as a child. They were able to reflect on how this pattern of behaviour had continued into adulthood and shaped their current need to be more present and self-assured in their daily life. Building on this moment of loudness, I encouraged November to shout their positive affirmations in the sessions, addressing the need to take up space through volume, while simultaneously promoting a positive self-image.

The creative process seemed a key element to this therapeutic journey, so I addressed the residual fear of music-making by allowing November to explore the instruments without judgement. Having noticed the common fear of 'getting it wrong' with my GSRD client base, I put aside the more difficult instruments, notably the keyboard, and November worked through a box of almost entirely percussive instruments and some simple wind instruments. November voiced reassurance that they would not be asked to make 'complex' music and was particularly drawn to the ocean drum. They declared it was 'the best thing ever' and went on to purchase a smaller drum for the infant they co-parent, with the intention of playing with the child. Co-parenting was a strong motivation for November to seek out a therapist, as they wanted to be a 'grown up', capable of being a good parent. To embrace an instrument, and use music-making outside the therapy space, felt like a significant development for November, as they continued their own healing and creative play to develop a parental bond.

Conclusion

LGBTQ+ people often have formative experiences of feeling and being the 'outsider'. This may cause trauma that results in poor physical and mental health. Consequently, many LGBTQ+ disabled people have experienced further trauma in medical settings. Being neurodiverse and having experienced familial rejection, or coming from a culture where being LGBTQ+ is illegal or forbidden, will inevitably exacerbate trauma. This trauma may affect the client's ability to form a therapeutic alliance with the art therapist, particularly if they are perceived as heterosexual, cisgender and perhaps unable to understand the lived experience of those under stress related to gender, sexuality or disability, which is often exacerbated by prejudicial social norms. These difficulties can be addressed through theoretically informed practice and practical adaptations, which may include the following:

- Recognizing who or what the therapist may represent personally and psychosocially, and the resulting transference, through a psychodynamic framework.
- Maintaining a strong person-centred framework that allows for cultural and generational differences to be addressed.
- Recognizing and understanding unconscious biases about the LGBTQ+ and disabled communities through an intersectional framework.
- Using the art form to build trust, gain understanding of the client and allow the client to be creative without feeling pressure to perform/produce 'high-quality' creative products.
- Acknowledging the client's use of unfamiliar terms, self-educating if necessary, addressing the client based on their wishes, and encouraging colleagues to do the same.

By using intersectionally informed practice, reflecting on our own unconscious biases as practitioners and understanding the complex intersects of where our clients' identities meet, we can recognize that their experience of identity is shaped as a multiple minority, but is much more than the sum of their parts. We can also raise personal and societal awareness as practitioners, engage in an ongoing process of self-education and validate the client as much as possible. As therapists, we must reassure our clients that every effort is being made to understand them and that we are striving to avoid the mistakes other health professionals may have made in the past. We must work with this reality, and continue to inform practice, challenge unconscious biases and provide positive and beneficial therapeutic experiences for everybody.

References

Albert Kennedy Trust (2015). *LGBT Youth Homelessness: A National Scoping of Cause, Prevalence, Response and Outcomes*. London: Albert Kennedy Trust.

Anderson, D., Irwin, J., Brown, A. & Grala, C. (2020). 'Your picture looks the same as my picture': An examination of passing in transgender communities. *Gender Issues, 37*(5), 44–60.
Arana, G. (2019). Gay men's obsession with masculinity is hurting their mental health. Them. Accessed 01/02/20 at www.them.us/story/gay-men-masculinity-mental-health.
Bachman, C. & Gooch, B. (2018). *LGBT in Britain: Trans Report*. London: Stonewall.
BBC (2020). Transgender people face NHS waiting list 'hell'. Accessed 02/02/20 at www.bbc.co.uk/news/uk-england-51006264.
Boggan, C., Grzanka, P. & Bain, C. (2018). Perspectives on queer music therapy: A qualitative analysis of music therapists' reactions to radically inclusive practice. *Journal of Music Therapy, 54*(4), 375–404.
Bradley, A. & Potter, A. (2017). *Women most at risk of experiencing partner abuse in England and Wales: Years ending March 2015 to 2017*. Office for National Statistics.
Bristowe, K., Marshall, S. & Harding, R. (2016). The bereavement experiences of lesbian, gay, bisexual and/or trans* people who have lost a partner: A systematic review, thematic synthesis and modelling of the literature. *Palliative Medicine, 30*(8), 730–744.
Brown, L. X. Z. (2016). Gendervague: At the Intersection of Autistic and Trans Experiences. National LGBTQ Taskforce Blog. Accessed 10/04/20 at www.aane.org/gendervague-intersection-autistic-trans-experiences.
Colledge, L., Hickson, F. & Reid, D. (2015). Poorer mental health in UK bisexual women than lesbians: Evidence from the UK 2007 Stonewall Women's Health Survey. *Journal of Public Health, 37*(3), 427–437.
Coombes, E. (2019). 'Re: Training.' Message to Naomi Rowe. 15 March. Email.
Cooper, K. & Jackson, T. (2019). Autism and Gender Identity. Autism, Gender and Sexuality Conference, 17 May. National Autistic Society, Leeds.
Creighton, S. (2001). Surgery for intersex. *Journal of the Royal Society of Medicine, 94*(5), 218–220.
Crenshaw, K. (1989). Demarginalizing the intersection of race and sex: A Black feminist critique of antidiscrimination doctrine, feminist theory and antiracist politics. *University of Chicago Legal Forum, 1*(8), 139–167.
Desmond, B. (2019). For years, gay bars were a vital refuge – but it's time we challenged the idea that LGBT spaces are synonymous with drinking. *Prospect Magazine*. Accessed 02/02/20 at www.prospectmagazine.co.uk/politics/gay-bars-alcohol-lgbt-alcoholfree-spaces.
Devita-Raeburn, E. (2016). The controversy over autism's most common therapy. Spectrum. Accessed 10/12/20 at www.spectrumnews.org/features/deep-dive/controversy-autisms-common-therapy.
Deweerdt, S. (2020a). Repetitive behaviors and 'stimming' in autism, explained. Spectrum News. Accessed 04/02/2020 at www.spectrumnews.org/news/repetitive-behaviors-and-stimming-in-autism-explained.
Deweerdt, S. (2020b). Autistic burnout, explained. Spectrum News. Accessed 02/04/20 at www.spectrumnews.org/news/autistic-burnout-explained.
Drescher, A., Schroeder, M. & Shidlo, A. (2001). *Sexual Conversion Therapy: Ethical, Clinical and Research Perspectives*. New York, NY: Haworth Medical Press.
Ghassemlou, P. (2018). LGBT suicide and the trauma of growing up gay. Psych Central. Accessed 03/03/20 at https://psychcentral.com/lib/lgbt-suicide-and-the-trauma-of-growing-up-gay.
Gibson, M. F. & Douglas, P. (2018). Disturbing behaviors: Ole Ivar Lovaas and the queer history of autism science. *Catalyst: Feminism, Theory, Technoscience, 4*(2), 1–28.
Gillies, T. (2017). *Rare Disease Scotland: Progress Report*. Scottish Government Publication.
Gov.UK (2018). *Autism Self-Assessment Exercise 2018: Executive Summary*. UK Government Publication. Accessed 01/05/20 at www.gov.uk/government/publications/autism-self-assessment-framework-exercise/executive-summary.
Grahame, R. (2015). EDS – Past, Present & Future. EDNF Learning Conference, 13–15 August. Ehlers Danlos National Federation, Baltimore, MD.
Guasp, A. (2015). *Gay and Bisexual Men's Health Survey*. London: Stonewall.
Gupta, A. & Silman, A. (2004). Psychological stress and fibromyalgia: A review of the evidence suggesting a neuroendocrine link. *Arthritis Research and Therapy, 6*(3), 98–106.

Heylens, G., Aspelagh, L., Dierickx, J., Baetens, K. *et al.* (2018). The co-occurrence of gender dysphoria and autism spectrum disorder in adults: An analysis of cross-sectional and clinical chart data. *Journal of Autism and Developmental Disorders, 48*(6), 2217–2223.

Hillier, A., Gallop, N., Mendes, E., Tellez, D. *et al.* (2020). LGBTQ+ and autism spectrum disorder: Experiences and challenges. *International Journal of Transgender Health, 21*(1), 98–110.

Hunt, R. & Fish, J. (2008). *Prescription for Change: Lesbian and Bisexual Women's Health Check.* London: Stonewall.

Kuyper, L. & Fokkema, T. (2010). Loneliness among older lesbian, gay, and bisexual adults: The role of minority stress. *Archive of Sex Behaviour, 39*(5), 1171–1180.

Martino, A. S. (2017). Cripping sexualities: An analytic review of theoretical and empirical writing on the intersection of disabilities and sexualities. *Sociology Compass*, 11(5), e12471.

Meier, C. & Harris, J. (2015). *Fact Sheet: Gender Diversity and Transgender Identity in Children.* Washington DC: American Psychological Association.

Parson, V. (2020). Liz Truss reveals 'shocking' plan to remove healthcare for trans youth, slammed as an 'extraordinary' attack on equality. Pink News. Accessed 25/04/20 at www.pinknews.co.uk/2020/04/23/liz-truss-trans-rights-gender-recognition-act-reform-healthcare-puberty-blockers-backlash.

Payton, N. (2015). Feature: The dangers of trans broken arm syndrome. Pink News. Accessed 03/03/19 at www.pinknews.co.uk/2015/07/09/feature-the-dangers-of-trans-broken-arm-syndrome.

Royal College of Surgeons England (2016). *Smokers and Overweight Patients: Soft Targets for NHS Savings?* London: Royal College of Surgeons.

Russo, F. (2018). The costs of camouflaging autism. Spectrum News. Accessed 03/03/20 at www.spectrumnews.org/features/deep-dive/costs-camouflaging-autism.

Sainty, L. (2016). Largest ever survey of intersex Australians shows high rates of suicide, poverty. Buzzfeed News. Accessed 14/01/20 at www.buzzfeed.com/lanesainty/largest-ever-survey-of-intersex-australians-shows-high-rates#.gib2WPEaNk.

Somerville, C. (2014). Unhealthy Attitudes: The treatment of LGBT people within health and social care. YouGov and Stonewall.

Talwar, S. (2010). An intersectional framework for race, class, gender, and sexuality in art therapy. *Art Therapy, 27*(1), 11–17.

The Trevor Project (2019). The Trevor Project Research Brief: Accepting adults reduce suicide attempts among LGBTQ youth.

Wenn, L. (2019). Autism and Gender Identity. Autism, Gender and Sexuality Conference, 17 May. National Autistic Society, Leeds.

Wigram, T., Pedersen, I. N. & Bonde, L.O. (2002). *A Comprehensive Guide to Music Therapy.* London: Jessica Kingsley Publishers.

Chapter 14

On the Outskirts: Founding an Intersectional Feminist Art Therapy Charity

NOA YEHESKEL BAUM, GILLIAN W. DATLEN,
— CORRINA EASTWOOD AND CHARLOTTE ELLISTON —

Introduction

An intersectional and feminist therapeutic approach inherently questions how art therapy responds to the needs of clients and communities in the context of complex societal, political and organizational structures. It explores beyond the individual and the family, privileging the voice of the client as expert, and prioritizing examinations of power as a relational entity. Acknowledging the intersecting and multifaceted nature of client identity and social location, as well as societal, structural inequality, supports psychodynamic thinking, informs the transference relationship and deepens self-reflexive use of the countertransference. In addition, it encourages robust exploration and challenges the impact of organizational and institutional policy driven agendas, which often contain and guide therapeutic work.

Intersectionality was first conceived within the context of autonomous grassroots movements, organizing from social change perspectives and addressing social inequalities (Carastathis, 2016; Collins & Bilge, 2016). Promoting the need for a synergy of ideas and action, this chapter will document some aspects of the launch of a small London-based art therapy charity, Outskirts, founded on intersectional, feminist values and as an act of social action. It will illustrate the ways in which a vision of art therapy meeting social action and activist-therapist work can be mobilized. Viewed through a lens of intersectional organizational thinking, the challenges and potential of art therapy practice to embed and adapt to the unique and complex needs of differing client groups and communities are considered alongside the conception of mission and ethos, partnership working, recruitment, therapeutic approach and evaluation. This chapter encompasses reflections from women who have contributed to the formation of Outskirts and includes client feedback and learning capture.

On the Outskirts and radical caring: A founder/director perspective – Corrina Eastwood

The idea of therapeutically difficult-to-reach communities extends to all communities that do not comfortably fit within socially dominant narratives of trauma and its 'treatment'. Considering the social imperative in art therapy research in her keynote speech at the International Art Therapy Practice/Research Conference in 2019, Lynn Kapitan spoke of the importance of acknowledging pain and trauma as socially constructed, and that as art therapists we can be limited in our explorations of what can help, viewed solely from Western perspectives. Kuri (2007) notes the way in which art therapy is rooted in White European ways of knowing and how practising from intersectional frameworks facilitates critical thought surrounding pre-existing knowledge and assumptions about self and other.

As a Romani Gypsy woman from the Gypsy, Romani and Traveller (GRT) community, I have often found myself at ethnic and gendered intersects of marginalization. My work is influenced by the ways in which Romanichal women may suffer oppression doubly, from within and outside their communities (Corradi, 2018). Outskirts was founded in response to the ways in which conceptions of mental ill-health, trauma and 'treatment' are predominantly formed within White, Eurocentric, patriarchal, cishet-normative traditions of normal versus abnormal, which impacts on the fabric of many 'helping' organizations and their approaches.

Central to Outskirts' values and ethos is the acknowledgement that identity and social location are historically specific and socially constructed and that related oppressions operate at both macro and micro levels (Weber, 1998). Such oppressions need to be scrutinized to enable greater ethically informed insight into the experiences of clients seeking support. Important to mission is the concept that political organizing can be seen as a radical type of community care, relevant to art therapeutic practice that supports individual clients at macro levels. This enables learning capture along with the ongoing assessment of organizational structures, advocating for clients and decolonizing the non-profit (Ravichandran, 2019) through radical caring methodologies (Rudrappa, 2004). Such an approach can challenge reductive perceptions of client demographics, implementing intersectional approaches to administrative, managerial and therapeutic interactions with clients and staff. Hocoy (2007) notes the boundaries of Western constructions of self and how this can obscure the intrinsic interrelatedness of therapeutic work and social action: 'doing clinical work that is cognizant of the societal implications *is* social action, and being politically active *is* doing therapy; these activities are understood to be interrelated processes' (Hocoy, 2007, p.29).

Outskirts' founding principles have been the formation of a therapeutic approach that 'includes the exploration of external realities impacting on an individual's experience, as well as the personal' (Eastwood, 2019, p.5), and outlining practice and providing supervision that is 'continually concerned with power, power imbalances and misuses, and its manifestations in the form of privilege' (ibid). This practice guidance incorporates political and societal concerns, while working from psychodynamic foundations. Working closely in partnership with organizations maintains art therapy practice that is conceived within the wider complexity of which it is a part, acting creatively and complementing other existing forces of change (Hocoy, 2007). This enables engagement with clients alongside utilizing intersectional approaches to assessment, including careful consideration of each individual's experiences and trauma, and engages clients who may otherwise not be able to access therapeutic support.

In context: A trustee perspective – Charlotte Elliston

Intersectionality has always felt like an essential framework to work within. As a woman from a working-class background rooted in East London, and the first of my immediate family to study at university, I have witnessed the need for intersectional feminist thinking in my education, and careers as an art practitioner and cultural administrator. Outskirts' homepage outlines its intersectional feminist ethos: 'Outskirts operates from a feminist perspective, valuing the contribution of all members of society equally and understanding the various different types of oppression many people face' (Outskirts, n.d.). This reflects Erin Kuri's definition that 'Intersectionality focuses on deconstructing how social identity and inequality (specifically racism) simultaneously shape one another, creating layered forms of oppression' (2007, p.118).

When Outskirts was founded in 2015, many of us working in arts organizations and charities were afraid for the future. With the first majority Conservative government elected in the UK since 1992, there were concerns that a move towards USA-style philanthropy models of funding (Battersby, 2015) combined with privitization models (Jones, 2015) would see the ruin of many arts organizations. Government policies of austerity were also seen to be negatively impacting women and other marginalized groups. Cuts to social housing rents led to cutbacks in provision of services, such as women's refuges for those fleeing domestic abuse (Foster, 2015). Cuts to local council budgets impacted the funding of smaller, more specialized services, such as those for BAME women which 'uniquely understand the situations they face' (Bates, 2015).

Since its formation, Outskirts has been awarded grants from Big Lottery Funds and through corporate funding initiatives. This is tempered by policies which are threatening many charities that offer support to the most disadvantaged. Reduced council budgets continue to disproportionately affect women, who are most likely to be public service users and carers (Reis, 2018). Cuts are currently impacting on BAME women's services in particular, and it has been shown time and again that reductions in public services impact these women more than any other demographic (Reis, 2018; Runnymede Trust, 2017).

A similar story of funding cuts is seen in the cultural sector. In a 2017 survey by ArtsProfessional, 85 per cent of organizations had lost, or were likely to lose, local authority funding (Hutchinson, 2017). Cuts to arts education are also expected to have a negative impact on those hoping to make a career in the cultural industries, from controversial curriculum changes (The Guardian, 2018), to centre-right think-tank Onward arguing for 'a reduction in low-value university degrees that deliver weak earnings for graduates and poor value for money for taxpayers' (Phillips, 2019). Their opinion decrees that the visual arts should be considered 'low-value' degrees.

Looking at the intersect of the arts and social care which Outskirts straddles, it is clear that the future holds challenges for the charity on two fronts. The therapy that Outskirts provides is an accredited form of psychotherapy and is founded in creative practice, requiring both a therapist's and an artist's skillset from its practitioners. It seems that the art world, already full of challenges for those who do not confirm to the 'somatic norm' of the White middle-class man (Brook, Taylor & O'Brien, 2019), is being made increasingly difficult to navigate for anyone who falls into the category of 'other'. Given that 'the very act of living in a society is bound up with a division between that which has value and that which does not' (O'Brien & Oakley, 2015, p.4), it seems clear that ongoing cuts to social services show that women, women of colour, disabled, working-class and LGBTQ+ women are not valued by our current government, making Outskirts' work with these groups even more vital.

Intersectional approaches to ethos and recruitment: A trustee perspective – Noa Yeheskel Baum

Working in charitable organizations, both as a psychotherapist and a service manager, I have witnessed, often silently, the systemic neglect of issues surrounding difference. As a clinical placement manager, I have been coordinating placements for students from various training backgrounds for many years, while working closely with numerous psychotherapy training bodies. It continues to be apparent that there is a significant lack in the discourse on difference. It seems that teams within therapy trainings are often resistant to a fundamental truth: that acknowledging issues of difference, potential prejudice, power and privileges is pertinent to psychotherapy. This omission in teaching also takes place where there is a majority White female, middle-class cohort. This truth in itself often remains unspoken, potentially indicative of unconscious defences and anxieties collectively held within the profession.

I have often reflected on the impact of the lack of considerations of difference from intersectional perspectives in the curriculum (Talwar, 2019). Without providing robust spaces for students to process and voice identity-related concerns, biases or traumas, how do we provide them with resources to manage difficult identity-related and ethical, clinical concerns? Psychotherapy trainees lacking thinking space to consider issues surrounding identity and subsequent societal positions, in a field where the primary concern is *people*, with the self being a fundamental tool in the use of concepts such as *countertransference*, continues to concern me.

As an Israeli woman living in England, I reflect on my own prejudice, biases and prejudgements. I know I must consider my social location and positions of power, and ethically challenge my internalized fears. I must challenge them from politically and personally informed places, from places of power, but also of trauma.

I was eight when the Gulf War began. We learned to hate and fear the Iraqi Muslims, while praying for American rescue. For me as a teenager, taking the bus was avoided, due to terror attacks on transport, leaving much trauma, followed by a harsh Israeli military response. I remember when I first arrived in the UK at the age of 22, fresh from military service, sitting on buses and trying hard to overcome my anxiety when people around me spoke in Arabic. The rule was obvious: stick to speaking in English in public places. This was due to both fear and guilt, as well as the worry of being targeted for our nation's actions towards displaced Palestinians. I can reflect now on the impact of my upbringing and culture on my internal world and of my identity-related fears and the complexities of feeling both oppressed and like the oppressor.

Years later, when I was training to become a psychotherapist, one of my peers was the daughter of Palestinian immigrants. It took her and me a long time to name our truth, and discuss its difficult impact on our experiences of each other. I had various uncomfortable thoughts: Would I be able to work with Muslim clients? How will my biases impact the therapy I will be offering? Are my own feelings of anger, guilt, hatred, distrust and remorse processed enough to work with this difference ethically? These anxieties were never voiced to my colleagues in training, and there was no curiosity from my training body in wondering about these issues with us. I experienced this lack of inquisitiveness as a lack of support, and wondered how one could be supported in something not seen or acknowledged (Crenshaw, 1989).

When I joined the board of trustees for Outskirts, I experienced a sense of relief related to a need for this acknowledgement. As mission, values, ethos and policy were built, the sense of possibility, of fully embracing the uncomfortable explorations of our own potential biases as practitioners, felt hopeful and important. I moved from 'silent witness' to what I refer to as an 'active practitioner' in response to Outskirts' ethos of considering therapeutic practice as part of social change activity. Here I will reflect on Outskirts' recruitment within intersectional frameworks.

A central part of the recruitment process has been to reflect on the encounters we as interviewers have with applicants, considering the intersecting ways in which our own identities and experiences may meet theirs. Given the integral role of intersectional thinking in shaping Outskirts' ethos, Corrina and I approached recruitment from the outset with exploration of our own intersecting identities, shaped by upbringing and culture. We also considered our relationship with one another, exploring collective ways in which relational and organizational dynamics impact on professional decision-making. Initially we asked ourselves: what makes us truly veer more towards one candidate rather than another? Is it realistic to aim to be 'objective' when decision-making? It felt important not to ignore these realities or, as is often the case with interviewing processes, to presume 'objectivity' is possible and disregard personal triggers that arise. For example, an interviewee with a strong accent evoked different associations for Corrina and myself. One of us felt captivated and could identify feelings of romanticism, while the other admitted associations of deprivation and violence.

Through recognizing and naming these thoughts and feelings honestly, we were able to reflect on their origins, and consider an applicant's work experience and response to interview questions around practice from greater intersectional and ethical perspectives. The ability to enter such conversation non-defensively, analysing judgements and recognizing blinkered spots, while supporting each other to think in self-reflexive ways, has been a vital component in the process of recruitment at Outskirts.

An art therapist perspective – Gillian W. Datlen

Before commencing work, the comprehensive induction to the Outskirts model revealed what I had been seeking, on a professional and personal level. I was eager to adopt the charity's perspective: valuing difference and intersectionality and analysing power differentials. This felt a positive shift away from models in which external realities such as social and political contexts were not acknowledged in a way I deemed containing, for my clients or for myself as a client of art therapy.

However, when approached about writing this chapter, I began to recognize my own confusion surrounding the definition of 'intersectionality'. I experienced an inability to think reflexively, which in hindsight may be a response to the continuing debate around the meaning and use of the term (Collins & Bilge, 2016). Furthermore, as a newly qualified art therapist, I realized intersectional theory was absent from my training. Talwar (2010) notes that art therapists have explored issues of difference in research, training and practice. However, I agree with her observation that issues of identity tend to be explored in isolation rather than as intersecting areas of difference. Intersectionality, albeit a 'progressive' term, appears not to have reached the field of art therapy.

After further exploration in supervision, it became apparent that I was often adopting an intersectional approach, but was not always conscious of doing so or adequately self-reflexive as to why. I questioned why I instinctively adopted this approach and what value this brought to the client in therapy. Describing time-limited art therapy, the following vignette may suggest some answers. This work took place as part of my work for Outskirts with a survivor of domestic violence (DV) whom I shall refer to as Stella.

Stella

The therapy took place in a refuge setting where Stella lived with her infant son, where we met within days of her arrival. She engaged easily, showing awareness of the factors that contributed to the abusive relationship she had felt so unable to leave. As a Black East African migrant, Stella found that financial pressures of living in an inner city, in a job where she was overqualified yet underpaid, meant that her relationship with her UK-resident partner progressed faster than she may have preferred. When co-habiting, Stella became pregnant and restrictions on her visa resulted in their marriage. On a spousal-visa, Stella became dependent on her husband on many levels, most predominantly financially. Alongside their mixed cultural expectations of her role as wife and mother, Stella believes this power imbalance was then exploited by her husband. She encountered various forms of abuse, most significantly psychological, leading to lowered self-esteem and isolation. It was fundamental for us to recognize her experiences as reflective of a much wider social frame and this seemed to ease the sense of shame we had been naming and exploring, and the personal responsibility Stella carried as we worked towards supporting her empowerment.

Essential in any therapeutic relationship, I held in mind our difference, aware of further power imbalances Stella may face in our relationship. I am a White, Scottish woman and come from a working-class background. I do not deny my privileges, including economic ones. Accessing free higher education in Scotland allowed me to become an educated professional, like Stella, and our shared level of education felt apparent to me. I also reflected on further shared experience; I myself am a survivor of DV. I did not disclose my experiences to Stella. I wanted to maintain a space focused on her experience. This felt important in response to her tendency to focus on the needs of others and in response to a potential maternal transference I had begun to notice. However, I explored this extensively in supervision, teasing out my personal experiences and their impact on clinical decisions. Despite shared experience, there also existed clear power imbalances in relation to our roles, race, culture and social circumstances. Stella shied away from such considerations, evidently uncomfortable. While I allowed Stella to direct sessions, I considered that recovery from abusive relationships must take place within the context of a healing relationship (Burt, 2012), hence the need to voice such power differentials.

When unable to verbalize feelings, Stella expressed herself through art-making. She hand-sculpted a clay head. I noticed Stella's natural skill and ability to capture something of identity, possibly celebrating the physicality of her features and richness of culture (Figure 14.1).

Stella dismissed these ideas, but linked the expression/pose to her need 'to hold her head high', regardless of circumstances. Here, it felt important to value Stella's thoughts more highly than my own, allowing a dialogue to open up around societal and cultural pressures on women, particularly mothers. We moved on to explore power relations between the sexes, a key component of feminist models (Hogan, 2012). I wondered whether our shared experiences as women allowed this conversation to take place more easily.

Figure 14.1: Clay head

After the clay had dried, the sculpture could not remain standing. Watching the weight cause the sculpture to fall down felt poignant. Stella identified with this, sharing her struggles. Though in a shared house with other families who had survived DV, Stella felt extremely isolated and was becoming increasingly depressed. She expressed relying heavily on her sessions, and talking dominated much of our time together. I was eager to understand why Stella was re-experiencing such isolation. Initially working in the transference, I considered the potential of Stella's past relationships to be affecting the present, yet felt this encouraged self-blame. However, considering psychosocial issues, Stella focused on new relationships such as the families within the refuge and the staff team. Having witnessed violence, Stella's son appeared to be externalizing his experiences through aggression, as were the other children (Mills & Kellington, 2012). Stella felt her son was unfairly held responsible and her parenting disproportionately criticized. This apparent blame in itself was a repetition of what Stella faced in her marriage, re-traumatizing her and making the refuge feel unsafe.

I felt Stella would benefit from the integration of psychoeducation into psychodynamic thinking, in keeping with the Outskirts model. We explored her 'freeze responses' to her son's behaviour (Van der Kolk, 2015) and Stella linked this to the recurrent trauma she had experienced. Compounding this was Stella's resistance to asserting herself with staff and co-residents. Stella identified the challenge of having a voice in relationships where she felt inferior. Examining each relationship, we uncovered the intertwining nature of race, class, gender and culture. As the only Black residents, I wondered whether Stella and her family felt discriminated against by co-residents who were predominantly not Black. Had her son already been unfavourably stereotyped? Voicing such possibilities brought relief for Stella. She too had wondered whether issues of race, consciously or unconsciously, were present in the difficulties. I felt saddened to hear Stella was unable to express these concerns in the refuge for fear of being perceived as 'playing the race card'. It seemed to reassure Stella to have these feelings validated and not dismissed in the context of psychodynamic work, where feelings of persecution related to past trauma could also be explored.

I wondered whether Stella felt adequately supported by staff. She did not. For me, this sparked an internal conflict. As a sessional therapist, I was not integrated in the staff team. I too was on the 'outskirts', bringing mixed feelings about my role. In a positive sense, Stella voiced her trust in the confidentiality of her sessions. However, it felt important to raise the unacknowledged refuge dynamics with staff and to advocate for Stella. I questioned my response in supervision in relation to my ability to bear and stay with the difficulties Stella brought. I felt powerless, my countertransference giving me a sense of Stella's isolation, past and present. Perhaps there was something collusive about my feelings or even an underlying motive for me; an unconscious attempt at being a 'white saviour' (Straubhaar, 2015)? This was explored both in supervision and with Stella, and the discomfort evoked was tolerated. I further reflected on my responsibility as a White art therapist to deconstruct the productions of White privilege and familiarize myself with concepts of intersectionality and decolonization (Hamrick & Byma, 2017). Following the end of the therapeutic work, I addressed some of the concerns transparently with the partnership organization following the end of therapeutic work, as an act of safeguarding, social action and advocacy.

Continuing dialogue surrounding power differences brought Stella increased confidence. Despite this, an ongoing challenge was the 'relentless criticism' Stella felt subjected to from staff. In a meeting about her son, Stella felt deeply disappointed that refuge staff, two Black women, had unfairly criticized her ability to parent without sufficient insight into her lived experience. I wondered whether their being Black heightened this disappointment. Given space to educate me, Stella stressed that a Black African, Black Caribbean and Black British woman's experiences are potentially different, particularly in their cultural beliefs surrounding gender roles, DV and parenting. Stella compared this difference to ongoing tensions between Scotland and England, based on historical conflict, seeking reassurance that I understood. I identified with her thoughts, particularly after my experience of being Scottish on a training course in England, where such differences or oppressions were denied and silenced. I was aware of the complex territory of our exploring sameness and difference, oppressions and privileges.

Although I did not voice this in our sessions, I noted in supervision the irony of my Scottish identity being seen in the context of allyship for Stella, when Scotland historically ran overseas slave colonies. This historical leap was hard to name, yet in many ways felt present in the enmeshment of our identities and considerations of imbalances of power and oppression. However, it is also possible that my personal, yet very different, experiences of denied oppression increased my level of empathy and that this could be felt and known by Stella. Our exploration of intersecting identities seemed containing and reassuring for her.

Intersectional thinking created in Stella an increased understanding of her experiences, naming an unnamed dimension and bringing some relief from the difficult dynamics she faced. Stella's voice had been heard and valued. From this, I have discovered the importance of intersectional approaches in raising an awareness of historical and current oppressions in the art therapist, as well as advocating self-reflexivity (Kuri, 2017; Talwar, 2010), power differentials and remaining with any discomfort surrounding privilege (Hamrick & Byma, 2017).

The Outskirts model acted as a container and framework for my existing focus in my work, with supervision usefully linking theory and practice. During my work with Stella, I reflected on my personal experiences to inform my practice, while integrating a perspective that included social and cultural difference of the client experience. As a survivor of DV, I used supervision to explore my own experiences in relation to my work with other survivors, ensuring ethical practice. My own art therapy has been important in the ongoing process of managing trauma. However, I have also encountered hurdles in challenging my therapist's denials of power differences. I have personally experienced the negative impact of this, which in turn has clarified my own practice. Using intersectional and feminist therapy perspectives informs my ongoing examination of my own intersecting identities, my clients' many social and cultural locations, and how these dimensions impact on art therapy practice.

Stella's evaluation methodology

Evaluation is vital in evidencing the impact of our work, but should also inform our insight into the lives and experiences of those we work with to guide future practice. In structuring methodologies to include potentially problematic existing social constructs such as diagnosis, or directing that which is deemed significant to measure, we continue to reinforce those constructs and potentially position the client as 'other'. Evaluation is led by a desire to acknowledge power imbalances between researcher and client-researcher, and be guided by the client's assessment of what therapy should respond to in their lives and what they perceive as problematic. A simplified version of Shapiro's Personal Questionnaire evaluates what each client identifies as problematic in their lives, and then measures change in these specific and client-tailored areas (see Table 14.1). Evaluation methodologies are built into the session structure, making space for exploration of identified 'problems'.

Stella: A client perspective

Stella requested to include her feedback statements alone in this chapter, declining the opportunity to provide further feedback.

Feedback statements provided by Stella:

> 'It has been helpful to have someone else voice the unspoken dynamics of power, abuse and discrimination.'
>
> 'Therapy has helped me through my current difficulties.'
>
> 'The refuge gives a lot of practical support but emotional support could be better.'

Table 14.1: Stella's personal questionnaire

Self-identified problems		Not at all 1	2	3	4	5	6	7	Variance
I feel powerless in relation to finances	START						6		−5
	END	1							
Others' reactions to my child's behaviour	START							7	−2
	END					5			
Loss of sleep to accommodate others	START							7	−2
	END					5			

Conclusion: Learning capture and the future

Challenges and successes were identified in this Outskirts pilot service. This chapter has explored the challenges in gaining funding for grassroots art therapy organizations and difficulties in partnership working when negotiating and holding practice accountable to intersectional and feminist thinking. Challenges in implementing feminist and intersectional approaches to managerial structures and clinical supervision have also arisen and been reflected on. A sense that there can be a tension between desires for egalitarian organizational structures, yet also for firm direction and containment, has been explored within staff dynamics, with some resolution and learning achieved. When considering power dynamics in supervisory relationships, Miller (2019) notes the grey areas of ethics that emerge as personal material arises and supervisees face particularly charged countertransference in relation to clients or supervisors. Attempts to create 'flattened' organizational structures while conceiving of therapist-activist work (Hocoy, 2007) should be carefully considered in relation to the tolerating and understanding of boundaries in the supervisor/supervisee relationship. Regardless of less hierarchical organizational structures, those that hold power or perceived authority are always ripe targets for projection (Miller, 2019). Therapist-activist work may well challenge traditionally held ideas of boundary transgression in the clinical supervisory or managerial relationship, with activist, political or creative identities being more visible or public to supervisees and clients alike. This can be particularly relevant when considering the use of online amplification and promotion of work and ideas. Careful consideration of the context and impact of facilitating 'power with others' type interactive dynamics with some supervisees, as opposed to more traditional 'power over' hierarchical structures (Miller, 2019), is important when considering containment and symbolic holding.

Learning was captured through evaluating patterns of client attendance of this pilot service, leading to insightful collaborative future planning with partner organizations. Linking the therapy service to existing support and awareness-raising groups offered by partner organizations has been assessed as a way of bridging identified existing gaps in emotional support. Positive qualitative client feedback has evidenced the value of intersectional feminist approaches to psychodynamic art therapy practice that have been illustrated in this chapter's case study. Psychoeducational interventions embedded in practice have also been evidenced as supportive and containing and have provided foundation for future planning of partnership working, conceptions of client empowerment and challenging social injustice. Critical client feedback has highlighted attendance issues, illustrating the difficulties faced by clients in relation to current lived experience and circumstance;

for example, finding ways to manage social care appointments and avoid sanctions related to accessing benefits and juggling childcare, while simultaneously exploring responses to and symptoms of trauma in art therapy. Childcare was provided by the partner organization and negotiated as part of the working contract. However, this still presented scheduling difficulties. Nevertheless, client feedback provided invaluable insight for service development, understanding of wider social and political contexts of client experience, and further exploration of the organizational embodiment of social change activity to empower.

Despite the challenges, Outskirts will strive to survive and thrive, as its clients do. The future is uncertain, but what remains clear is that survival relies on the need for services such as Outskirts to assimilate to the needs of individual clients, communities and existing forces for change, challenging the lines of deviation between the personal and the social and developing opportunities to greater advocate for and empower from intersectional perspectives.

Acknowledgements

Gillian would like to thank Stella for consent to write about her.

References

Bates, L. (2015). Women's support services save lives. So why is the Government cutting their funding? *The Guardian*, 30 November. Accessed 28/01/20 at www.theguardian.com/lifeandstyle/womens-blog/2015/nov/30/womens-support-services-save-lives-so-why-is-the-government-cutting-their-funding.

Battersby, M. (2015). What will happen to the arts under another Tory government? *The Independent*, 8 May. Accessed 28/01/20 at www.independent.co.uk/arts-entertainment/art/features/what-will-happen-to-the-arts-under-another-tory-government-10237076.html.

Brook, O., Taylor, M. & O'Brien, D. (2019). Art Workers, Inequality and the Labour Market: Values, Norms, and Alienation Across Three Generations of Artists. In A. Glauser, P. Holder, T. Mazzurana, O. Moeschler, V. Rolle & F. Schultheis (eds) *The Sociology of Arts and Markets: New Development and Persistent Patterns*. London: Palgrave.

Burt, H. (2012). Women, Art Therapy and Feminist Theories of Development. In S. Hogan (ed.) *Revisiting Feminist Approaches to Art Therapy*. New York, NY: Berghahn Books.

Carastathis, A. (2016). *Intersectonality: Origins, Contestations, Horizons*. Lincoln & London: University Press.

Collins, P. H. & Bilge, S. (2016). *Intersectionality: Key Concepts*. Cambridge: Polity Press.

Corradi, L. (2018). *Intersectional Politics, Alliances, Gender and Queer Activism*. London: Routledge.

Crenshaw, K. (1989). Demarginalizing the intersection of race and sex: A Black feminist critique of antidiscrimination doctrine, feminist theory and antiracist politics. *University of Chicago Legal Forum, 1*(8), 139–176.

Eastwood, C. (2019). *Outskirts Therapist Handbook*. London: Outskirts.

Foster, D. (2015). Cuts to women's refuges are a matter of life and death. *The Guardian*, 6 November. Accessed 28/01/20 at www.theguardian.com/housing-network/2015/nov/06/cuts-womens-refuges-violence-death-social-housing.

The Guardian (2018). British artists: Ebacc will damage creativity and self-expression. *The Guardian*, 8 May. Accessed 28/01/20 at www.theguardian.com/culture/2018/may/08/british-artists-ebacc-will-damage-creativity-and-self-expression.

Hamrick, C. & Byma, C. (eds) (2017). Know history, know self: Art therapists' responsibility to dismantle White supremacy. *Art Therapy, 34*(3), 106–111.

Hocoy, D. (2007). Art Therapy as a Tool for Social Change: A Conceptual Model. In K. Kaplan (ed.) *Art Therapy and Social Action*. London: Jessica Kingsley Publishers.

Hogan, S. (2012). Problems of Identity. In S. Hogan (ed.) *Revisiting Feminist Approaches to Art Therapy*. New York, NY: Berghahn Books.

Hutchinson, J. (2017). Arts professional survey highlights impact of local funding cuts on grassroots arts. 19 October. Accessed 28/01/20 at www.a-n.co.uk/news/arts-professional-survey-highlights-impact-local-funding-cuts-grassroots-arts.

Jones, J. (2015). Five more years of the Conservatives will reduce the arts to a national joke. *The Guardian*, 6 May. Accessed 28/01/20 at www.theguardian.com/artanddesign/jonathanjonesblog/2015/may/06/conservatives-arts-national-joke-gallery-cameron-britains-cultural-sector.

Kuri, E. (2007). Toward an ethical application of intersectionality in art therapy. *Art Therapy: Journal of the American Art Therapy, Association 34*(3), 118–122.

Miller, M. (2019). Multiple Roles in Art Therapy Supervision: Using El Duende One-Canvas Process Painting. In A. Maria & J. Rubin (eds) *Exploring Ethical Dilemmas in Art Therapy: 50 Clinicians for 20 Countries Share their Stories*. New York, NY: Routledge.

Mills, E. & Kellington, S. (eds) (2012). Using group art therapy to address the shame and silencing surrounding children's experiences of witnessing domestic violence. *International Journal of Art Therapy, 17*(1), 3–12.

O'Brien, D. & Oakley, K. (2015). *Cultural Value and Inequality: A Critical Literature Review*. Arts and Humanities Research Council. Accessed 28/01/20 at https://ahrc.ukri.org/documents/project-reports-and-reviews/cultural-value-and-inequality-a-critical-literature-review.

Outskirts (n.d.). *Home Page*. Outskirts. Accessed 28/01/20 at www.outskirtscharity.com.

Phillips, S. (2019). Art under threat: The growing crisis in higher education. Royal Academy, 20 March. Accessed 28/01/20 at www.royalacademy.org.uk/article/art-under-threat-crisis-britain-higher-education.

Ravichandran, S. (2019). Radical Caring and Art Therapy. In S. Talwar (ed.) *Art Therapy for Social Justice: Radical Intersections*. New York, NY: Routledge.

Reis, S. (2018). The impact of austerity on women in the UK. Women's Budget Group. Accessed 28/01/20 at www.ohchr.org/Documents/Issues/Development/IEDebt/WomenAusterity/WBG.pdf.

Rudrappa, S. (2004). Radical caring in an ethnic shelter: South Asian American women workers at Apna Ghar, Chicago. *Gender and Society, 18*(5), 588–609.

Runnymede Trust (2017). Intersecting inequalities: The impact of austerity on Black and minority ethnic women in the UK. Accessed 28/01/20 at www.runnymedetrust.org/uploads/Executive-Summary-Intersecting-Inequalities-October-2017.pdf.

Straubhaar, R. (2015). The stark reality of the 'White Saviour' complex and the need for critical consciousness: A document analysis of the early journals of a Freirean educator. *Compare: A Journal of Comparative and International Education, 45*(3), 381–400.

Van der Kolk, B. (2015). *The Body Keeps the Score: Brain, Mind, and Body in the Healing of Trauma*. New York, NY: Penguin Books.

Talwar, S. (2010). An intersectional framework for race, class, gender, and sexuality in art therapy. *Journal of the American Art Therapy Association, 27*(1), 11–17.

Talwar, S. (2019). *Art Therapy for Social Justice: Radical Intersections*. New York, NY: Routledge.

Weber, L. (1998). A conceptual framework for understanding race, class, gender and sexuality. *Psychology of Women Quarterly, 22*(1), 13–32.

Chapter 15

Traversing the Unknown: Group Analytic Approaches to Intersectionality within Tertiary Education

— HAYLEY BERMAN —

Introduction

This chapter proposes a methodology of psychoanalytically informed arts-based group work to address the deficit of meaningful engagement with intersectionality within higher education. This can be understood both as internalized psychic manifestations of fragmentation and separatism as well as externalized divisions within culture and society. It is written from a perspective that acknowledges that the 'forms of cultural life we are born into serve as enabling constraints – [that] shape us but do not determine us' (Dalal, 2008, p.19).

Examples are drawn from working with students and academics within informal and formal art psychotherapy programmes in the UK and South Africa to inform methods of best practice within higher education. It challenges ways of 'coming to know', embracing the need to decolonize academic curricula, thus enhancing opportunities for democratic engagement. This work focuses on the group as the 'developmentally needed object' (Winnicott, 1956) and the 'transformational object' (Bollas, 1987). This approach of collective inquiry, co-production and participatory visual research invites a return to community engagement as a way of addressing social inequality. The education and modelling of these core capabilities help to develop strong intrapsychic and intersubjective relationships within both training (educational) and therapeutic group formations.

Contributions of Freud, Bion, Winnicott and Bollas will be introduced alongside Foulkes, offering psychic textures that make up the qualities of an intersectional art psychotherapy practitioner. It is essential to note that these are all white men, who inform the majority of the foundations of psychoanalytic and group analytic thinking. As Mandikate powerfully asserts, 'psychoanalysis was born out of and into a world which constituted a "colonial mindset"' (2002, p.221). With this in mind, acknowledging the often-unconscious overt omissions, they have provided valuable contributions that have been and continue to be built on within a critical discourse. These theoretical foundations have been consciously adapted and re-contextualized within an intersectional framework, distilling the beauty and potential they offer in our work as therapists.

Included in the core capabilities is the creative capacity to bring both the analysis and integration of the 'here-and-now' and 'there-and-then' of the manifest and latent content of the group process to provide a robust, transformative and democratic model of practice.

Background

Engaging with the concept of 'intersectionality', as coined by Crenshaw (1989), presumes entering a realm of unresolvable paradoxes. Being invited to write a chapter in a book on privilege, power and politics immediately defines my identity. It suggests a presumption that as a practitioner and academic I come from a place of 'knowing', a place of privilege and power within the wider socio-political context.

I was born in 1968 in Johannesburg, South Africa, at the height of apartheid, into a society that was fundamentally constructed on the premise that being white allowed you access to privilege and power. Prejudice was the cornerstone of the white South African experience. I will refrain from trying to articulate the experience of a Black South African, as there is no homogenous experience. As Dalal contends, 'In its most extreme form any expression of a view about the other's culture, any stance short of complete acceptance, is construed as an act of imperialism' (2008, p.8).

While I am neither black nor economically or politically marginalized, I understand something about living in a context of extreme inhumane racist discrimination. Within this context, many white children were raised by their biological mothers, while also being raised by and having significant attachments to their carers/domestic workers who were often treated unequally and with far less value. I was one of those children. These beginnings informed my complicated identification with blackness rather than whiteness.

In reaction to the oppressive divisive apartheid segregation and enforced racism, and layered with the intergenerational trauma of my Jewish identity, I was propelled to provide alternative democratic 'potential spaces' (Winnicott, 1974). Together with the intergenerational transmission of trauma and the residue thereof, I carry traumatic moments in utero, infancy, childhood, adolescence and adulthood, as many of us do. Furthermore, perhaps being part of a fairly large family where the divisiveness of pairing was a prominent feature, I gravitated to the more democratic practice of a whole group that meets in a circle rather than a more singular or pairing approach to therapy.

I carry with me an acute sensitivity to inequality and injustice. I attempt to address this explicitly and implicitly within all the groups I encounter, as both participant and conductor. Working within multiple and diverse contexts within the complexity of identity, gender, race, class, culture, the notion of difference is a core component. This invites a continual need to name, make overt and engage with these issues. In my work, I encourage my clients to articulate feelings of otherness, sameness – belonging, not belonging and the opportunities for feeling part of, and not 'other' as a means of feeling contained. I wonder if opportunities to create our own histories and relationships with our identities are lost, when for example acronyms such as BAME (Black, Asian, Minority Ethnic) are created in the spirit of equality, yet may evoke an antithetical experience of othering.

Furthermore, I would concur with Bollas's understanding that:

> to affirm a special and separate identity, there [is] always the risk of losing sight of a wider and more embracing goal: a collective alliance of humanism with science, politics and religion, which might bring together millions of people with otherwise disparate cultures and identities, joining forces to face the challenge of the wider societal psychodynamic. (2018, p.124)

My history is complex, with threads of colonialism as well as a spirit of activism that flows in my veins and those of my ancestors. 'Colonialism was many things, but perhaps above all it was the march of absolute ignorance invading rather than understanding the human universe' (Bollas, 2015, p.540).

As a pioneer in art psychotherapy in South Africa, before group analysis was formally introduced, I founded a non-government organization, Lefika La Phodiso[1] (the rock of holding/healing in Sotho), to address the deficit of mental health resources within the complexity of a stressed and traumatized country post-apartheid in 1996 (Berman, 2019). Access to tertiary education was unavailable to the majority of the population, riddled with 'drivelling paternalism with regard to the blacks and the loathsome idea derived from Western culture that the black man [and woman] is impervious to logic and

1 www.lefikalaphodiso.co.za

the sciences' (Fanon, 1967, p.130). In response to this, and in collaboration with the communities I was working with affected by the brutalities of apartheid, we developed and built a community of learning through analytic group-based practice with an intention of responding to individual and societal reparation. This model of practice forms the foundation of my philosophy and practice as an intersectional art psychotherapist (Berman & Lefika La Phodiso, 2016).

Methodology

In 1964, Foulkes wrote: 'the spirit in which these groups are conducted, and the qualities required on the part of the conductor have an essential affinity to education according to the concepts of a democratic way of life for good world citizenship' (p.64).

Foulkes's statement encapsulates the potential and power of these applied qualities to catalysing social and political change towards 'a democratic way of life for good world citizenship' (ibid). I would argue that the qualities of the conductor are synonymous with providing the capacity to promote democracy. Particularly at this time within our global crises of an increase in fundamentalism, xenophobia and separatism, embracing and engaging Foulkes's notions of democracy and global citizenship as a fundamental function of the group analytic tradition calls for further emphasis and attention.

The qualities of the conductor can be translated into multiple potential contexts where these qualities may have an impact on growing democratic practice and global citizenship. I inhabit the positionality of a transformational object, where meaning is not fixed but continually evolving, making 'himself [or herself] an instrument of the group' (Foulkes, 1964, p.57), a developmentally needed 'mother' that models and invites the replication of a 'good enough' object, thus becoming the environmental mother (Winnicott, 1974). This 'object' can adapt and transform the frame in response to the political, social, organizational and individual needs of any group, small, medium or large. I bring myself, my learning and my experience into the space and adapt to the group's need. I offer my capabilities as a conductor which may require offering more or less theoretical input, interpretation, analysing, exchanging, resonating, modelling, mirroring. I am an educationalist, teaching through experience of being in a group, bridging the outside world, the global, society, community.

The approach of my role as an educator challenges the idea that the teacher is the one that teaches and transmits knowledge and the student is the one that receives knowledge. Rather, my approach engages the interchange of ideas and ways of coming together, challenging and critiquing models of learning that privilege power relations. It embodies Paolo Freire's philosophy of the pursuit of liberation through education. 'Hence, the teacher-student and the student-teachers reflect simultaneously on themselves and the world without dichotomizing this reflection from action, and thus establish an authentic form of thought and action' (Freire, 2005, p.83). There is a constant interplay between the intrapersonal, interpersonal and social matrices.

I encourage and try to impart a capacity to bear the unknown and embrace ambivalence, a vital quality of an art psychotherapist/conductor. Negative Capability is a phrase that Bion adopted from Keats, alluding to the capacity to sit with uncertainty and contradiction without reaching after fact or reason (1970). The majority of my work within education contexts mirrors my analytically informed individual and group work. Foulkes's group model provides a theoretical framework of analytic holding which enables the growth and capacity of disparate individuals to form relationships within a group, shifting internal, interpersonal relationships within the group, within their communities, thus impacting society.

It is important to locate Foulkes's contribution to group analysis within the context in which it was born, since his critique and reformulation of the idea of leadership emerged as a reaction to the political milieu following the Hitler and Mussolini regimes of authoritarian dictatorships. Foulkes's approach overtly offered a revolutionary contribution to the development of democratic ways of working within groups and challenged the notion of leader as the one who knows, determines and directs the way people think, feel and engage. He offered clear guidelines and methodologies for disrupting traditional forms of leadership, empowering the group with the capacity to lead over time. The quality the conductor offers the group 'is like a loan, wisely administered, helping recovery, but stimulating activity and self-help on the part of the receiver, not delaying it or making him even more dependent' (Foulkes, 1948, p.170).

The group itself operates as the main 'agency of change' offering a simultaneous activist stance of social engagement together with a therapeutic function of holding a capacity to think and feel in the presence and democratic practice of the group. 'Our main challenge as therapists is that area of relating which lies beyond the transference, deep within the social unconscious in all of us' (Mandikate, 2002, p.222). I would argue that the techniques and theoretical foundations of psychoanalytic/group analytic thinking and the use of objects and images invite a mindful democratization of a collaborative working through, rather than repeated patterns of divisive and destructive leadership styles.

My model of practice developed within the South African context, training community workers to replicate the function of a conductor that can model a way of being in a group to assist in the transition from autocratic, racist, divisive ways of engaging to inclusive, horizontal and democratic systems of engaging. This coincided with Nelson Mandela's inauguration as the first democratically elected president in South Africa with a vision for an inclusive, rainbow nation. He had a capacity for holding ambivalence, and a capacity to hold different states of mind. He was able to create an ethos of inclusivity encouraging diversity, metabolizing disparities in a form that felt safe. Mandela modelled the qualities of being a conductor, the purveyor of true democracy. He did not retaliate; he did not discriminate, yet provided 'the immanent presence and protection of a father figure in whose impartiality and justice they have confidence' (Foulkes, 1964, p.63).

The lack of mental health resources demanded a creative, adaptive approach. This took the form of a training institute, created to bridge the function of education and therapeutic engagement. This was a large group of 20 diverse trainees traversing race, class, gender, each with a commitment to conducting a supervised group in their communities, held in the vernacular, thus widening reach and sustainable opportunities for inclusive global citizenship. This was replicated over 20 years, increasing mental health care significantly. The initiatives undertaken by Lefika continually addressed questions of race, gender, power and so on. The work took place in schools with educators, offering work discussion spaces to address latent and overt trauma and residues of corporal punishment. Work within rural communities included facilitating national dialogues around gender-based violence, using community mapping as a participatory research model and opportunity for large therapeutic group work.

This model challenged specialization, diagnostic criteria of working with 'illness', and worked with complexity, using the group as a preventative, reparative and elaborative object. People accessed a therapeutic holding and containing space, not because they had a medical diagnosis but because their lives had been impacted by difficult economic, familial, social injustices, including violence, poverty and neglect.

Freud's method of free association, and Foulkes's corollary of free-floating discussion in group analysis, can be seen as the cornerstones of democracy. Barratt emphatically argues in his book *Radical Psychoanalysis* that 'the free-associative method has a powerful potential for the critique of all modalities of fundamentalism, fascism and fanaticism (indeed all the ideologies and hegemonies of domination that infuse our intrapsychic, interpersonal, cultural and socio-economic lives)' (Barratt, 2016, p.6). Furthermore, Bollas (2018) corroborates this in describing the analytic method as a process that invites all of the self's parts, comprising what he calls the personal idiom (1992). The analytic relationship invites an open mind comprising conscious and unconscious, democratic and totalitarian, manifest and latent, all without censorship. These parts may be contradictory and nonsensical yet are invited and received in a non-judgemental way by the art psychotherapist/conductor within the relational domain, creating a 'psychological democracy' (Bollas, 2018, p.81). While there is critique of the Eurocentric and racist origins of psychoanalysis (Gordon, 2004), there are compelling counter arguments and evidence that 'its roots are rich in one ethnic group, but it touches on universal human dynamics' (Bynum, 1999 in Mandikate, 2002, p.220).

The group is the developmentally needed object mirroring the developmental phases of moving from dependence to interdependence (Nitsun, 1989). It is an object 'space' with boundaries of respect, lack of criticism, openness to learning, punctuality, regular attendance and confidentiality. It is a space where conversations can be had with diverse groups about race, racism, histories and herstories.

Over the years, my personal experience of this function has kept changing according to the social and political milieu of HIV and the AIDS pandemic, crime, corruption, nepotism, popularism and neoliberalism, and most recently adapting to online engagement in response to the global pandemic caused by COVID-19 (Wu, Chen & Chan, 2020, p.217). The group transforms to adapt to the needs of the society, offering the potential for society to simultaneously adapt to the needs of the group. The basic premise and approach to this work is about enhancing opportunities for democratic engagement and social justice.

The education towards developing and cultivating the qualities of a mindful art psychotherapy practitioner enables the facilitation of a 'potential space' (Winnicott, 1974) to not only 'lift the barrier of repression' (Bhurruth, 2008) but to make available the 'receptive unconscious' (Bollas, 2009), to re-find parts of ourselves, and in so doing begin to liberate the life force in traumatized or autocratic societies. Foulkes says, 'the energies set free through the analytic process are being used in the service of this integration' (1964, p.57). Potential space is a space, internal and external, including a third 'intermediate space', where symbol formation, creativity, play and imagination become possible (Winnicott, 1974).

I would suggest that this psychic space and real space with an extended vocabulary of the group as potential material, together with the potential of real materials and objects, offers a creative democratic arena. Bollas believes that 'objects have an integrity of their own... [F]or the unconscious there is no difference between a material and a non-material evocative object;

both are equally capable of putting the self through a complex inner experience' (2009, p.79). These elements invite transcending the neat professional categories and hierarchies of experience towards a more intersectional approach, not only in relation to who we work with but how we work in a congruent and inclusive way.

Applied practice within the UK

It is important to provide a context for my transition to the UK in 2016 and the challenges I faced coming from a traumatized country. The political climate at the time of my leaving paralleled my journey of handing over leadership of Lefika La Phodiso, in collaboration and with the support of a sabbatical programme initiated by Rand Merchant Bank to increase black leadership in the non-profit sector. This was in line with the implementation of black economic empowerment (Arya & Bassi, 2011), giving black South African citizens economic privileges previously only available to white South Africans.

The political situation was rife with protests calling for the decolonizing of the curricula at schools and universities. 'Fees Must Fall' graffiti populated the walls of the city, and the political party Economic Freedom Front leader Julius Malema was creating fear and demonstrations to drive the whites out of South Africa. 'Such practices amount to a denial of the rights of white people as citizens – a situation no different from the very racism we are trying to consign to the dustbin of history' (Ramphele, 2008, p.86). The political terrain is complex, where reparation and redress are essential, yet factions repeat familiar patterns of splitting, precluding an inclusive and mindful anti-racist society (DiAngelo, 2019).

Libraries at universities were being burned and public sculptures defaced, which destabilized my confidence in access to tertiary education for my white children. At the same time, I was approached to apply for a position as an academic on a master's in art therapy programme in the UK and was offered the position. I had a strange fantasy that I was entering a progressive, democratic and functioning country and institution where I could relax into the job, share my knowledge and experience, and innovate a more socially engaged globalized programme impacting the training and practice of future art therapists within a holding and established environment.

However, this transition coincided with the Brexit referendum in June 2016 – an extended debate mobilizing an increased separatism determining whether the UK should remain a member of, or leave, the European Union. Soon after, in January 2017, it was the US presidential election, with

Donald Trump inaugurated, creating an international rupture and further threatening democracy. These global displays of racial, class and gender injustices betray and undermine complexity and intersectionality in the broadest meaning of the word in favour of a return to autocracy.

This disillusionment was mirrored within the microcosm of a university with a dominance of white educators, white students and a Eurocentric curriculum, within this particular programme. My desire and capacity to implement a change of thinking to a more psychosocial approach, embedding intersectional thinking and practice within a higher education training programme, became the 'location of the disturbed object' (Foulkes, 1983). I had the experience of being the disturbing outsider and subject of hostile othering. This put me in touch with the experience of abjection.

> There looms, within abjection, one of those violent, dark revolts of being, directed against a threat that seems to emanate from an exorbitant outside or inside, ejected beyond the scope of the possible, the tolerable, the thinkable. It lies there, quite close, but it cannot be assimilated. It beseeches, worries, and fascinates desire, which, nevertheless, does not let itself be seduced. Apprehensive, desire turns aside; sickened, it rejects. (Kristeva, 1982, p.68)

I brought with me what I know, and more than that: what I didn't know and needed to learn. I was tasked with re-visioning an existing curriculum, in a foreign context, without a history of living there, and so approached it like an anthropologist 'watching the English' (Fox, 2014, p.20). Having co-created the curriculum in South Africa over many years, bringing together what people felt was helpful, integrating multicultural facilitators, debunking the hierarchical, patriarchal and racist methods of practice, I attempted to replicate this.

This began with a consultation process with staff and students, other UK-based and international training organizations, stakeholders and service users to attempt to represent the current climate and needs. The co-creation of the curriculum mirrored the model of 'communities of practice', of how the curriculum within the non-formal education sector in South Africa developed which now forms the basis of the Honours in Art Therapy at the University of Johannesburg. Decolonizing education demands engaging with the complexity of the deep-rooted transgenerational residue of racism and trauma and finding new ways of learning and teaching. While it is important to have protocols and trainings to promote 'cultural competence' and 'unconsious bias', there did not seem to be a sustained, embedded and active stance of a psychosocial and anti-racist agenda. 'To understand racism, psychoanalysis is necessary but in itself insufficient and must be welded to social and political theory' (Gordon, 2004, p.14).

I brought an internalized model of practice where leadership is about collaboration and not hierarchical structures of relating. This was received by colleagues and management as poor leadership, as alien, other and unwanted. For the first time in my professional life I became defensive, afraid and uncertain of myself or my worth, and I chose to step aside in this role and find spaces that I could more comfortably inhabit.

Experiential spaces have evolved across different sectors within higher education with the objective of increasing and building on intersectional practice to be 'in the service of the group' (Foulkes, 1964, p.57). Within this context, this offering aims to challenge what some now call 'epistemicide' to describe the cognitive injustice involved in the marginalization and, on occasions, extermination of different ways of knowing to those based on measurement and calculability (Hoggett, 2017).

This is demonstrated in the following vignettes.

Vignette 1

In a tutorial group for final-year trainee art psychotherapists, students were expected to bring drafts of their case studies. However, in checking in with them, I realized that there was a considerable unexpressed distress and I enabled the group to transform into a therapeutic space to contain and hold some of the complexity of their life events, including car accidents, an anticipated bereavement, financial difficulties, displacement – all experiences that in the moment needed to be heard, witnessed and reflected on by the group. Holding the function of an empathic educator with an implicit therapeutic capacity frees up the propensity for learning. I made my shift in role overt, as an opportunity for teaching and modelling a way of being that could be a transferable quality they could internalize as trainee therapists. Hoggett (2017) suggests we need to come outside our bubble and find ways of making common political cause with those who otherwise feel excluded by our 'fine ways of talking, thinking and behaving' (p.14).

Vignette 2

I worked closely with staff wellbeing and offered several large and median groups to staff in response to key national events pertaining to racial awareness and mental health, as well as offering smaller groups to doctoral students across the university. Participants expressed a need for ongoing creative spaces to engage meaningfully together. Hopper contends, 'the ways in which the environment of large groups influence structures and processes within the group...also affect structures and processes in their environment' (2003, p.65). A research project was developed to establish the efficacy of group work in higher education, offering therapeutic services within the university for staff. This was the first time a therapeutic service was offered internally and not outsourced to employee wellness services that traditionally offer short-term cognitive-based therapy (CBT) as individual therapy.

There is an exponential increase in mental health problems within UK universities among staff and students. In 2019, statistics revealed that 43 per cent of academic staff exhibited symptoms of mental health issues, almost double the prevalence within the general population (Morrish, 2019). Mental health needs cannot be addressed without extensive research into what creates such vulnerability. What factors impact learning and teaching and how do we address this on a preventative level? Mental health cannot be seen in isolation, it is systemic and the result of political, economic, social and historic circumstance. Health is created by the systems we inhabit. Taking group analysis, sociology and psychosocial thinking into account, 'there is no such thing as an individual that exists apart from and outside the social' (Dalal, 1998, p.12).

The dynamic administration and formation of these groups held the core values of promoting heterogeneous groups privileging intersectionality, the objectives being as inclusive and diverse as possible, across hierarchies of role, class, race, gender as criteria for membership. Ellison, in her paper on promoting public scholarship beyond the academy, posits the 'importance of multiplicity and complexity in work in the arts and humanities that is jointly created as a public good by academic and community collaborators' (Ellison, 2008, p.463).

I will provide a brief example exploring the group function as disruptive yet potentially transformational. Within a closed group in the context of working with staff in higher education, a group member disclosed her recent diagnosis of obsessive compulsive disorder (OCD). The last 50 years have witnessed a profound proliferation of psychiatric disorders referenced by the *Diagnostic and Statistical Manual for Mental Disorders* (*DSM*) (American Psychiatric Association, 2013) that has both reflected and caused the over-diagnosis and medication of individuals afflicted with social rather than psychological problems.

This group member felt shame, humiliation and a resignation that her diagnosis was evidence of her 'mental illness', for which she had been given medication. In describing her early childhood of economic impoverishment, domestic violence and living in a dangerous community, her terror manifested in her checking doors, making sure they were locked over and over again.

I wondered aloud if this was an adaptation to what she had experienced rather than a pathology. The hypothesis/formulation was that this adaptation was in reaction to traumatic residue, perhaps the 'return of the re/opp/ressed' (Bollas, 2015). It was a moment of unsettlement and recalibration that generated further free-floating discussions from the group members about ways in which they have adapted to early personal and social trauma. This demonstrates the analytic and integrative processes that complement one another in de-escalating the hierarchies of diagnostic criteria to social responses and adaptations to systemic and structural violence (Young, Lee & Lee, 2018). Perhaps her diagnosis and fixity of a sense of identity could be liberated and become generative. She could be given permission to move, into a more inclusive and democratic domain of being. She created an image in the next session using colours associated to childhood, revisiting and playing in this refound freedom of just being human in response to adverse circumstances.

Vignette 3

During the COVID-19 pandemic and in lockdown, this group function was replicated virtually with the medium of Zoom video conferencing. This has simultaneously highlighted disparities and social inequalities, while offering opportunities for individuals to meet across continents and circumstance and share in the 'unsettlement', trauma and grief. People's homes have become their safe enough spaces, with the potential for multiple group configurations of educating, therapy, consulting to teams and organizations.

It is an intersectional experience of multiple frames/sections that sit side by side, or one on top of another. The technology allows for a speaker view that privileges the view of one person, or a gallery view that is horizontal and inclusive in the spirit of democracy. Exchange of imagery, sound, mirroring and witnessing people's personal spaces brings a strange dissonance and intimacy. In an art therapy training group in South Africa, students were asked to bring an image, object, photograph or poem representing something of what they are experiencing in lockdown. Two participants in mourning were both wearing black. On my screen, they appeared alongside one another. There was literally an actual death in the room as one was at their parents' home in a rural community, which doubled up as a funeral service, and coffins were in the space on screen. The connection died, one of them vanished. They were there and not there, existing and not existing. There is an equality in shared real and anticipatory trauma and grief of death and dying, of economic instability and terror. A primal fear of non-being and abandonment was embodied and enacted within this session.

Conclusion

In this chapter, I have been confronted with questions and a deep sense of not knowing. My reflections are gathered from experiences in countries where inequalities of access due to race and power can be challenged within a space of collaboration and difference. The invitation is for educators and researchers to be effective communicators who can effect change and generate knowledge.

I have focused on a group analytic and psychoanalytic theoretical contribution which informs the cultivation of the qualities of an art psychotherapist/practitioner and promotes intersectional thinking in all we do. These qualities are acquired through 'continuous mutual interaction' (Foulkes, 1964, p.56). These qualities are continually becoming, they are not fixed but imbue thoughtful, free associative and flexible selves. These selves are creative and curious, playing in the social matrices of dreams, reflections and reveries. The learning spaces have included being a member of an analytic training group, being part of a large group, the didactic forms of learning through lectures, seminars, supervision, work reflection groups, readings and academic writing and teaching. My work as an art psychotherapist, learning from my clients and learning through my practice as an artist, is a form of knowledge creation that disrupts, unsettles and questions binaries and orthodoxies. These competencies of coming to know/not know within the tradition of Foulkes rely on the intrapsychic and intersubjective processes at play within the group matrix, promoting a spirit of democracy and curiosity.

The invitation that Foulkes lays the foundation for seeks to challenge the neoliberal malaise of increased separatism and the increased relinquishing of governmental responsibility and societal accountability for structural disadvantages in society. Continuous mutual interaction includes the interaction between disciplines, communities of learning, the intersectionality of individuals, modalities, materials, theoretical contributions and conflicting parts of the self that provide a rich potential space of possibility. With increased accessibility of spaces in higher education and training in small, medium and large groups promoting intersectionality, we will be better able to achieve the goals and vision to promote a healthier society in the spirit of democratic engagement and global citizenship.

> The evolution of democracy, over thousands of years, is among our greatest accomplishments. Although it may come and go according to the emotional state of a person or a nation, the democratic process remains the potential in all human beings, even within the most totalitarian self. If we sustain a democratic frame of mind, we may take solace in knowing that, given the right group conditions, it can return. (Bollas, 2018, p.91)

References

American Psychiatric Association (2013). *Diagnostic and Statistical Manual of Mental Disorders: DSM-5* (fifth edition). Washington, DC: American Psychiatric Publishing.

Arya, B. & Bassi, B. (2011). Corporate social responsibility and broad-based black economic empowerment legislation in South Africa: Codes of good practice. *Journal of Business and Society, 50*(4), 674–695.

Barratt, B. (2016). *Radical Psychoanalysis*. London: Routledge.

Berman, H. (2019). Redressing Social Injustice: Transcending and Transforming the Borders of Art Therapy Training in South Africa. In A. Di Mara (ed.) *Exploring Ethical Dilemmas in Art Therapy: 50 Clinicians from 20 Countries Share Their Stories* (pp.68–75). London & New York, NY: Routledge.

Berman, H. & Lefika La Phodiso (2016). *Body of Work*. Johannesburg: Lefika Publications.

Bion, W. R. (1970). *Attention and Interpretation*. London: Tavistock Publications.

Bollas, C. (1987). *The Shadow of the Object: Psychoanalysis of the Unthought Known*. London: Free Association.

Bollas, C. (1992). *Being a Character*. London: Routledge.

Bollas, C. (2009). *The Evocative Object World*. London: Routledge.

Bollas, C. (2015). Psychoanalysis in the age of bewilderment: On the return of the oppressed. *The International Journal of Psychoanalysis, 96*(3), 535–551.

Bollas, C. (2018). *Meaning and Melancholia. Life in the Age of Bewilderment*. London: Routledge.

Bhurruth, M. (2008). Matriculating the matrix: A different understanding of psychic structure, resonance and repression. *Group Analysis, 41*(4), 352–365.

Crenshaw, K. (1989). Demarginalizing the intersection of race and sex: A Black feminist critique of antidiscrimination doctrine, feminist theory and antiracist politics. *University of Chicago Legal Forum, 1*(8), 139–176.

Dalal, F. (1998). *Taking the Group Seriously. Towards a Post-Foulksian Group Analytic Theory*. London: Jessica Kingsley Publishers.

Dalal, F. (2008). Against the celebration of diversity. *British Journal of Psychotherapy, 24*(1), 4–19.

DiAngelo, R. J. (2019). *White Fragility: Why It's So Hard for White People to Talk About Racism*. Boston, MA: Beacon Press.

Ellison, J. (2008). The Humanities and the Public Soul. In K. Mitchell (ed.) *Practising Public Scholarship: Experiences and Possibilities Beyond the Academy* (pp.113–121). Oxford: Wiley Blackwell.

Fanon, F. (1967). *The Wretched of the Earth*. London: Penguin Books.

Foulkes, S. H. (1948). *Introduction to Group-Analytic Psychotherapy*. London: Maresfield Reprints.

Foulkes, S. H. (1964). *Concerning Leadership in Group Analytic Psychotherapy*. London: George Allen and Unwin.

Foulkes, S. H. (1983). The Location of a Disturbance. In S. H. Foulkes, *Introduction to Group-Analytic Psychotherapy*, revised edition (pp.127–131). London: Routledge.

Fox, K. (2014). *Watching the English: The Hidden Rules of English Behaviour* (revised edition). London: Hodder & Stoughton.

Freire, P. (2005). *Pedagogy of the Oppressed* (trans. M. B. Ramos). London & New York, NY: Continuum.

Gordon, P. (2004). Souls in armour: Thoughts on psychoanalysis and racism. *British Journal of Psychotherapy, 21*(2), 277–292.

Hoggett, P. (2017). Shame and performativity: Thoughts on the psychology of neoliberalism. *Psychoanalysis, Culture & Society, 22*(4), 364–382.

Hopper, E. (2003). *The Social Unconscious*. London: Jessica Kingsley Publishers.

Kristeva, J. (1982). *Powers of Horror: An Essay on Abjection* (trans. L. S. Roudiez). New York, NY: Columbia University Press.

Mandikate, P. (2002). Different culture: Different treatment? *Psychodynamic Practice, 8*(2), 219–228.

Morrish, L. (2019). *Pressure Vessels: The Epidemic of Poor Mental Health Among Higher Education Staff.* Accessed 20/06/20 at www.hepi.ac.uk/wp-content/uploads/2019/05/HEPI-Pressure-Vessels-Occasional-Paper-20.pdf.

Nitsun, M. (1989). Early development: Linking the individual and the group. *Group Analysis, 22*, 249–260.

Ramphele, M. (2008). *Laying Ghosts to Rest: Dilemmas of the Transformation in South Africa*. Cape Town: Tafelberg.

Winnicott, D. W. (1956). Primary Maternal Preoccupation. In D. Winnicott, *Collected Papers: Through Paediatrics to Psychoanalysis* (pp.300–305). London: Tavistock.

Winnicott, D. W. (1974). *Playing and Reality*. London: Pelican.

Wu, Y., Chen, C. & Chan, Y. (2020). The outbreak of COVID-19: An overview. *Journal of Chinese Medical Association, 83*(3), 217–220.

Young, J., Lee, B. & Lee, G. (2018). From Human Violence to Creativity. In J. Adlam, T. Kluttig & B. Lee (eds) *Violent States and Creative States. Volume One. Structural Violence and Creative Structures* (pp.29–43). London: Jessica Kingsley Publishers.

The Contributors

Noa Yeheskel Baum has worked with children, young people and families for over ten years in the UK in a wide range of professional and clinical roles. She gained a master's in integrative child psychotherapy and a Diploma in the Therapeutic Application of the Arts at the Institute for Arts and Therapy in Education, and a Certificate in Counselling Skills at the Mary Ward Centre, London, UK. Noa works with children and young people and is passionate about working with children in the foster care system. She is a clinical supervisor at Terapia, and also works for a UK children's charity as clinical placement manager and in private practice.

Hayley Berman is an art psychotherapist and artist, with specialist expertise in contexts of trauma and social and political upheaval. She has a PhD in psychosocial studies and is a senior lecturer in the UK at Hertfordshire University on the MA Art Therapy Programme, a researcher, supervisor for Public Health, and examiner for psychosocial studies and visual arts doctoral students. She is Visiting Professor at the University of Johannesburg and founding Director of Lefika La Phodiso (www.lefikalaphodiso.co.za), the first psychoanalytically informed art therapy training in South Africa. She is a group work practitioner and trainee group analyst (IGA). Hayley has worked with individuals, groups and businesses in the UK, South Africa and several other countries. She has a private art psychotherapy practice, supervises mental health professionals and consults to organizations.

Sejal Chad is an arts psychotherapist, facilitator, writer and campaigner, with long-term experience in the mental health and community support fields, based in the UK. She is part of the Survivors Collective and Not the Only One project, offering training and support to university staff and students around issues faced by survivors of sexual violence, including child sexual abuse, and facilitates survivor consent workshops and support groups. She was part of the organizing team for Clear Lines Festival in 2015, the first event of its kind solely focused on issues of sexual violence and consent. She has offered therapeutic support and management in a range of community and educational settings, and also runs a private practice at London Creative Psychotherapy.

Jessica Collier is an art psychotherapist and clinical supervisor who has worked primarily with violent offenders in prisons, secure hospitals, a modified forensic therapeutic community and women in the criminal justice system. She has lectured widely to national and international audiences on forensic art psychotherapy and has contributed to MA Art Psychotherapy trainings in the UK as a visiting lecturer and senior lecturer. Jessica is co-convenor of the Forensic Arts Therapies Advisory Group and sits on the executive board of the International Association for Forensic Psychotherapists. She is co-editor of the *International Journal of Forensic Psychotherapy* and has published extensively on forensic art psychotherapy with a special interest in the experiences of female offenders.

Gillian W. Datlen is an art psychotherapist, artist and writer based in the UK. She began her career as an art educator working in secondary schools with adolescents with extended additional support needs and social, emotional and behavioural difficulties. Gillian now works as a lecturer in further education and as an art therapist. She has worked in paediatric and refuge settings and currently works with those with learning disabilities and physical conditions.

Corrina Eastwood is an art psychotherapist, supervisor, artist, lecturer and activist based in the UK. She qualified as an art therapist in 2005 and since then has worked in a variety of third-sector settings, including charities supporting survivors of domestic abuse, and adults experiencing homelessness and addiction, in medium secure settings working with women given personality disorder diagnosis, and in children's charities where she managed several therapeutic services within schools. She has worked as a lecturer on MA and Foundation Art Psychotherapy trainings in the UK since 2014 and has lectured widely on intersectionality and acknowledging power, privilege and potential prejudice in art therapy practice. Her art practice is central to informing her work as an art therapist and she has an interest in the meeting of art and activism, co-founding the intersectional feminist arts organization Sweet 'Art in 2012. In 2015, she founded the feminist art therapy charity Outskirts and in 2021 was appointed equality, diversity and inclusion (EDI) advisor for the *International Journal of Art Therapy*, while consulting on EDI policy for the British Association of Arts Therapists.

Charlotte Elliston is an arts administrator working in the museum/gallery sector in the UK, with an education in visual art. She is co-director of the feminist arts organization Sweet 'Art. Prior to this, she worked for ten years as a fashion retail buyer for a luxury boutique. Charlotte sits on the board of trustees for the art therapy charity Outskirts and on the Steering Group for the East End Women's Museum.

Georgina Obaya Evans is an art psychotherapist, artist and associate lecturer. She currently works as an art therapist in NHS adult mental health services and with young people in higher education. She has lectured on undergraduate psychology, professional art therapy and fine art training courses at various universities in London. She has a background of working in support services for women overcoming gender violence. Georgina's therapeutic and creative practice is informed by her personal research centred at the intersection of gender, embodiment, cultural identities, creative self-enquiry and 'dialogues of difference'.

Sarah Furneaux-Blick is an art psychotherapist based in the UK who qualified in 2017. Her art therapy practice sees her working with children in schools and adults in community mental health settings. She is also an artist and graphic designer whose practice is influenced by social activism and she focuses on working with organizations wishing to incorporate ethical person-centred approaches into their work in the commercial sector.

Jaspal Kaur Lotay is an art psychotherapist living and working within the Sikh Punjabi community in the UK. She initially studied psychology and following further training as a psychiatric nurse worked in the NHS for 13 years across various sectors, including forensics and perinatal specialist services. During this time, she also worked in India for a large charity. In 2018, she qualified as an art psychotherapist and as part of her studies piloted an art therapy service within the Sikh faith community with a focus on raising mental health awareness, breaking the taboo around mental health issues and promoting art therapy as a form of therapeutic intervention within this community.

Wabriya King qualified as a dramatherapist from the University of Roehampton in 2019. While maintaining her work within the mental health sector and private practice, she has quickly established a portfolio of work within the theatre sector. Having trained as an actress herself, this work feels particularly nourishing and important to her practice and freelance career. Wabriya is proud to be part of the growing number of global majority dramatherapists and feels honoured to be a contributor to this very necessary book.

S. J. Langer is a writer and psychotherapist in New York City, where he maintains a private practice. Along with psychotherapy, he provides clinical supervision and mentorship as a World Professional Association for Transgender Health (WPATH) Global Education Initiative (GEI) Standards of Care 7 (SOC7) Certified Mentor. He is part of the faculty at the School of Visual Arts in both the MPS Art Therapy and Humanities & Sciences departments and is the Principal Investigator studying embodiment and trans phantoms. His article 'Trans bodies and the failure of mirrors' was the co-winner of the Symonds Prize from Studies in Gender and Sexuality. He is included in the edited volume *Sex, Sexuality and Trans Identities: Clinical Guidance for Psychotherapists and Counselors*. His first book, *Theorizing Transgender Identity for Clinical Practice: A New Model for Understanding Gender*, was a finalist for the Lambda Literary Award in 2020.

Kairo Maynard is a dramatherapist and aspiring child psychotherapist. She is also an executive member of the British Association of Dramatherapists (BADth) and a scholar of the Stuart Hall Foundation. She has worked in child adolescent mental health services (CAMHS) for a number of years and is passionate about improving access and creating better outcomes for young people and families from minoritized communities, as well as the impact of intergenerational trauma and attachment on Black families. Kairo is active in pursuing anti-racism work and leads on two race equity working groups within her NHS trust and BADth Inclusion and Visibility Subcomittee.

Naomi Rowe is a practising music therapist, vocalist and social activist based in the UK. She has worked in special education and now works with both children and adults, many of whom are neurodiverse and/or LGBTQ+. She is Chair of Brum Bi Group, one of the most active regional bi groups in the country. She served as access lead for Bi Camp in its first two years, serves on the anti-racism committee for Bi Continuity and is co-chair of Limmud Midlands 2021, a regional Jewish one-day conference.

Savneet K. Talwar is a professor and chair in the graduate art therapy and counselling programme at the School of the Art Institute of Chicago. She is a member of the Critical Pedagogy in the Arts Therapies organizing group. Her current research examines feminist politics, critical theories of difference, social justice and questions of resistance. Using an interdisciplinary approach, she is interested in community-based art practices; cultural trauma; performance art; and public cultures as they relate to art therapy theory, practice and pedagogy. She is the author of *Art Therapy for Social Justice: Radical Intersection* and has published in *Arts in Psychotherapy*, *Art Therapy: Journal of the American Art Therapy Association* and *Gender Issues in Art Therapy*. She is also the founder of the CEW (Creatively Empowered Women) Design Studio, a craft, sewing and fabrication enterprise for Bosnian and South Asian women at the Hamdard Center in Chicago. She is a past Associate Editor of *Art Therapy: Journal of the American Art Therapy Association*.

Eleni Tsolka is a qualified music therapist and an advanced trainee in the Bonny method of guided imagery and music (BMGIM) and neonatal intensive care unit (NICU) music therapy. She is also a primary school and special school teacher and a music teacher. As a music therapist, she has worked with children facing social, emotional and behavioural difficulties, with people on the autism spectrum and refugees in Greece, Palestine and the UK. She is HCPC (Health and Care Professions Council) registered and a member of ESPEM (Greek Association for Music Therapy). Eleni's work has been presented and published at music therapy conferences and in scientific journals.

Subject Index

Author Index